BLACK BOY POEMS

An Account of Black Survival in America

by

Tyson Amir

Freedom Soul Media

Sis Eman,

I hope & pray you are well.
I really respect + appreciate
what you do. You're out
there inspiring people daily.
Accomplishing your dreams,
keep getting it. I hope
you enjoy this work. Let's
keep building. Tyson
Amir

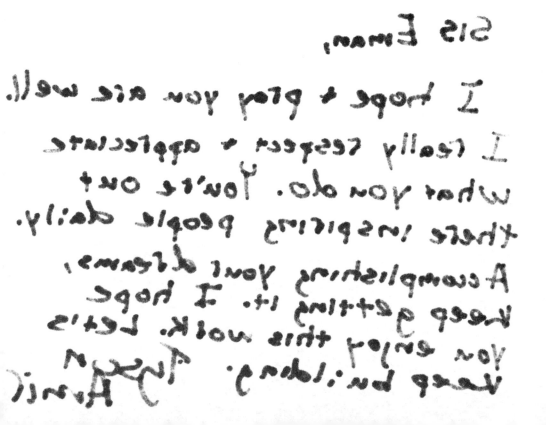

This work is dedicated to the struggle for liberation of my people.

Table of Contents

Acknowledgements	6
Introduction	9
41 Shots (1999)	54
Family Tree (2000)	64
Under a Different Light (2001)	78
Dream Revisited (2001)	91
Between Huey and Malcolm (2015)	103
Out (2005)	116
Blue Devil (2002)	124
War Zones (2002)	139
The Rose (2015)	148
"The Dirge" (2014)	167
"Letter to Johnetta" (2015)	178
Material of Martyrs (2015)	199
Black Child (2015)	207
Death Toll (2015)	218
You (2009)	229
A Word on Mario Woods	237
A Poem for Mario (2016)	238
Aftermath, Thoughts, and Reflections	248
Bibliography	272
About Tyson Amir	276

Acknowledgements

I'm thankful and grateful for the opportunity to present this work to the world. It is truly an honor to be used as a conduit to carry forth the traditions of my people. I sincerely pray these words convey the truths of our story with a clarity that inspires us as we struggle on our path toward freedom. We will win!

It is said in my spiritual tradition that the one who doesn't thank others doesn't thank the creator. This project is only possible because of the contributions of many. It is only right that I take a few moments to acknowledge those who played a role in making this work a reality. The first thanks is to the creator. I must also give thanks to my mother and father for their love, guidance, and support. To my sister Kira who always encouraged me to pursue greatness. My nieces Indira and Olivia, I thank you both for your love. You inspire me to want to fight long and hard for our family, and to make you proud. And a very special thank you is for the woman who holds my heart. She's the Betty to my Malcolm and has supported me every step in this journey. Alia, there aren't enough words to express my deep sense of love and appreciation for who and what you are. Thank you. To my sister from another mister, Mya, you've been down since day one and are partly to blame for my career as a writer. To sister Nora who completed the first edit of this work, thank you for your mind, eye, and belief in this project.

To our ancestors whose shoulders we stand upon. Thank you for your sacrifices, we have been made better by what you've left for us. To my people, thank you for being your black beautiful selves. We are a people that have experienced some of the worst of what humankind is capable of, but it is our strength, resilience and resolve that has allowed us to remain and continue to fight. I am in awe of our people's fight for survival. It is that very fight that is present in these pages. I thank you all for daring to be beautiful and daring to live in the face of ugly hate.

To my family, my grandma, uncles, aunts and cousins, I love and thank y'all. You've put up with my crazy militant behind all my life. It's your love and support that has nourished me throughout these years. And now to the homies, Jay Walker, Agin, Ise, Anas, Lloyd, Big B. Jake & Vanessa, B.J. Dooley, Oscar, KP, Chris, Jose, Noel, Prime, Istock, Soul Glo Fam, Jake Mason, Q, Shawn Green, Dre the 6th member of NE, illTrax, Rid, Mik, Ishaq, Kumasi, Erik Rico, Stevie, March, Marlon, Uthman, Mike, Kamilah, Vanessa, Kai-Ti, White Jake, Adisa, Khalil, Amir, Lil Anas, Saeed, Blue, Remarkable Current Fam, Midnight Basketball Fam, San Quentin Fam, the brothers on the yard, San Bruno and CJ 5 folks, my 5 Keys colleagues, Football Fam, Sylvandale, Leyva and Piedmont Fam, The Justice 4 Mario Woods Coalition, and all community groups organizing for the survival of our people. I can't forget the sisters, Big sis Phelicia, Ayoola, Nyimah, JoJo, Shana, Dahlia, Sabeen, Kamilah, INVST, Stella, Pam McCali, Mother Cristina, Kelli, Tanesha, Hana, and Fatima. Thank you for the love and support.

To my teachers, Malik, Fred McCoy, Jeff Heard, Mrs. Malcolm, Ms. Munson, Prof. Rycenga, Dr. Harris, Imam Zaid, Imam Shuaibe, Imam Anwar Muhaimin, Sidi Yassir, Shaykh Alaeddin, Shaykh Hamza, Shaykh Abdullah Ali, Br. Siddique Abdullah, 850 Sinbad, San Jose, The Bay Area, and Cali. I'm indebted to you all for your knowledge, wisdom, examples, and guidance. Thank you.

To Sista Elaine Brown and the brothers and sisters who are alumni of the Black Panther Party for Self Defense and other political movements of the 60s and 70s. I thank you all for your sacrifices, dedication, and bravery. It was not in vain. That spirit of struggle has taken root in your offspring. We will carry it forward.

A sincere thank you to the team at Self-Publishing Services LLC. I've learned a lot through this process and your work has brought this from vision to reality. A quick thank you to the folks at Brown Sugar Kitchen, Arizmendi on San Pablo, Cosecha, Sukho Thai, Grato Burgers and Los Cantaros Taqueria for the nourishment. And to the Vitamin String Quartet and their renditions of Tupac's "Dear Mamma" and "To Live and Die in L.A." I wrote most of the book to those songs.

Lastly, I want to thank all those who granted me permission to use their material in this book. Special thanks to the Amaru estate, Lorne Cress Love, Tommie and Delois Smith, Equal Justice Initiative, Dr. Kapperler, Brooks Permissions, Faith Childs Literary Agency, the estate of Dr. Martin Luther King Jr., Penguin Random House, Ron Hussey at Houghton Mifflin Harcourt, Richard Hazboun at Pathfinder Press, and everybody else who was kind enough to allow me access to their material for this text. Your contributions are greatly appreciated. Thank you.

And thank you for taking the time to read this book.

Introduction

First, I dedicate this effort to my creator and my mother and father; they are the ones the creator selected to be my first instructors in this world. They taught me how to love; they taught me knowledge of self and of my people. For that I am a better man and eternally grateful.

Second, I dedicate this effort to my sister, my two nieces, and my family. My sister, my womb-mate, was the first person to challenge me to become better. She never accepted anything but greatness from me. I love you, Kira. My nieces, Indira and Olivia, and my family, you all have provided me with the strongest of foundations to stand upon. You've given me the greatest motivation and support. Your stories have filled my heart and soul with love and adoration. I am you, and I am nothing without you.

Third, I dedicate this to my ancestors who struggled with all their power and ability to make a better world for me to inherit. Your lives were not in vain. Your hopes and dreams live on in me. I honor your existence with my words and my work. Through these words may your struggles be known and celebrated, for it is your sacrifice that made this moment possible.

Last, I dedicate this to my people. We are the proud offspring of sons and daughters unfairly and unjustly stolen from their homes in Africa. We are the children of those who were forced into the most wretched and inhumane system of slavery ever invented. We are the children of those who survived the tragedy of slavery and created the most intelligent, beautiful, strong, resilient, suave, stylish, charismatic, soulful, and memorable people on this planet. This is the blood that pumps through our veins. Our genetic inheritance is precious. It is not a badge of inferiority for us to be ashamed of. On the contrary, we carry the struggles of our ancestors with pride. We carry the sacred traditions of our people in our hearts and souls. May they forever guide us and instill in us a deep sense of self and purpose. We are survivors, and we will win.

An Homage to Richard Wright

As an artist, educator, poet, man, and now author, I have had mentors and role models who have influenced and, from time to time, guided my development. My mother is responsible for my introduction to Richard Wright. I cannot recall which birthday it was, but my mother gave me an unwrapped gift with a simple yet powerful disclaimer. She put a book in my hand and told me, "This is my favorite book." In my young hands was a copy of *Black Boy*. I remember staring at the cover for days. The book seemed to carry an ancient power that I didn't quite fully understand. I was intimidated by the energy emanating from the text, so much so that I didn't know how to approach it. Eventually I peeled the cover back and cautiously began to explore the content of the pages. Keeping it as real as possible, I wasn't ready! Wright spoke of his world in a voice that was superhuman to me. His words flew off the page with a strength and focus that I had never experienced before.

My initial read left me broken, fragmented into millions of pieces by the raw power and eloquence of Wright's pen. I felt like I was a sorcerer's apprentice attempting to perform a master incantation, and being the novice that I was, it blew up in my face. I was moved by the text in a way I had never experienced before, and, due to my novice status and Wright's literary sorcery, I had not been able to fully assimilate the data.

It took several years before I attempted to understand Wright's magic again. This time when the pages opened, I was invited into the master's inner sanctum. The growth and maturity I had undergone made me worthy of the secrets buried beneath the words, and Wright patiently explained the source of his magic to me. I was present in every line, critically analyzing every movement, and, as a result, I was forever transformed. I inhaled every phrase and made it part of my being. I traveled the dusty roads of his childhood walking barefoot through racist Mississippi. I felt the pangs of his ever-present hunger turn my stomach upside down. I stood next to him as he suffered silently watching his mother's illness worsen. He shared his schemes for escaping that dark southern night and his hopes and dreams for a better life in Chicago. More than anything else, he shared the power of his analysis with me. Like any great teacher or sorcerer he taught me how to find the power and ability to do the same for myself. In this exchange he became something like a literary father to me. Like him I wanted to harness the power of my pen for the benefit of my people. Wright's words are weighted with the experience of hundreds of years of black suffering. His magic is the result of his refusal to be conquered by the strictures of his society. Like a true sorcerer, he conjured a new world for himself, and in the process shared that magic with millions of black men and women in his stead.

I did not share the same path as Wright, but our souls possess a similar unapologetic and unyielding desire to not be controlled by the world around us. I too am a black boy. I too have inherited this shortsighted and belligerent racist culture of America. I too, in the face of the hate of my society, wear the title of "Black Boy" with pride. It is mine, and it will always be mine. However, I will define the reality of what it means to be a black boy; America will have no sway over that. America and the larger world can try to deploy any and all machinations to serve as obstacles, but like Wright the master sorcerer taught me, black men and women possess a magic; it is an old and powerful magic, and that magic in the hands of a master sorcerer carries the power to conjure new realities and possibilities the world has never seen. It is an honor to have learned from the hand of Wright. The honor is weighted with the responsibility of carrying forth this tradition and practicing this black, bold, and beautiful magic for the benefit of myself and my people.

The love for reading and writing was passed on to me by my mother. I've yet to meet a person who has the ability to read more than she did. Almost all of my childhood memories of my mother place her not far from a book. I honestly do not know how she was able to read so much in such a short period of time. Along with working full-time and being a wife, she had to raise two energetic kids with active extracurricular lifestyles, and still was able to finish multiple books a month. Through her I was introduced to the world of black authors. My mother read all different types of books, but her favorite thing to read was anything from a black author. She introduced me to Wright, James Baldwin, Walter Mosley, Octavia

Butler, Maya Angelou, Audre Lorde, Phyllis Wheatley, and so many others. From her example I was thrown into a literary world that would help define who I was.

And just like my momma, Richard Wright's *Black Boy* became my favorite book as well. His cutting insight helped shape my world view. I have been forever changed by the power of his pen and analysis. That is why a portion of the title of my work is an homage to the literary genius of Richard Wright. But it is also an homage to my beautiful mother because it was her who felt *Black Boy* would speak to me, and she was right. It was her who saw me pick up a pen and encouraged my attempts at writing. This is part of the reason why this book is so important to me. It's a celebration of what my parents, specifically my mother instilled in me. Momma, you were the first to believe in me. I'm truly grateful for that. This is for you.

Home Life

My upbringing was the furthest thing from a typical black family experience. At the time I was growing up, I didn't realize that, but it started to dawn on me as I approached my mid- to late teens. It was clear to see that my sister and I had a unique home life. Both of my parents participated in the civil rights and black liberation movements. My father was a member of one of the most "revolutionary" groups of that time, the Black Panther Party for Self Defense. There was no question that it would be my birthright to forward the struggle. I came out the womb, head first, into a world of deep black consciousness.

Before I knew many things about the world, I knew I was black; this knowledge was more than a biological or scientific understanding of the term. I knew I was black culturally, spiritually, politically, and mentally. I was so entrenched in my knowledge of blackness that at the age of five, I started to question other people's blackness. My momma was the first to be questioned because I had to figure out what was going on with her. My mother was fairly light on the scale of blackness, but still very black. My five-year-old mind had a difficult time understanding how my father, sister, and I were all our deep hues of brown (which made us visibly black in American society), and she was light bright. This puzzled me, so one day curiosity got the better of me, and I had to ask. She, startled at the question, chuckled a bit, but assured me that she was certifiably black and that a light complexion did not mean that a person wasn't black. What I would later come to learn is that in America it did not take much to sentence one to a term of immutable blackness. As little as "one drop" of "black blood" was all that it took. As light as my mother was, she and others of her complexion still faced the institutional racism and discrimination pioneered and perfected here in America.

At the age of ten, my family moved from the home I was born in on the East Side of San Jose to another home still on the East Side but in a "better" neighborhood. This house gave us four bedrooms, and immediately my father commissioned that extra bedroom, "The Black Room." He filled it with artifacts, posters, pictures, and memorabilia from the movements of the '60s and '70s. It was our own museum to the black struggle. I would spend hours in there looking at old Black Panther Party newspapers or trying to understand the messages on various protest posters. Malcolm X, Muhammad Ali, Marcus Garvey, Angela Davis, Amilcar Cabral, Dr. Martin Luther King Jr., and others decorated our walls. I remember when my parents brought home these giant portraits of Malcolm and Nelson Mandela. We put them both on the front facing walls of our home so every guest who walked in would be greeted by Brother Malcolm and President Mandela. Off top, you knew you had just stepped into a universe governed by blackness.

My parents did everything they could to manufacture a black community for us in San Jose. I didn't understand how difficult a task it must've been for them, but they relentlessly endeavored to perform what might seem the impossible. I grew up in a city that had a black population of between 6 percent and 8 percent, but I couldn't tell that. They took that small percentage of folks and wrapped it around us like a thick black blanket, enveloping us in warm nurturing blackness. My sister and I went to a black dentist, had a black eye doctor, were taught by strong black teachers, and had mentors who were black firefighters, black actors and actresses, and computer engineers. They even created a black school for us and other children to learn the ways of blackness. Instead of going to Sunday school, my sister and I went to what we called "black school" where we studied black history and culture from a revolutionary perspective. Our classes were always held on a college campus or at a black community center. We had a textbook and other additional readings and assignments to do for homework. We even took field trips. Our goal was to learn and experience any and everything black.

One of the most memorable events I recall from my childhood took place when I was about ten years old. Nelson Mandela had just been released from prison and started a world tour calling on leaders of nations to aid in the South African fight against apartheid. I was excited because my household had been practicing a boycott of all companies that supported the apartheid regime. My parents would call out brand names as we walked through stores and explain how they supported the apartheid that was hurting our South African brothers and sisters. We would not spend money on those products to help them hurt our people. I learned the power of boycott early on. To this day, I boycott some companies who sent money to apartheid South Africa.

Mandela was free, and it seemed like the entire world was rejoicing in his release. He was to speak in Oakland at the Coliseum on his tour, and my parents made sure we were there to witness history. I don't remember much of his message, but I know we sat close to the front of the stage, and I stood up on my seat and raised the black power fist that was the symbol of Mandela's organization, the African National Congress (ANC). Mandela acknowledged my fist with a point and a nod. One of the greatest freedom fighters of the twentieth century shared some of his revolutionary energy with me. The light from this son of South Africa, the pride of the Xhosa and Thembu, the future president of the Republic of South Africa, shined forth black and proud. He shared some of that revolutionary shine with me, and I absorbed it all like melanin skin absorbs sunlight.

Another memory that shaped my revolutionary childhood took place on an August evening in 1989. My sister, Kira, and I were doing homework when a story appeared on the five o'clock news. I wasn't watching the television, so the name drifted from the voice on the screen and filtered through my ears. I had heard the name many times before and a face appeared in my head. The voice from the television was telling me that the name and face that was in my head had been shot and killed earlier that day in West Oakland. The man was Huey P. Newton.

Without much conversation or prompting, my father gathered us up in his brand new but always about to break down Chrysler with license plate reading Finn2Go, and we made a forty-minute drive up to west Oakland. Throngs of folks were already on the scene: Some were helping to create a vigil to honor the passing of our fallen soldier, brother, and comrade; others were crying in disbelief. That memory is still vivid for me to this day, and the hurt and pain in the people present on the scene was heavy. I recall seeing what I thought were traces of his blood still visible on the street. At that early age I could not understand the depth of the message of Dr. Huey P. Newton and the Black Panther Party but I knew they fought and many died or were incarcerated for the sake of my people. I would later come to understand some of the philosophy of Huey, he had coined the term "Revolutionary Suicide," which could be described as living and dying for the people in a way that advances the struggle for liberation. We will all die, but not all of us will truly live lives that honor our people and our commitment to the struggle. Although Huey's death was tragic, his legacy would live on, and that day was the first time I learned to mourn for a fallen comrade.

My teenage years added more depth to the lessons I was to receive as a black boy in America. My parents still did all they could to keep me in the comfort and safety of the black community. I attended Black Nationalists' rites of passage programs where I learned black politics, black economics, and other skills for surviving America as a black boy who would hopefully one day grow to become a black man. We attended just about every event that had something to do with blackness on the West Coast, including black plays, concerts, festivals, and National Association for the Advancement of Colored People (NAACP) gatherings; we were regulars at the black cultural center; and eventually Kwanzaa slowly replaced the remnants of Christmas celebrations in our home. We were raised at the epicenter of blackness and consciousness, guaranteeing that there was no possible way that my sister and I would ever not know that we were black.

High School Years

My entire freshmen year in high school I spent listening to a collection of speeches by Malcolm X. Folks would see me on the 71 bus riding down White Road with my headphones bumping some Malcolm from 1962. I studied his accent and cadence; I was enthralled by the way he would articulate the plight and condition of the so-called "Negro" people in America. I would sit in the hallways before class and write speeches to America about how she was currently treating her black sons and daughters. Maybe my classmates had similar thoughts and were creating a similar collection of essays and speeches; it is possible, but I knew in my thirteen-year-old body that I was very black and proud, and that America had to be told about the wrongs she was committing against my brothers and sisters. I knew that I had been drafted into a struggle that predated my existence and that I would eventually play a role in this fight. Unquestionably and unapologetically black, and constantly exuding blackness, I would play my role when my contribution was demanded of me.

It was pretty much assumed that I would attend an Historically Black College or University (HBC or HBCU). Like many black students, one of the highlights of my high school career was being sent on black college tours to showcase the excellence of the Historically Black College experience. Carl Ray was a community organizer, activist, author, and comedian who would host college tours for Bay Area students. He graduated from Tuskegee University and showed a little bias for Tuskegee because our longest stay on the trip was at his alma mater. I didn't mind at all; I soaked up all the blackness I could find at every stop we made on the tour.

Before going on the trip, I already wanted to attend an HBC(U); it was fulfillment of the plan that was laid out for me. Once completing the trip, there was no doubt in my mind that I would not go anywhere other than an HBC(U). I was so certain that I would attend an HBC(U) that when approaching graduation from high school, I only applied to one school, Morehouse College. I wanted to attend the historic and hallowed halls of Morehouse; no other college or university mattered. It was Morehouse or bust.

The happiest and saddest moments in my young life occurred on the same day. Morehouse said it wanted me. After reading those words, I was picturing myself walking the grounds of the campus with all the other brothers I'd meet. I thought about the beautiful sisters I would see at Spelman College, too. I rushed home and shared the letter with my parents and learned that the package Morehouse was offering me wasn't going to be enough to allow me to attend. Just like that, I had to say goodbye to the dream I had been holding onto for what seemed like my entire life. I can't describe the pain of that moment. Morehouse seemed so close; I was holding in my hand my letter of acceptance, but finances denied me my chance at realizing that dream. Growing up as a kid here in America, it is hard not to be inspired by predominantly white colleges and universities with exciting athletic programs. I cheered on certain college teams, but the excitement went no further than that; I had no desire to attend any of those schools. I wanted to assume my position next to the educated black men and women who were the proud byproducts of so many historical black institutions. In a matter of seconds, that dream was snatched away from me. I didn't quite understand why; I thought I had done something wrong. Somewhere in the process, I must've missed a step. It was supposed to work out for me to attend Morehouse. I was destined to be a Morehouse man, but apparently my destiny was to lead me down another path.

This was the first time I actually felt like I failed at something in life. Consequently, it was also the first time I began to search for wisdom and blessings in the moment. I don't know what path I would've ended up on had I gone to Morehouse. I would like to think that I would've been successful at whatever I chose to do. That I would've found a way to take part in the struggle and help advance the cause of my people as well. However, none of that was to be. I tucked my dream of Morehouse away and started taking steps down the road that would eventually bring me here.

After dealing with the heartbreak of losing Morehouse, I decided I would stay local. My path would be to attend San Jose

City College and then transfer to San Jose State University. The spirit of revolution was still on my side because SJSU is arguably the birthplace of one of the most lasting symbols of the Black Liberation Movement. In the summer of 1968, two SJSU students named Tommie Smith and John Carlos made an emphatic gesture on the medal stand in Mexico City. Dr. Harry Edwards is known as the founder of the Olympic Project for Human Rights that initially called for all black athletes to boycott the '68 Olympics and then eventually facilitated discussion and debate around how to use the Olympic platform for voicing a political message. Smith and Carlos both took the medal stand shoeless in black socks to symbolize black poverty and raised their fists clothed in black gloves for human rights and in solidarity with the Black Power struggle.

Smith would later go on to say about his 200-meter victory and protest on the medal stand: "If I win, I am American, not a black American. But if I did something bad, then they would say I am a Negro. We are black, and we are proud of being black. Black America will understand what we did tonight."

SJSU was one of the breeding grounds for the spirit that helped contribute to that movement, and I planned to immerse myself in every remaining revolutionary particle on the campus.

It was my time at SJSU that allowed me to focus more on my music and experiment with poetry. Saying good-bye to Morehouse and eventually to playing basketball afforded me the time to concentrate my energies on my art. I actually wrote my first poem on the encouragement of one of my instructors. That poem is where *Black Boy Poems* begins. When I picked up my pen that day to write, I knew a few things; I knew I was already a proud member of a storied people in America. I knew the strength and power of my people. I also knew without a shadow of a doubt that I was a Black Boy, replete with all the potential, challenges, greatness, fears, anxieties, and promises. I was black in America, a land that has practiced an unbridled hate for my kind for centuries. I knew I was one of the fighters selected to carry forth the banner of struggle for my people. All of this was present in my heart, mind, body, and soul on that day I put proverbial pen to paper to write. I am a black boy, I will forever be a black boy, I am blessed and thankful to be a black boy. My name is Tyson Amir, a black boy in America, and these are my poems for my people.

Overview of the Text

In *Black Boy Poems* I use my raps and poetry in conjunction with various social, historical, political, cultural, and academic analyses to speak on the state of black life in America and make an emphatic statement on the need for revolutionary action to safeguard the present and future of black people the world over. This is not simply a collection of poetry. This is a work that truly endeavors to harness the original revolutionary power of the hip hop art form and use it to spread healing and inspire the spirit of 66, that revolutionary fervor that led to the Black Panther Party for Self Defense.

The presence and importance of hip hop in this text cannot be overstated. There is no cultural medium more powerful than hip hop in the world today. This generation which finds itself under attack for being black in the Western world consumes information and media differently than the civil rights and black liberation generations. If a revolutionary message is to be crafted, it has to be done in a language the people can understand. We were raised off complex rhyme schemes and punchlines that blew our minds. It is quite possible that we learn as much, and possibly more through social media and song, than "traditional" learning experiences. Point blank, there can be no revolution without hip hop playing an essential role. This is the first revolutionary manifesto produced by hip hop.

My approach in this work is formulaic. I begin each chapter with an original composition, either a poem or lyrics from a song. I've selected fifteen different pieces that span 17 years of writing to feature as windows into the black experience. Each composition is followed by brief reflections or quotes that provide a segue between the poetry and main text in the chapters. The main text in each chapter will expand on the content and subject matter of the poems/lyrics and segue selection. Upon completion of the main body of the text I added an additional chapter in response to the killing of a student of mine, Mario Woods. I finish off the book with a conclusion of sorts to synthesize the major points made in the book and focus them once again to reiterate the main point of the text, the need for revolutionary action to secure the freedom and liberation of black people.

What primarily informs my writing is my existence in America as a black man. I simultaneously embody multiple experiences that contribute to my life and my art, but my first lens as a writer is that of a black man. I know that the concept of race or human beings representing different races is scientific fiction. Race is the brainchild of ideologically blinded pseudo-scientists who sought to justify their flawed worldview through a gross misappropriation of the scientific method. I know that the terms "white" and "black" are false constructs that have no true meaning in any real scientific understanding of the world. This is what makes the sting of racism that much more painful to bear because the premise for all that will be discussed in this text is rooted in a social fallacy supported by greedy individuals clinging to outdated prejudiced "science."

Differences attributed to simple minute shifts in the allele of a person's genetic makeup are not what should grant one access to a privileged existence and force others into a third-class existence. None of us is able to choose what we will be at birth. Some of us have the means and privilege to change our characteristics, but from birth we are biologically what we come out of the womb with. Western society has valued certain qualities over others, and as a result doles out differential treatment to members of specific social groups, be they gender-, race-, or ability-specific. I know for a fact that "race" is scientifically and biologically false. This is a fact the scientific community attests to, but I also know all too well that this once-scientific fact, which is now largely viewed as a social fabrication, is responsible for millions of deaths, injuries, traumas, and my people's continued social torments in America and the larger Western world.

Purpose of This Book

The stories that follow are authentic depictions of the black experience from my vantage point. I'm writing in the early part of the 21st century but the reality for blacks in this country in many ways is the same as if I were writing in the early 20th or 19th century. The racism that existed during the days of chattel slavery is still here. The devaluation of black life that was written into the constitution is still with us. The disenfranchisement of blacks is evident almost everywhere you look in the western world. All of this means that our fight goes on. I've been asked numerous times whom I write for. First, I write for myself. It is a clichéd response, but for me it is a very true response. It is imperative I give voice to these stories that have manifested in me. Part of the imperative is for self-healing. My cousin Prentice Powell, who is actually the best poet in our family, said this in one of his pieces:

"Being a black man in America
is to be a black man in America.
And unless you are a black man in America,
You will never understand what it's like
to be a black man in America.
But please, don't pity us,
Envy us.
We are whole pieces of broken.
Some too shattered to care,
and some just trying to put the pieces back together."

This writing is one of the ways that I'm trying to take these "whole pieces of broken" and put them back together. That is why, first and foremost, the "whom" I write for is me. There is plenty of pain in the black experience, and that pain has to be exorcised in a healthy way. If nothing else, I am an optimist. I have to synthesize what I see, feel, and experience, and filter it through a matrix that allows me to still remain positive and believe that change is possible. Like many artists before me, my art and my writing are an important part of that process. The synthesis becomes cathartic for me as the processing allows me to go from coping with pain to making it a tool for learning and healing that can be shared with others. This is where the artistic process becomes transformative; it's borderline alchemic. The artist is able to take the raw elements of feelings and emotions and convert them into a powerful healing force and share it with the world. This is the alchemy in the artistry.

The evolved artist/alchemist knows that story, when transmitted from heart to heart, carries the potential to change the world. It is the responsibility of the initiated to wield that power wisely.

Second, I write for my people. These are stories for and about black people. Being as clear and as unapologetic as possible, I do not write for White America. This compilation of work is for healing, empowerment, strategy, critical analysis, awareness, and paradigm shifting in the minds of black people worldwide, especially my brothers and sisters here in America. To accomplish this, the message of the text will be written in the language/vernacular of my people. This text could've easily been written in a more Western/academic form, but I am not interested in praise from the world of academia. I'm interested in the freedom of my people. Channeling the spirit of "The Dragon," George Jackson, this piece of work is not literature; it's a weapon for the liberation of my people. My people are my family; in our intimate closeness, we speak with relaxed tongues; this allows the message to penetrate heart, body, mind, and soul. It's not to make some "institution of higher learning" look good, or earn respect in the eyes of an "educated" elite. This is about freedom and liberation, everything else is of no importance.

The language of the youth and the people is hip-hop. That is why rap and spoken word feature so prominently in this work. It's a siren sound that goes out, summoning the ears of the people. Once ears are open, they must be fed with a potent message tailored specifically for them.

That is exactly why this work is not some attempt at race relations. I actually believe the idea of "race relations" is a backward undertaking that is counterproductive to pursue. The idea of "relations" is something that presupposes equality between those parties relating. As if both parties are equally open to dialogue and listening to concerns from the other party and possibly making changes or agreements based on said discussion. This is nowhere near the reality for America between black and white. Black people have been victimized by the American system since its inception. The only group that has received worse treatment than blacks in America are our indigenous native brothers and sisters. European migration to the Americas has meant almost complete annihilation of indigenous peoples, cultures, and languages. In what is now called the United States of America, native populations have been completely marginalized and victimized to levels of epic proportions.

The black struggle for liberation will forever be in solidarity with native peoples because their oppressor is our oppressor. The main difference between our experiences is that blacks have been thoroughly oppressed within the system of America, while the Indigenous peoples have been kept on the boundaries of American political and social life but have been exploited and oppressed all the same. Native Americans were not considered part of the United States of America until the early 1900s. Black people have been considered part of the U.S. as property, beasts of burden, and beings with no political rights since the beginning of the colonial era, and we've been forced to exist within the system ever since.

And it is precisely for this reason that race relations is such an idiotic endeavor in my opinion. My freedom, equality, dignity, and human rights in my society are not a matter of round table discussion for white overseers to ruminate over. I do not need to negotiate for your intellectual approval of what is rightfully mine and my people's. My people and I, like anyone else in "civilized" society, have a right to exercise our freedoms, and that is a fact that is not dependent upon anyone else. I am not a fan of simple dualistic binaries, but White America and those who ally with the privileges of White America are either actively working to make full freedom and equality for blacks and all oppressed groups a reality, or they're on the wrong side.

Black freedom and equality is a must, and you either recognize that and work toward making that a reality, or you're in the way, simply another obstacle for us to maneuver through as we work to manifest our liberty, dignity, and freedom by any means necessary. Hence, no need or reason for "race relations" conversations; the time for talking has passed. We've talked and petitioned for almost 400 years; it is beyond the time for action now. Please note that any who choose to ally with our movement and who honestly wish to work to help make freedom and equality for all a reality can join at anytime. For those who wish to stand on the wrong side of history and cling to an immoral and unethical system, be forewarned that you will be seeing us shortly, and there are some who hope you do not move out of the way when we come to take what is rightfully ours.

Understanding Racism

Many attempts have been made to qualify racism, but most definitions are terribly inadequate. The main reason for this inadequacy is because this entire conversation is taking place in what can be called, "the language of the colonizer." This is borrowing a concept from Frantz Fanon, who spoke at length about the experience of a people being colonized by an outside force. To paraphrase Fanon, colonization can be more than just physical. We often think of borders, personal liberty, and resources, or things that are tangible being taken when discussing colonization, but colonization can be mental as well. In the example of Native Americans in what is now known as the United States of America, despite their best resistance efforts, some groups were so thoroughly colonized that they were forced to no longer practice their native religions. For other indigenous peoples, the colonization was so extensive that people were prevented from speaking their native languages and using their native names.

These are all markers of mental colonization. Africans who were brought here to the Americas as slaves experienced a similar mental colonization. They were prevented from speaking their native languages and practicing their original religions, and were forced to accept various forms of Christianity, which were used to justify their subservient position. The mental colonization effort was so thorough that laws were passed making it illegal for blacks to learn to read and write, in essence, forcing them to remain in a state of ignorance that would make them "easier" to control. When you are unable to educate yourself independent of the power structure, you are forced to accept the reasons and meanings the system gives to you via its word symbols.

Language

We'll briefly examine language in the abstract. What is language? How does it work? Language is arguably the greatest tool that human beings have to use. Historians and archeologists use written language as one of the markers signifying the "birth of civilization." Language allows us to pass information from one person to another. It has allowed humans to make meaning out of our experience in life. We can do that with verbal symbols (spoken words), written symbols (written words), and nonverbal communication (sign language or other forms of nonverbal communication). When one has access to a language, they are able to use that language to convey meaning and develop understanding through the lens of that language.

Not all languages are created equally. Some languages have hundreds of thousands of words and others a few hundred. Each word gives you a window to explore and understand the world. That window comes with a context that is embedded in the language that can enhance or limit the scope of experience one can have in the world. This is something people who have learned a language outside of their native tongue can attest to because they'll find that some words do not translate into other languages or certain languages do not have words for certain experiences.

Who defines these words? People do, and at times modern people do because language is constantly evolving. We create meaning and new words all the time, be they slang, or terms that are influenced by social media and technology, or pop culture references. Thus, language is alive and evolves over time. Most of us inherited our language from our ancestors. It is something that is passed on to us, and in that process of receiving language, we also receive meaning for the symbols given to us. That meaning is reinforced in our home life and our outside world. Quick note, English is the language spoken by the most nonnative speakers, which is a direct result of the colonization efforts by the English. They exported their language and culture all throughout the world. Hence my non-English self is able to write this book in English, and you are able to read it even though most of us are English speakers by force and not by birthright of being born English in

England. We are all by-products of their colonization, and the language we speak, think, and write in is one of the lasting artifacts of that colonization.

English was superimposed on global populations, and it included a particular view of the world. One of the core values of that English cultural worldview became the supremacy of English people over all other groups of people. Their false reading of events in the world led them to believe they were the most "civilized" of all the nations. Their language began to reflect this cultural arrogance, and we still can witness it in the English language to this day. Case in point, examine the definitions for the words white and black. It is no mere coincidence that the people who felt they were the best of all people defined a word that is used to describe their skin color with all the positive attributes they could pile into the word.

The Merriam-Webster Dictionary defines the words white and black as follows:

"White -

    a. (1): free from moral impurity innocent (2): marked by the wearing of white by the woman as a symbol of purity <a white wedding>

    b. not intended to cause harm <a white lie> <white magic>

d: favorable, fortunate <one of the white days of his life— Sir Walter Scott>

Black -

    4. dirty, soiled <hands black with grime>

      a. thoroughly sinister or evil: wicked <a black deed>
      b. indicative of condemnation or discredit <got a black mark for being late>

7. connected with or invoking the supernatural and especially the devil \<black magic\>
8.
   a. very sad, gloomy, or calamitous \<black despair\>
   b. marked by the occurrence of disaster \<black Friday\>
9. characterized by hostility or angry discontent: sullen \<black resentment filled his heart\>

11
   a. of propaganda: conducted so as to appear to originate within an enemy country and designed to weaken enemy morale
   b. characterized by or connected with the use of black propaganda \<black radio\>
12. characterized by grim, distorted, or grotesque satire \<black humor\>
13. of or relating to covert intelligence operations \<black government programs\>"

These definitions are not figments of my imagination; I did not make them up, they are "real" definitions in a popular English dictionary. To be fair, English is not the only language that attaches meaning to colors, but the Europeans via Johann Blumenbach and other pseudo-scientists began to equate skin color with position in social hierarchy. According to Blumenbach and his pseudo-scientific observations, white skin was the highest and black skin was the lowest in terms of social hierarchy in the eighteenth and nineteenth centuries. Other "respected" voices of the scientific community chimed in, and coincidently the dictionary definitions began to parallel the "educated" judgments of the day. These definitions are very telling; one can clearly see the positive definitions assigned to the word white in stark contrast to the word black. White carries meanings of purity, favor, innocence, and good fortune. These definitions are completely arbitrary, subjective, and baseless, but the English people believed them to be true and assigned them to the color that defined them. Thinking of the claims of their definitions critically, we quickly find there is no empirical data to suggest white is pure. White in terms of science is a color produced by combining all of the color frequencies. This scientific fact in no way connotes purity, goodness, favor, or fortune. That is a completely subjective conclusion based on societal biases, or as we might say on the street, "That's that BS!"

Conversely, a black anything is almost always negative. Black carries meanings of dirty, sinister, evil, deserving condemnation, devilish, gloomy, hostility, anger, and other pejoratives. In fact, there is really only one positive connotation associated with black in the English language and that is in the financial context. Being in the black is being profitable. This supposedly comes from accountants who would note positive financial gains in black ink. That is why it is always better to be in the black than the red. Critically examining the English claim to defining black with such pejoratives leads one to see there is no scientific or objective reason to correlate black with negative, but there it is, in English, in black and white.

The impact of this type of bias in the construction of their language is not benign. What do you think this can do to a people who are identified in their society as white or as black? If all the meanings associated with how you are described are positive or negative, it will have an effect. Dr. Kenneth B. Clark conducted his famous Doll Test in the 1930s on young children and found that black kids believed that black dolls when compared with identical white dolls were evil, ugly, or bad because of the difference in skin color. There are multiple factors that contribute to what Clark found in his tests, but one thing that definitely contributes is the language that frames the understanding of the society those kids lived in.

When you analyze the recent spate of whites, especially cops not being indicted for the killing of black bodies, the power in these definitions may provide some insight. White is innocent, pure, and without harm or ill intent; it's free of moral impurity. Black is evil, connected with the devil, is dirty; it is indicative of condemnation. Maybe this linguistic context has something to do with juries finding it difficult to convict white men or white officers, or grand juries failing to find reasons to indict white cops who kill black bodies. White man or white cop can be understood through definition as man without ill intent or a cop who is innocent, and black person could be understood through definition as person who is dirty, evil, angry, hostile, or discontent. How does a black person find justice when the very language used to describe them frames their existence with guilt and evil?

The colonization effort went way beyond stealing our native languages and vilifying black bodies in the words they speak. It's also present in what we eat, where we stay, what we see, learn, and believe. Religiously, Western society has colonized the mind and soul of black folks. The most popular image of God in Western society is a white man. How is it that Jesus, who tradition tells us was born in the Middle East and was Jewish, can be drawn with no noticeable Jewish or Middle Eastern features and instead looks like he was born in Scandinavia? It doesn't stop there. At times, the West will take gods of other cultures and turn them white. Hollywood just finished white-washing ancient Egyptian gods in the film *Gods of Egypt*. For black people, even the "sacred" space of religion isn't immune to color-politics, and blacks are told on a daily basis that "God" does not look like them. That's only possible in a world where people are redefining their reality. They are actively shaping language, symbols, and religious imagery to their benefit and to our detriment.

Many of us do not question the symbols we've inherited, but these symbols are not innocent; they are powerful and must be confronted when they are destructive to one's mental, physical, and spiritual well-being. Fanon alluded to this when he articulated his points on the language of the colonizer. All of this has to be said because I'm writing to you in English, which is my native tongue by conqueror. This is not the language I would have received from my ancestors had certain historical events played out differently.

English as a language is full of meanings that can be confusing when delving into social and political topics. This is something that we have already seen; English is a language that carries deep bias with no empirical foundation for justifying that bias. Even though I have studied other languages, I am still left with discussing the trials and tribulations of my people in the language of those we were colonized by. The power to name and define is immense; you literally have the ability to say what is and what is not. With that in mind, the civilization that perfected the system of racism that is prevalent in almost every corner of the world today might not be the best "authoritative" or "unbiased" source for defining racism. Just like the civilization that thought it was the best of all people on the planet probably wouldn't be the best source to seek out if you want to know about the greatness of black people or other civilizations.

If we acknowledge all of these implicit and explicit biases in the English language, then how can we fully explore a topic such as racism while using the terms and the definitions of the oppressor? It is my belief that racism from the lens of the perpetrator is going to be explained away and justified in a fashion that won't demonize the perpetrator. Just like a "white lie" or "white magic" is intended to cause no harm, racism perpetrated by whites is going to be defined in a way to minimize the harm. This is exactly what we see when trying to analyze racism as a word symbol from the hands of those perpetrating racism. Racism gets defined in such a way that the inherent evil and pernicious nature of the system is neutralized. What does this do? It causes confusion, and it victimizes those who are the victims of racism over and over again, while exonerating, through obfuscation, those who are responsible for it.

To prove this point let's examine some definitions. Merriam-Webster's online definition of racism states:

"poor treatment of or violence against people because of their race"
"the belief that some races of people are better than others"

Let us examine the second definition, the belief that some races of people are better than others. If racism were simply a belief, we'd all be fine. There would be no need for this extended discussion. Racism, if it were simply a belief, would essentially be a moot point. People are free to believe whatever they choose to believe, and freedom of belief should be protected. You might believe your favorite team is the best team ever assembled to play their sport. With all due respect to your belief, your belief in your team's superiority does not guarantee their victory. Win or lose, you are still entitled to hold onto that belief for as long as you want. Another related example is in the world of religion. People believe many different things due to their religious preferences. Some religions claim certain groups of people are slated for eternal damnation. Others believe in no afterlife, or that you can only find salvation or release through a certain set of principles. Regardless of the faith orientation, another person's belief does not detract from your way of life. Their personal belief alone does not prevent you from having a job or a family, or from obtaining an education. Your quality of life remains intact regardless of the personal beliefs of others. We even have a term in modern slang for people who believe false things about you or want to see you lose; we call them "haters." Haters can hate on you all they want, but that doesn't mean that you won't be able to shine. They can attempt to throw "shade" in your direction, but you are still going to do you. This is why belief in and of itself is not the problem. What is a problem though, is the fact that the people at Merriam-Webster's haven't the slightest idea of what racism is and are in the business of passing out false definitions to people. Someone needs to tell them that they are guilty of obfuscation, which can be defined as making things harder to understand or unintelligible.

Merriam-Webster's is not the only major English dictionary guilty of this very thing. The Oxford English Dictionary, which claims to be the most-accurate English dictionary ever produced, has committed the same offenses.

The Oxford English Dictionary states:

"Racism: Prejudice, discrimination, or antagonism directed against someone of a different race based on the belief that one's own race is superior."

Here we have the mention of discrimination that is somewhat similar to the poor treatment that was part of the Merriam-Webster's definition. One common point between both definitions is the mention of racism being tied to belief in superiority. Sadly, we see obfuscation again because this is not racism. Discrimination is an issue, but if a person discriminates against me because they think they are superior, that doesn't really detract from my quality of life. Maybe a person chooses to call me a nigger. Or maybe they attempt to insult me using some other racial epithet. This is very common, but before, during, and after the epithet, I still have a job and I still have my life and all things that matter to me. And it is possible that the person who used the epithet might be more in danger because they are now at risk of losing life or limb by attempting to insult me.

The quality of life piece is very important because we will all encounter people who might not like us for whatever reason, but if you can still take care of your family and live a fairly decent life, then you're actually in a good place. Sure, the discrimination or hate is certainly unwanted and unmerited, but it can be neutralized and then life goes on. That type of discrimination could result in some loss; I might not have too many white friends or friends who espouse similar discriminatory/prejudicial opinions, but if they held those opinions about me or my people, I wouldn't want them in my circle of friends anyway. The discrimination is an unwanted inconvenience, but personal discrimination doesn't result in loss of life or major changes to quality of life.

What both of those definitions are missing is the sole most important piece when discussing racism, and that is power. Discrimination and prejudice become problematic when they are paired with power and authority. When a government, state, or society discriminates against a group of people through institutional means in a way that impacts the quality of life of people in said group, you are now beginning to examine the underpinnings of racism. Discrimination/prejudice articulated and exercised through directed state power evolves into racism that restricts the quality of life of the targeted group. This is what these definitions need to say and are clearly lacking.

Why is it that these definitions perpetuate obfuscation instead of truly defining the problem accurately? Why am I so easily able to refute the feeble claims of these meaning-making institutions? In my opinion, the answer as to why they are lacking an objective and thorough understanding is because a true definition of racism is counterproductive to Western society. They have no need to author a real critical definition of something that they continue to profit from, especially because they hold the power of defining their language. There is nothing holding Western society accountable for its racist practices, so therefore there is no reason for it to critically analyze and correctly define its racism.

To further debunk the gross inadequacies of these definitions, we'll deal with the concept of "superiority." Both definitions cited superiority as one of the major components of racism. Believing in one's superiority does not create institutional discrepancies. Furthermore, belief in superiority doesn't account for the staggering disproportionate statistics surrounding black incarceration, poverty, and other areas where racism rears its ugly head. Belief in superiority does not explain why crack cocaine related offenses receive much harsher penalties than powder cocaine offenses, even though they are the same drug in different forms. Belief in superiority doesn't explain why poor underfunded schools are found all throughout black communities, and it doesn't explain the process of redlining that 'legally" forced blacks to live in certain parts of cities. Each one of these previous examples is the result of some deliberate action taken by people who hold the reins of power. This is why racism is more than a belief and more than the idea of racial superiority. One can believe they are better than someone else; that belief does not directly lead to a system where the person who falsely believes they are superior will always have more than the one who is believed to be inferior.

I can believe I am the most superior basketball player alive. That belief does not change the fact that Steph Curry is the greatest player on the planet at this moment. I can believe that as much as I want, but the reality is he is that dude. But if I used my institutional power in conjunction with a belief to create a system that reinforced my belief that I was better than Curry, all the while limiting opportunities for him to showcase his talent, then we begin examining the basics of a system of discrimination. In the event that he is able to showcase his talent, I'll then use my resources to tell him that his talent is worthless and that actually my talent is still more valuable. Then we're beginning to approach what a total system of institutional discrimination looks like.

Why is it that the definitions of racism we use in English don't even venture near a correct understanding of the phenomenon of racism? In my opinion, it is because these definitions are created by the society guilty of racism, and that society is not interested in holding up a mirror to itself to account for the atrocities it has committed. Instead of objective analysis, society elects to blur the understanding to avoid the truth. Defining racism accurately in English is akin to a rapist defining what constitutes rape or the equally absurd reality of police officers policing themselves regarding miscarriages of justice. Somehow officers keep finding a way to explain away the actions of their colleagues and friends as justified. The general public can see an unarmed black person who posed no threat being illegally executed, but somehow when police analyze the actions of their officers, that black person becomes "life threatening" and the extermination of that black life is deemed justifiable. In the context of racism, it is the perpetrators of racism and the language that gives meaning to their society defining racism. The racist defining the racist or policing the racist. Just like the rapist would most likely justify his or her actions, the police often find no violations in police misconduct investigations. The system of racism is equipped with this mechanism that allows itself to not see racism in its institutional practices. This is what the Western world looks like when it continuously defines racism in a way to limit its culpability.

So many of us do not arrive at this level of understanding because we are so thoroughly wrapped up in the narrative provided by our society. The confusion and misdirection is a full-time, full-scale operation. Black people have to be aware of the fact that the social tools, words, and symbols that we use within our societies can actually be harmful to our self-development. Likewise, using Western definitions of racism will have you confused as to what the real problem is. How can you successfully deal with and possibly fight against something if you don't even know how to define it properly? Many people will say they know what it feels like when they are a victim of racism, but developing a strategy to combat racism will require an understanding of the rules of the system, according to the great work by Sun Tzu, *The Art of War*.

"It is said that if you know your enemies and know yourself, you will not be imperiled in a hundred battles; if you do not know your enemies but do know yourself, you will win one and lose one; if you do not know your enemies nor yourself, you will be imperiled in every single battle."

If you place any value in this ancient text on stratagems of war, then you'll see the importance of not only knowing your enemy but also of knowing yourself. Sun Tzu cites both as imperative if you want to guarantee victory for yourself. How can you understand the system of racism that is your enemy when it's not defined correctly? How can you truly know yourself if you only understand yourself through the lens of the system that has colonized and oppressed you? Not knowing your enemy or yourself relegates you to that third category in Sun Tzu's example, the one who never wins. If we are not careful, we will not be able to see that racism is so imbedded in our culture that people are violated in the very words that come out of their mouths. Furthermore, this society does not equip us with education and tools to accurately know ourselves, leaving us violated in that sense, too. These are the people who, according to Sun Tzu, are destined to lose in every battle.

Real Definition of Racism

If you are interested in a more accurate definition of racism, then you must go to the good doctor. I defer to the definition by Dr. Frances Cress Welsing, who in *The Isis Papers: The Keys to the Colors* puts forth the best definition of racism I've ever studied. For those unfamiliar with Cress Welsing, she was a psychiatrist who specialized in creating a framework for combating white supremacy. She is famous for her work in this field and her other published works. Her two most popular publications are *The Cress Theory of Color Confrontation and Racism* and *The Isis Papers*.

According to the good doctor: "RACISM (white supremacy), is the local and global power system and dynamic, structured and maintained by persons who classify themselves as white, whether consciously or subconsciously determined, which consists of patterns of perception, logic, symbol formation, thought, speech, action and emotional response, as conducted simultaneously in all areas of people activity (economics, education, entertainment, labor, law, politics, religion, sex and war); for the ultimate purpose of white genetic survival and to prevent white genetic annihilation on planet earth – a planet upon which the vast majority of people are classified as non-white (black, brown, red and yellow) by white skinned people, and all of the nonwhite people are genetically dominant (in terms of skin coloration) compared to the genetic recessive white skin people."

This is what the Merriam-Webster Dictionary and Oxford English Dictionary are for some reason reluctant to or unable to say. This definition allows one to fully see the extent of the racial apparatus at work in America and globally. This definition also demonstrates that racism is not a one-to-one matter, which is a common misnomer. Yes, a person can engage in racist activity, but racism, i.e. a system based on race, is only possible through systemic power. To state it another way, racism is the systematic empowerment, and the institutional advancement of one group over the systematic/institutional degradation and disenfranchisement of another group in all areas of human interaction or "people activity."

Any attempt at providing a solution to the problem of racism will have to address and work to dismantle the institution of race as a whole. The problem our society faces is daunting because racism is deeply entrenched within the bone marrow of America and the larger Western world. The corrective procedure to remove what can be considered the social terminal cancer of racism from our society will be highly invasive, and it is possible that America might not survive the operation.

In the light of the doctor's definition, the concept of "race relations" in no way is a prescription for removing this malignancy that has caused so much death and destruction over the past four centuries. I have had close family members and friends face cancer. Imagine a doctor advising healthy dialogue as the way to best treat the cancer. It's preposterous, and it demonstrates a clear failure on the part of our society to grasp the immensity of the problem we face. Some may still argue that you can't change the system without conversation. It is a good point, but an even better counter is the fact that there is no liberation struggle that has been successful via petitioning the oppressors for freedom in the form of conversation/race relations. None!

Never in the history of human beings has power abdicated as a result of conversation, especially in the recent history of the Columbus era and Industrial Age. Appealing to the moral center of an oppressor who rules while ignoring morals has not once resulted in a change of direction by the oppressing group. Those struggles that have found their way to being liberated most often treaded a path paved with blood and bone or some other form of organized protest movement that dealt major social/political/economic blows to their oppressors.

Once "liberated," there's no guarantee that liberation will lead to freedom. There's a long list of examples of peoples and countries that have fought for independence but are still controlled by, or at least heavily influenced by, outside Western forces. Still, the point remains; to even arrive at a place where political "freedom" or "independence" was a reality, it took the power of the people through military force or concentrated protest movement, and not dialogue, to lead to the changes. Let those who wish to race relate do so. I stand firmly with those who seek to mobilize and take direct action to manifest freedom and liberty for their people. This body of work is a contribution to that effort.

Black Boy Poems is not an appeal to the intellect to solve the problem. It's not an appeal to the good nature in every man, woman and child. *Black Boy Poems* is a reflection of my firm belief that concentrated force, which can manifest in multiple ways, is the only way to combat those who profit and benefit from a system of white supremacy and force them to relinquish the *accoutrements* they receive. Racism is not about belief in superiority of white people over all else—that belief does exist and contributes to the perpetuation of the system—but most importantly racism is about wealth, power, and access to resources, and the transference of all of the above to a people's offspring. Those who have developed the system have acquired huge amounts of wealth, power, and resources, which they will not voluntarily give away until a powerful force either strips them of the above or compels them to change.

Freedom Fighter versus Career Race Relations Expert and Allies

A phenomenon I feel I've witnessed in the world of "race relations" is the emergence of specific personality types who have either self-selected or through some other means have been "appointed" to a position of spokespersons on all things race related. I see them as wannabe race-relations experts and out-of-position allies. Both can become problematic because they turn the issue of race into an opportunity for profiting off the very real pain and suffering of black people and other people of color. The Western world, via "free market" capitalism, has found a way to create industry out of just about anything. The social reality of race is no exception. The industrialization of race has led to the development of personas that are able to make a living off of race in America.

In the colonial era or Jim Crow South, North, East, and West, there was no career in race politics. State-sponsored racial domination was the rule of the land. If you resisted the system, you faced consequences, mainly death. This was the reality of revolutionaries and freedom fighters before race became a career path. Not too many people want to make a career out of something where death is a potential reality. There were people discussing abolition or enfranchisement and rights for blacks, but you could not make a career out of race politics in colonial or Jim Crow America without having a price on your head. The people who did find a way to profit off of the racial dynamics that existed during the colonial, constitutional slavery or Jim Crow eras were blacks who helped support the system that enslaved blacks. It was possible to fetch a pretty penny as a slave catcher, or if you snitched on a plot to kill the slave master, or helped squash an uprising, or told on some escaped slaves. If you endeavored to preserve the white status quo, then the system might confer favor upon you and give you a little something for your troubles.

Immediately after the end of the Civil War, the Freedmen's Bureau began to lay foundations for the rise of black institutions of higher learning. Not all of Black America was uneducated; there were a substantial number of educated blacks prior to Reconstruction, but most black people were enslaved and for them education was illegal and therefore hard to come by. The rise of public schools, colleges, and universities for blacks led to the development of black academics. Some of them began to set their sights upon the fundamental problems facing blacks in America, including institutional racism. That is one of the truly liberating things about knowledge. Once blacks in masses began to master letters, theory, philosophy, and numbers, they began to use these new weapons to take shots at the system that oppressed them. Names like W. E. B. Du Bois, Booker T. Washington, Mary McLeod Bethune, Ida B. Wells, Anna Julia Cooper, and many others whom history hasn't remembered with similar acclaim, labored to improve the condition of Black America. Not all agreed on their strategies for facing the problems blacks experienced in America, but each one knew that their stand against white supremacy could cost them their lives. With that knowledge, they did not approach their work as a "career" for the sake of a paycheck. The advancement of a people was the reward, and to the descendants of slaves, that was worth the ultimate sacrifice.

That context is important to establish because we are now living in an age where race politics has been monetized and commodified. It is "cool" to be against the system. There are examples of people who have parlayed their fame and notoriety from being a "revolutionary" into a lucrative financial opportunity. I'm not hating; we all have to survive, but freedom fighting does not come with a promise of fame and fortune. Dr. Huey P. Newton mentioned in his autobiography how he received a letter from a Hollywood studio after he was released from prison. The studio wanted Huey to use his "star power" for the sake of selling Hollywood TV shows and movies. Huey could've made that decision and capitalized on his fame for the sake of fortune, but the "servant of the people" was more focused on revolution for the sake of liberating his people.

In today's world, it is quite possible to live fairly well being a race commentator. Write a few books, do some show appearances, secure speaking engagements, participate in some demonstrations from time to time, maybe even have a university position as a lecturer. If you do all that, you might be able to enjoy a comfortable existence by material standards.

I'm trying to be cognizant of not making sweeping statements of certain personalities in the main. I do not want to paint with a broad brush because it prevents you from tending to the nuances and finer details. To be clear, I am not saying all who are race scholars, commentators, and authors are not helping to fight for the liberation and independence of Black People. It is foolish to make such a blanket claim. It is possible to occupy a space in academia and the media, as well as in the field, working to bring about change. Academia, media celebrity, and tangible movement work are not mutually exclusive.

There are a number of examples of people who push the academic envelope and have a foot in the street, fighting the good fight. The movement is made better by their contributions. However, there are some who have no real action behind their words at all. They occupy no tangible space in the movement unless there is a chance for a photo-op or some other advantageous move to boost their visibility. They are skillfully able to exploit movements for their own personal gain. They might contribute as a critical voice or simply echo what the establishment wants to hear. Either way, they are able to profit off of the social discord present in our society.

This new realm that accompanies race in America should make one question whether these people are sincerely and genuinely interested in a solution, or if they are more focused on their status and paycheck. In searching for an analogy to this phenomenon, I've come across several that I feel warrant the same type of questioning. When examining the privatized American health care system, one has to question whether the industry is genuinely interested in health of patients or maintaining a system whereby bodies keep moving in and out of hospitals for high premiums. Does the health care system really want to see all Americans happy and healthy? Related to and equally deserving of question is the pharmaceutical industry. Does it really concern itself with curing customers' conditions, or is it more interested in a revolving consumer base that grows more and more dependent on high-priced drug treatments? The shareholders for major pharmaceutical companies want to see big profits every quarter; they are hoping their drugs fly off the shelves, which means people are in need of those drugs. Regular people are not in the habit of collecting medicines like memorabilia; they either develop a habit that makes them dependent on drugs or are prescribed them by their doctors and physicians. Is it really about health and cures, or is it about consumption?

Similar questions should be asked of military contractors and gun manufacturers. Their business is war and death. Are the gun manufacturers at all concerned about the more than 400,000 Americans killed due to gun violence since 9/11, according to numbers from the Centers for Disease Control and Prevention? War and fear are very profitable. Are these institutions of death concerned about the blood on their hands or is their financial bottom line more important? The Prison Industrial Complex (PIC) deserves questioning as well. Is the PIC really about rehabilitation and ending incarceration, or is it about warehousing majority black and brown bodies for profit? One must wonder.

This is what can happen when industry is built around a thing. I am not claiming those who exploit what has become the industry of race politics have the same blood on their hands as weapons contractors or the PIC does, but the commonality in all of the previous examples is the pursuit of profit that can potentially blind the industry to the moral and ethical implications of their work. Race politics in the modern world has become an industry. That is something that has to be acknowledged. We have our celebrities and "professionals" who are called upon anytime something erupts in America that is race related. People get their airtime. They get a chance to plug their books and most recent articles. It really makes you question if these people are genuinely interested in seeing an end to what is putting money in their pockets, food on their plates, and fame behind their name. Some may even probe deeper with the question and examine who has been granted a voice in the world of "race relations" and why. Certain voices don't exist anymore; they are either dead or in prison, and other voices loudly and proudly ring out. History has clearly shown us that there is a price to pay for true liberation work, not a check to be made and fame to be had, but that's for an entirely different discussion.

Allies

In the work of movement building, it is important for people involved to understand their role and play that role to the best of their ability. It almost seems a moot point to explain, but any organized effort can be ruined by an ineffective approach stemming from mismanagement of resources. A brief historical analysis of liberation struggles will show you the importance of organization and structure. Not all are arranged using the same hierarchical structure, but organized movements need clear delineations for efficiency's sake. In the American context, the movement/struggle for freedom has always been structured. Slave rebellions, the abolitionist struggle, and resistance to Jim Crow all had an organized base. Any study of the Underground Railroad will reveal it was a complex web of people and places conspiring together to help smuggle black bodies to freedom. Leadership was integral to the success of the movement, and people were conferred the title conductor, which illustrated their position as one who helped steer people to freedom. The NAACP, Universal Negro Improvement Association, various factions of the civil rights movement like the Southern Christian Leadership Conference and the Student Nonviolent Coordinating Committee, or the Nation of Islam, and the Black Panther Party for Self Defense, and even organizations such as the Crips, Bloods, Vice Lords, and Gangster Disciples, all have well-defined leadership structures. There is no way to ignore the fact that leadership and structure is crucial in any organized effort.

Although different, they each possessed a process for becoming part of an organization and a period of acculturation to learn the ways of the movement. Once you become part of an organization, you have to learn your role in it. There is also a mechanism in place for dealing with people who intentionally or unintentionally attempt to represent the movement without going through the prerequisite training. The modern world has, via the Internet and specifically social media, introduced a wrinkle into this praxis because people are able to garner attention and espouse critical viewpoints that are reflective of a struggle without being plugged into a particular outlet of the movement.

Their fame or status can make them feel entitled to a position of leadership or importance in the struggle even though they haven't paid their dues or gone through the necessary training that in a traditional sense would allow them a role in the movement. Not everybody can lead; not everybody should be looked at as a mouthpiece of the struggle either. All must work for the common good of the movement, but not all perform the same work.

My writing this book is not a claim to be a leader. I play my role, whatever that may be, in the struggle. If I am called upon to lead, then I hope and pray that I join the ranks of those in a position of leadership who have led with wisdom and humility. If I am to follow, then I hope and pray that I follow and execute whatever tasks are mine. Most importantly I hope to work to establish a foundation ensuring that the next generation will eventually be able to take up the struggle and keep the movement alive for as long as it is needed.

These next few passages are designed to address issues that occur at times with folks who are allies. An ally is someone who is not of the community directly affected by institutional discrimination but wishes to work with the community to help them find solutions to their problems. Some allies find themselves out of position. Many of us are familiar with the term white ally, people who are white who wish to assist in the movement for black liberation. But we have other allies as well who are not white who sometimes violate their position.

Examples of allies who assisted in the black liberation struggle with a level of excellence are names like John Brown, who gave his life and the lives of his sons for the abolition of slavery. He never attempted to co-opt or appropriate the movement. He found a way to work within the boundaries of the movement by using his white privilege to enhance the struggle and died a heroic death. Another example is Grace Lee Boggs, who worked tirelessly in various movements, especially the black liberation movement throughout the twentieth and the early part of the twenty-first century. She was of Chinese descent but loved and lived for the struggle of oppressed people worldwide. She was an instrumental figure in the black liberation movement and a looming presence throughout the Detroit area.

A woman who I was blessed to meet who was an incredible ambassador and ally is Yuri Kochiyama. Kochiyama was a Japanese-American activist who dedicated her entire life to liberation movements. She organized in the Japanese community combating Japanese internment and other political and social issues her community faced. She also supported other struggles for freedom and independence outside of her community. She shared the same birthdate as Malcolm X and became a member of Malcolm's organization, the Organization of Afro-American Unity (OAAU). Kochiyama was present on the day he was assassinated and was one of the first people to rush to his side after he was shot. She later became involved with the Black Panther Party for Self Defense, continuing her commitment to liberation struggles. She served as an important figure in multiple struggles within and outside of her ethnic community.

These are examples of allies. Due to their proven commitment, at times their role may have been to lead, but they always worked within the context of the movement. In today's world, a voice who I would say is representative of the term ally is Tim Wise. He's a scholar who is described as an anti-racism activist. He's written several books on various aspects of racism and white privilege, and he tours widely educating predominantly white audiences on the realities of the oppressiveness of the American racist apparatus. He pulls no punches in explaining white supremacy and white privilege and has a very matter-of-fact approach to debunking the colorblind American hero narrative that is pervasive in American society today. He has a very powerful voice and uses it to support the movement. This merits him ally status.

If you are not familiar with any of these previous examples, then you need to be. All found their role in the movements that they were assisting and performed their duties to the best of their ability, but most importantly they did not attempt to co-opt the movement and in the process silence the black voice of the movement. They worked in conjunction with the movement to enhance the struggle and not to put themselves at the forefront of a struggle that belongs to another people.

It is important to understand allies who have worked to enhance the movement to be able to understand allies who make contributions that, at times, detract from the movements they claim to serve. All examples above were allies who played their position effectively and efficiently. Allies who are out of position do the exact opposite. They might place themselves in positions of leadership in a movement that is not theirs or find ways to occupy space that should be held by a black voice and attempt to advocate the direction, wants, and needs of a struggle that is not their own. This is a message to the "allies" who wish to assist in the liberation struggle. In an age where cultural appropriation is at an all-time high, it is important for black people to not allow allies to appropriate our struggle. We have precedent for allies who worked with us in the struggle, and we hold to that tradition; these other folks who are out here out of position need to be "gently" reminded as to how they can best assist our struggle, and that is not by exploiting it for their own personal gain.

Problems with Allies in the Modern World

Dear Allies, be you white or some other color, your desire to support our movement is appreciated, but it is important for you to know that you are not and will never be leaders of our struggle. Throughout history, there are far too many instances where the black voice was marginalized or deliberately muted. You cannot support liberation of black people if you contribute to the silencing of black voices. You cannot be the voice of our people or our struggle. That should be a given, but just in case it is not, then it needs to be said. Maybe nobody has told you that before, so let me be the first to do so. As an ally you play a role. At times it is an important role, but you are never to lead. You may stand with us on the front lines but always in the capacity of a support role. We are the ones who bear the full brunt of this racism and oppression. You have the privilege to walk away from our struggle at any time and go back to your regular life. We are the ones whose ancestors have been striving for generations to find their way to freedom, and whether or not we fight, we are still affected by the racism and institutional discrimination of America. You on the other hand, depending on what type of privilege you have in society, still benefit from the institutional discrimination. This is our fight. We do not need you to speak for us or on our behalf. We are more than capable of articulating the direction of our movement on our own. We've been doing so for hundreds of years without you. You are not our saviors, and you will not save us. You can be an important asset to the struggle if you are willing to support it in ways that are most effective.

What you need to do, if you wish to assist black people in their struggle for freedom and liberation, is first, listen and learn from those around you. Second, recognize that your role is ancillary; you provide support and play your part when your role is required. Third, know that if you are interested in fame and status, this not the place for you.

Our struggle is not something to build your resume up with or to be used as a stepping stone to bigger and better career goals. In our struggle, you will never have a starring role. It will be more the role of a support actor or an extra. If hearing this does not appeal to your aspirations for getting involved in the movement, then feel free to walk away now. Our struggle most likely didn't need your support in the first place. Fourth, being on the front lines with us is important and needed, but your greatest utility will be served in your own community, actively working to organize members of your community to assist in the struggle and, most importantly, mobilizing them to deconstruct the pillars of white supremacy or other forms of ethnic/cultural supremacy that affect blacks. That is a major contribution you all can make. And there are some great white allies and other allies as well. They know their place in the movement and play their role to perfection. I send out much love and respect to those who occupy that space.

Note: This is not directed solely at white people or white allies. There are quite a few allies from other backgrounds who think they are entitled to positions of leadership in the black struggle. It doesn't matter who you are or where you come from, if you're not black, then you have no position of leadership in our struggle. It doesn't matter if you've married into the black/African diaspora, been raised by black folks, or identify with black culture. You do not have any ownership over our struggle. You are not us; therefore, this is not about you. The struggle is for black lives and freedom. This is about black people. If you support, then you support under our leadership and direction, and offer your skills and expertise within the confines of our movement.

There are some voices out there that hijack the black struggle for their own personal gain. That's a violation of everything necessary for supporting the struggle. If you have ever committed one of these gross violations, then consider this your long overdue "Black Card" pulling moment. It's essential that this takes place for your sake and for the sake of what matters most, which is the liberation of black people and not your pocket or ego.

Do this simple exercise for me. Look in the mirror, look at your parents, and look at your upbringing; if all of those things tell you unequivocally that you are not a member of the black community, then you are not us and don't speak for us. In case there is some confusion, I'll explain a little further because there will be some who read these words and feel themselves exempt. Listening to hip-hop and being inspired by *The Autobiography of Malcolm X* or some other famous black literary work does not make you worthy of carrying the banner of the black liberation movement. I repeat, dating or marrying somebody who is of the black experience does not make you black by association and eligible to carry the banner of the black liberation movement. There is no blackness through osmosis or what Rachel Dolezal made a brief national debate in minds and hearts of people who carry privilege, "transracial." Black folks have tried for centuries to solve the problems they faced in America. If the solution was simply changing their "race" by declaring themselves a member of another race, then we would've solved all this generations ago. Black folks know all too well that we are black, and there is no changing that fact in America and the greater Western world. In light of the wisdom of the Godfather of comedy, Mr. Paul Mooney, we know that white folks and other non-blacks are all in for black culture and pretending to act black when it's convenient but none of them want to be black when it's time to face those black problems that black people deal with daily. With all that said, it doesn't matter what your orientation to the black community is, if you are not of us, then you are not us. And nothing that you can do or believe will change that fact.

So for my people out there who feel some deep connection to the black experience, it is cool to feel a connection, but you are not black and cannot and will not speak on behalf of black people on black matters. Best-case scenario, you are still an ally. The reality of that ally status needs to be confirmed upon a thorough vetting process to ensure said individual is authentically interested in black liberation and not cultural appropriation. If ally status is conferred to you, then report to your nearest black liberation organization and follow steps one through four which were laid out above.

Some of you still might not understand this is referring to you. I'll attempt to present a few scenarios where "allies" have violated their role and have attempted to lead when they needed to be following. If you've ever been a keynote speaker at an event discussing problems in the black community or African diaspora, and you're not black, then this is for you. If you've ever been in a position where you've been asked to speak on the black struggle and did not find issue with the fact that you instead of a person of the experience was speaking for the experience, then this is for you. If you've ever taken part in some action relating to the black struggle, and you are constantly trying to interject your voice into the discussion and not allowing those who live the experience to speak, then this is for you. Just like it wouldn't be proper for a man to attempt to be the voice of a feminist organization, the same is true for allies when it comes to the black experience. Or for a black man or woman attempting to speak on the liberation movement for the indigenous peoples of this land. That is their experience, and they are the leaders of that struggle. I can ally and support as much as they allow me to, but I should never attempt to put myself in a position that eclipses their voice.

Aspiring allies who find themselves out of bounds in this way are guilty of appropriating our struggle—exactly how Iggy Azalea has made her living via "cultural smudging" according to Azealia Banks. Banks went in hard on Ms. Iggy, whose claim to fame is doing a horrible black faced/black voiced interpretation of a southern female rapper. This woman is the farthest thing from black; she's a super-white Australian, accent and all. Azalea has exploited black culture to garner fame and wealth but shows no connection to the people and struggles of the people who created her path to short-lived fame. This Iggy Azalea-like cultural smudging happens in movement work as well. "Activists" can be found using the black struggle and culture of black liberation movements to forward their own agendas. These cultural smudging activists take up space that should be held by a competent black man or woman or true dedicated allies.

In 2015, we also saw another phenomenon in our communities of struggle. We have a few people running around the black struggle movement who are experiencing Dolezal syndrome. That statement is not meant to belittle Dolezal, but what she did was wrong. In the abstract, one can respect her active contribution to black liberation. She did put in time and work to better the condition of blacks in America. However, her contribution wasn't in the abstract; it was in a context of white supremacy and white privilege. She used her white privilege to become a crusader for black folks and eventually began to masquerade as one. That's the violation. Blackface is blackface; it doesn't matter whether you are putting on blackface for beneficial or harmful intentions. It is still blackface. The only real exemption would be for scientific reasons. A few researchers have attempted to darken their skin to live as a black person to publish their experiences with race in America.

Dolezal was not doing this for science. She black-faced herself to a position of leadership in a community that would've accepted her and her contributions as a white woman. They would've accepted her as a white woman who loved black people and culture and wanted to be surrounded by all of the above for the rest of her life. Instead, she falsely claimed to be black. In doing so, she used the privilege she has as a white woman to exploit the experience of black people. That's a huge problem. It is not to be excused because it was well intentioned. She could've accomplished much of what she aspired to achieve in the black liberation struggle as a white ally, but she co-opted, violated, and perpetrated one of the craziest blackface episodes witnessed in American history. There are others who are on their Dolezal, co-opting and taking up space where they are not needed or simply doing too much when they can perform similar tasks as an ally.

And this is one of the problems of movements in the modern world. Social media and technology make it easy to become a hashtag revolutionary. Our struggle at times is so thirsty for a voice that folks will listen to that we sometimes allow this to take place. This is dangerous because we know our movements have been infiltrated in the past by informants and government agents.

COINTELPRO was very real. The federal government has actively worked to prevent the rise of strong black liberation movements. We can't afford to be so naive and believe all folks who step up have our best interests in mind. We don't know these people, nor do we know where they came from. We can't trust their intentions. We must control the message and direction of our movement. With all sincerity, aspiring allies, you might have an audience, and when you speak people listen, and that is a great resource, but it does not entitle you to anything. If you thought this, then sadly you are ill informed. You are not of us, and therefore don't speak for us. It's a trip that black people seem to be one of the only, if not the only oppressed group that others feel they have a right to speak up for in advancement of their struggle. This is completely antithetical to anything that ever happened in the history of the black movement.

A very elementary lesson that can be learned from arguably the two most-celebrated figures of the black liberation movement in the twentieth century, Dr. King and Malcolm X, is they put work in. Neither one of them became who history knows them as now upon day one of entering their movements. Malcolm worked his way up through the ranks of the NOI and was eventually granted the position of national minister by the Honorable Elijah Muhammad. MLK spent time organizing in southern communities and was eventually selected by his community to lead. That's organic leadership. Both men were under heavy surveillance by the government and dealt with informants in their organizations. There are informants and surveillance now. If both Malcolm and King had to go through a process of acculturation and were held accountable by the communities they were selected to lead, then white allies or other allies are way out of bounds for thinking they can use their privilege to advance in any movement without going through the process of paying dues. They are sadly mistaken. Take your privilege and move to the ally section and wait your turn. If this is not to your liking, then you can leave.

Race Relations Enthusiasts

A smaller but still related issue to that of the race scholar and the out of bounds ally is that of the race-relations enthusiast. All of these types are problematic in their own way, but this one is uniquely flawed. The race-relations enthusiast is a person who enjoys or finds satisfaction in the discussion of race-related issues. The subject matter of race is fascinating to them. It's something like a hobby; race is intriguing and stimulating discussion material, an interesting conversation piece. Miss me with all of that. They want to discuss racism like some discuss their favorite athletes or favorite movies. You might hear one say that they like to hear other people's opinions on the matter of race. Others like to broach the subject to elicit a certain response in others they are talking to. Either way, the relegating of a very real matter to that of a sport or topic of interest is insensitive and idiotic.

The reason why I think I despise this type so much is because they have the audacity to trivialize a "subject matter" that literally means life and death for millions of people. This illogical, selfish, uncivilized madness of racism is my reality, and the reality my people are faced with. You do not get the right to trivialize it into a subject for leisurely coffee table debate. Millions and millions of black people and other peoples have lost their lives, cultures, minds, and ways of life over the horrific abomination of racism that was created and patented by white Western civilization. We are not here for your academic review and theories. We are not here for you to pontificate over whether or not racism is real or if reparations are necessary. Racism is real, and reparations are definitely necessary. Our lives are not for your intellectual entertainment or for you to pass time with a robust clash of differing opinions about race. My people and I are in the field trying to survive while you sit comfortably at places of privilege or fire off comments online. Your posturing is pathological and disgusting. To sit and do nothing but talk for sport while people literally die is hideous and barbaric. And no, I will not be talking to you about this book.

That's why these words are solely directed at the hearts, minds, and souls of my people. As Ms. Toni Morrison told the Guardian's Hermione Hoby in 2015, "I'm writing for black people, in the same way that Tolstoy was not writing for me, a 14 year old colored girl from Lorain, Ohio. I don't have to apologize or consider myself limited because I don't write about white people."

I know white people and other non-blacks will read this text. Upon reading, they might experience a shock. The shock will be felt more by white society because the stories are not about them. Western civilization has fooled them into believing everything begins and ends with white people, but once they are able to get over that initial shock, they can find nourishment. That nourishment is necessary because we can all learn to be better, and there is a growing number of white and other non-black parents who have mixed and or black children. Ignorance is not an excuse, nor is it a shield from the plight your black child may face once they step outside your door. Your privilege might protect you, but it will not extend to your black loved ones. You better know the potential dangers that await your child. Their lived experience will be different from yours, all because the larger society perceives them as black. That simple fact is the very reason why the hatred that America holds for black bodies just might show up at your doorstep draped around the neck of your child. You better pay attention and do what you can to arm and protect your offspring. This is exactly what black families have been trying to do for four centuries. Welcome to our world.

Although the words that follow are for black people, the undeniable reality is these are stories about people. The human condition is the same, regardless of degree of melanin, time, place, and space. The one empirical fact that we as a society have yet to accept is that we in the human species are all the same. Western society has falsely chosen to erect imperialist dichotomies that have led to the stories that follow. So regardless of who you are and what you look like, if you look deep enough in these words, you'll find you.

However, *Black Boy Poems* is for my fellow brothers and sisters who have been kissed by the sun, and covered in all the hues of that sublime blackness from head to toe. There is no word or form of manmade art that can truly describe our beauty and greatness. This is for us. I humbly present to you all, my family, the poetic fruit buried deep in my bosom by our loved ones who came before us. The themes of the narratives will be familiar because it is our experience. We know our problems extremely well because we've been confronted with them in the American context since

1619. We are almost 400 years into the experience of black in colonial and constitutional America. We are still fighting for the same things that we were stripped of once we were placed on those slave boats and shipped from our motherland to this new land, which held never-before-seen horrors and terrors that we would have to survive. We are still here! We are still surviving despite every attempt the system has ever made to ensure our demise. We are living and breathing miracles. We have found life in the most inhospitable of soils. We have thrived in a land that has envied and attempted to stifle our greatness. A land that has taken steps to silence our importance to the growth and development of this society. We are the hated bastard offspring of America. And to America's surprise, her hate and disdain for us has only made us stronger and more exceptional. We have been fashioned into the personification of black excellence. We will continue to be just that well beyond the days her hateful ways can no longer touch us. I am a proud Black Boy, and these are my poems for my people. May they be filled with the wisdom of our ancestors and enriched with a spiritual medicine to heal us all.

41 Shots (1999)

I speak to beats composed of African cries,
spilled indigenous blood,
horrified shrieks,
prison doors locking,
legalized lynchings
police ammunition flying through the skies
to contact black skin.
Let's examine that last line once again.
Police ammunition flying through the skies
to contact black skin.
My name is Amadou Diallo
41 shots
hit
19 times
these are simply the facts,
now we are forced to ask a question
what was my crime?
Some say guilty of being black
I agree.
I see 4 plainclothes police officers
I mean pigs
approach me and ask me for my I.D.
I oblige
they reply
with 41 shots
I was hit
19 times.
The first shot severed my spine in 4 different places
paralysis starts to set in
I can no longer stand,
an unarmed black man
lying on the floor,
never to them was I a threat

but they still
feel the need to fire 40 more shots.
Stop!
Whatever happened to
innocent until proven guilty
yet I am fatally wounded and filthy
covered in the blood of my ancestors.
I came in search
of a better life
the American Dream
but Immigration never told me about the 500 year history of this
racist nation
I never heard about brothers and sisters like
Rodney King,
Tyisha Miller,
Abner Louima,
Fred Hampton,
George Jackson,
Bobby Hutton,
Emmett Till
Still I say
I've committed no crime
but it's illegal to be black in this country
where they call me
monkey,
coon,
and baboon,
and scientists create theories to prove the inferiority of my skin
tone,
and police officers named
pork-chop,
piglet,
pork rind,
and swine
legally lynch me
and assassinate my 46 chromosomes,
That's state sponsored genocide
I can't even safely walk into my home.

41 shots
19 hits
that's a 46% hit ratio,
now do you see how these stereo-typical
beliefs affect me here
with the fears they associate with black people
on movies, television, and radio.
Black people are dumb,
black people are addicted to drugs,
black people are thugs with guns
this is how come
4 armed pigs can be afraid
and fire 41 standard state issued nigger killers
with the intention to kill just one
innocent, unarmed brother
I say it's because
I'm a Black Man!

Reflections of a Black Boy

What does one do when compliance and disobedience can merit the same response, i.e. death? What move should one make when doing all the "right" things while in black skin can be just as fatal?

How does one cope with the ever present and crystal clear reality that the greater society deems the destruction of your body as inconsequential?

In the United States of America the control, torture, and extermination of black flesh and blood is akin to a national pastime.

Where does one go mentally, spiritually or in any other way when the all too frequent reminders of the devaluation of black life come to visit?

Amadou Diallo was killed in February of 1999. I was attending San Jose State, and one of my professors, Dr. Kwasi Harris, encouraged me to write something about Diallo's assassination. He knew I was an emcee, so he told me to put pen to paper and give voice to this public execution of a black man. Up to that time, I hadn't written poetry before, but I went home and returned the next day with this piece, "41 Shots." Death is painful to deal with, murder is tragic, the constant murder of black lives is both tragic and traumatic. For black people in America we know that our death can be waiting for us at any place, any time. When one of our brothers and sisters is killed we feel the pain in knowing it could've been us. In essence we die a bit every time one of us is killed. As a result some of us have died thousands of times. I wasn't there on the street when the officers stopped brother Amadou. I didn't witness it with my own eyes, but the pain and anger I experienced in this event is clear in the words that I wrote.

The black experience in many ways is lived vicariously because what happens to one can happen to any of us at any given time. I wasn't on the steps with police revolvers pointed at me, but I still experienced the trauma of an unarmed man reaching for his wallet upon directive from plainclothes law enforcement agents and ceremoniously being executed for doing so. I don't think I even knew at the time of writing the piece how hard his murder hit me. One of the survival strategies we've learned through generations of American racist hate is to compartmentalize feelings in order to keep moving. We bottle up the hurt and the pain and put it somewhere inside our soul to deal with at another time. Periodically those bottled up emotions are triggered by an experience, and they break through the safety glass, spilling out over any and every thing. This poem was that spill of emotions, the glass shattered from the weight of the fragility of the black life. Amadou's death would not be the only time the safety glass was broken to pieces; I would experience more pain and trauma as more bodies were buried for similar "reasons" right next to Amadou.

This was not the first time American hatred manifested in brutality or murder of black lives in my lifetime. I had witnessed the beating of Rodney King on television when news channels covered the story for days. I recall the feeling of disgust I felt when all officers were acquitted of any wrongdoing in mercilessly beating King for twenty-plus minutes for a traffic violation. That too, hurt. I was young but not too young to realize in that moment that the black life was undervalued. I couldn't fully comprehend all the dimensions of the racial hatred present in that brutal act, but I knew it was wrong.

Amadou's murder happened when I was nineteen. News reports flashed his age, and I realized that I was only three years younger than he was. The scariest part was knowing that I could see myself in a similar situation. I've been stopped by police officers and asked to produce identification. Many black and brown folks have experienced that multiple times. Brother Amadou was at his doorstep when he was stopped by officers that were not in uniform. He reached for what officers asked for and was gunned down. That's what makes it so painful. The fact that no response is correct because your blackness makes you wrong all of the time.

What is one to do when obeying the law/law enforcement agents can merit the same response as disobeying the law/law enforcement agents? This is part and parcel of the Black American experience. Correct or incorrect behavior can produce the same results, and far too often that result is fatal.

The world and the treatment blacks experienced in post 13th Amendment America is similar in many ways to the world that Black people still live in. It is important to note some of the differences, but the state of black life is sadly pretty much the same. We don't fear death/violence from average white citizens like the ever-present fear of lynchings in the first iteration of Jim Crow. Violence perpetrated on black bodies by the local citizenry does still happen, but it's a little more rare for regular whites to conspire to bring death to black bodies. What has taken the place of civil lynchings are executions by police and security professionals, coupled with the insane amounts of men and women incarcerated in the Prison Industrial Complex (PIC). Black incarceration is nothing new in America. During slavery days, before the Thirteenth Amendment, it was rare to see blacks incarcerated because it was more advantageous to use their labor on plantations. After the legal abolition of slavery, America began to see a rise in black incarceration because that was the only legal avenue to enforce slavery. Since then, America has seen large numbers of blacks incarcerated, but what we see today is staggeringly unprecedented. Once people enter the PIC, the system does a thorough job of disenfranchising its "clientele," legally relegating them to the status of second-class citizens. Most lose their right to vote, opportunities for employment, housing, and participation in certain social services programs. Essentially branding these men and women with a mark akin to leprosy that mainstream America does not want to touch.

This is completely unfair. Yet, it's the system we live under. This is an all-too-common piece that has become part of the fabric of American society. This treatment paralyzes the progress of black people and the black community in America. There has never been an equal playing field at anytime in America, and this guarantees that no equal playing field will be seen anytime soon, if at all. The American propaganda machine wants us to believe that the dream is for all, but the black sons and daughters of America have long known the dream doesn't include us. The dream that White America clings to so proudly is a nightmare to Blacks, funded and fueled by the withered carcasses once clad in black flesh. Like any good story, there is the hero and the villain; black people have been cast in the role of villain and as a result suffer to the upmost under this American social order. And as long as they keep producing this dream, we know that the villain will always lose in the end.

The dream was on display when these four officers killed Diallo. If I was the author of the dream, our brother would be alive with his family, and those murderers never would've polluted the planet with their presence, but this is not my dream, it's theirs. Our brother's blood all on their hands, faces, hearts, and souls, and still all the officers involved were acquitted of any and all wrongdoing. They go on with their lives and go on with their careers. Meanwhile, we're left to bury and mourn for our dead. The dream hasn't stopped working for the cops involved in the shooting; in fact, just recently one of the officers received a promotion. I can't make this stuff up. For some, dreams come true, and for others dreams are deferred indefinitely.

Around the time of Diallo's death, some were calling him my generation's Emmett Till. For those who don't know about Emmett, he was a 14-year-old black boy from Chicago who was lynched while visiting family in Mississippi in August 1955. The reason for his lynching was that he allegedly flirted with a married white woman. The husband of the woman and his half-brother abducted Emmett, beat him for hours, and eventually put a bullet through his skull. After all of this, they dumped his body in the Tallahatchie River. His body ballooned up, making the savagery behind his lynching that much more pronounced. There was no justice for his murder as the murderers went unpunished, even though it was common knowledge who was responsible. Till's mother insisted on an open casket, so the world could see the evil that killed her son. The image of Emmett's mutilated, bloated body seared itself into the conscience of America and the collective souls of black folks. Every parent knew that any black child was an alleged flirt away from death.

It's a sad commentary that every generation of Black America has its own equivalent of a hate or fear motivated murder of a black body. No generation of black people is safe from savage acts of terror and brutality at the hands of American citizenry or the state. A quick point to add here is for our black African brothers and sisters who are migrating to parts of the Western world due to various issues "back home" that have pushed their families into the diaspora. This awareness of your black skin in the Western world is essential to understand quickly because Western racism does not discern between black American or African black. Black skin is the base requirement to elicit a hate- or fear-motivated response. African brothers and sisters, your sons and daughters are at risk of the same brutality that has been raining down on the heads of your long-lost brethren and sistren via the triangle trade, and you cannot afford to think yourselves immune. You might view yourself as different ethnically or culturally; your family might have left west, central, south, or east Africa, but the blessed hue in your skin tone is viewed with hate and suspicion here in America and other parts of the Western world. Brother Amadou and his family came to these shores from Guinea in the Gold Coast searching for opportunity, I don't know if they knew the potential consequences that came with black skin in this new land. Black American and African black cannot hope to survive in this society ignorant of that fact and find a way to come together to support each other in the war being waged upon our people.

One of the reasons why this poem is so important is the simple fact that it still continues to this day. Just recently a new Emmett Till has been crowned for this generation. That most unwanted distinction goes to 12-year-old Tamir Rice, who was gunned down by Cleveland police for playing with a toy gun in a park. The ironic part of Tamir's story is that in the state of Ohio, it is legal for a person to carry a gun, so by decree of the state he wouldn't have been in violation of the law if he had a gun, and he certainly wasn't in violation of the law with a replica toy gun. Just like Emmett was killed for allegedly flirting, which isn't a violation of any legal code, and Diallo was killed for complying with directives of an officer, Tamir was killed for being a law-abiding black boy. Even in our committing no wrongdoing, the state will find excuse for execution.

In the poem I repeat the phrase "41 shots 19 hits" multiple times. I do this intentionally because I want the listener to feel the brutality displayed in that moment. I want them to feel the malice, hatred, and complete disregard necessary to fire 41 shots and place 19 individual bullet holes in another human being. What drives a person or people to see so much of a threat and so little value in a life that they are capable of firing "41 standard state issued nigger killers with the intentions of killing just one?"

Just recently, an officer named Michael Brelo was acquitted in Cleveland of all charges after firing forty-nine out of a total of 137 shots at an unarmed couple whose car backfired. Police mistakenly took the backfire for a gunshot. The couple, Timothy Russell and Malissa Williams, had allegedly led the officers on a police chase. Brelo and his twelve colleagues fired 137 shots into the car. Brelo went so far as to hop on the hood of the car and fire an entire magazine of fifteen rounds into the couple at point-blank range. And of course, neither he nor his fellow officers were found guilty, and 137 shots in a residential area was not considered excessive force.

It doesn't matter how outrageous the situation is, people will explain it away. America will find a way to exonerate the murders socially and legally. As if the taking of a black life while wearing a specific uniform doesn't violate the same code of 187 for murder the rest of us are subjected to. The reason for this is because our system has built itself upon a solid foundation of white supremacy, fueled by artificial black stereotypes that drive America to a manic state whenever it encounters a black body. White supremacy mixed with racial mania is the deadly cocktail America takes to the head multiple times a day. This narcotized state makes it easier to injure and or kill a black life. In an attempt to protect America in its perpetual drunken state, the system has evolved to include fail-safe protocols, which is an age-old American tradition. One of the most striking historical examples of these fail-safes is the slave codes enacted in many states during antebellum America. The purpose of specific codes was to shield slave masters and other whites from prosecution in the event that he or she took the life of a slave. The state of Virginia, which gave us slave-owning founding fathers such as George Washington, Thomas Jefferson, and James Madison, granted this protection to their slave owners and citizenry.

Virginia, 1705: "If any slave resists his master ... correcting such a slave, and shall happen to be killed in such correction ... the master shall be free of all punishment ... as if such accident never happened."

The execution of a slave by a slave master did not merit punishment in the homes of our Founding Fathers and the death of that black man, woman, or child was ignored by white society as if it didn't happen. This is eerily familiar because police officers firing forty-one shots at Diallo, two shots at Tamir, and 137 shots at Williams and Russell, are considered accidents or following procedure. The officers' actions do not merit punishment in a court of law, and the black man's, woman's, or child's death is largely ignored by mainstream society as if it never happened. These murders were no accident. These are blatant examples of murder, but when it comes to "justice" being meted out by a racist state apparatus with its patented fail-safes, murdering a black body is termed an accident and therefore swept aside with no regard either for the life lost or those connected to that person, who will never be the same as a result of their loss.

We've all watched these scenes play out so much that we have the entire script memorized as to what will happen when white badge kills black body. We'll have a media firestorm; the community will be out in the streets demanding justice, and social media will be alive with various messages about injustice and accountability. The state will use multiple maneuvers to delay any court proceeding. Their new favorite tactic is exploiting the grand jury process to escape indictment, which throws out any attempt at reaching "justice." In the event we do find our way to a court trial, the most likely all-white jury will find it hard to prove guilt or ill-intent on the part of the murdering officer(s). The legal precedent is clear, and the story is already written. America has stated definitively that we are not all equal before the law, and for some of us, the law works to limit our life's potential. We change out the faces, the names, and the hashtags, but the conclusion is always the same. The American system specializes in dehumanizing the black body, incarcerating the black body for the sake of labor for profit, and in killing the black body out of "fear" or sport. This is simply a reality that anyone who wears the black skin uniform in America must understand while the rest of America has the luxury and privilege to ignore it.

Family Tree (2000)

This is the story of my Grandfather
You see,
when my Mom was still a toddler
her mother married a man named John Oliver
And like many black men
he worked in the armed service
it's hard to determine
what made him nourish
his habit
of alcohol which made him an addict
the travesty
of alcohol dependency
which led to a tendency
for a beast to surface
he would eventually
begin to
beat,
kick,
choke,
fight,
cuss,
whip,
inflict
pain
A young black man
intelligent and handsome
but destined
to reclaim the anthem
of souls destroyed by those liquid phantoms
he consumed demons and spirits
with stickers and labels
liquor,
in tinted glass containers

became a stranger to self
it changed his mentality,
became hellish
a drunken zealot
without any inhibition,
his mission
to satisfy his selfish desires
he struggled with his sobriety
even denying that he
had a problem
when off the liquor,
sober,
he was one of the nicest men you could ever meet
he was kind,
generous,
considerate
but you see those times were
few and far
in between
he developed a routine
on Fridays
to be gone for a few days
return home early Sundays
the booze he paid for
stayed on his breath
and the bruises he made became sore
and stayed on her flesh.
As he led his family through the church doors
and played the role of the righteous father,
pious
When he really had a dark side
of a pirate a tyrant
I call him a domestic terrorist
all that violence and abuse
sanctioned
under the guidelines
of legal marriages.
My grandma sought counseling

she went down to the local parish
and the church father told her like this,
to simply, "grin and bear it"
as if
God wanted her to be a punching bag for this man
through
sickness and health
until death do you part.
But she stayed strong
knowing something was way wrong
and kept praying to God for help
because this man couldn't control himself,
her mental health and life on the line
and at times
when intoxicated
you could see the devil in his eyes
my aunt, uncles, and mom would huddle and cry
hearing muffled blows on my grandma's flesh
not knowing if she'd be alive at the time of sunrise.
His inequities then spread to his seeds
you see,
my aunt and two uncles began to emulate his deeds.
They started with the drinking and smoking
but two of them didn't let it control them
they conquered the monster
but the addiction was so much stronger in my Uncle Johnny
named after his father
he took after his father
he sought something to curb his addiction.
He started experimenting
injected heroin into his system through his forearm
one shot was all that it took,
hook,
line
and sinker
destined from the womb
to be a casualty of this chemical warfare
the family noticed he drastically changed

his parents already gone their separate way
you see
my grandma finally got the divorce
John Oliver Sr.
he out in Mississippi
he tipsy of course.
Little Johnny was fidgety
he wasn't into as much physical activity
as he used to be
and what could it be the family would ask,
Nothing!
is what he'd snap back
but it became all apparent when he forged his mom's signature to
get cash
that he had smack tracks
on the other side of his elbow.
He got into a rehab
and started getting back to the Johnny we used to know
but then them chemicals
began to call him back
by way of this one fast sister he used to holler at
you see,
she slipped him a bag of smack
that wasn't cut clean
set to wreck havoc in his recovering bloodstream
still he cooked it
he drew it up slow into the syringe
tied his arm off tight
pushed that needle through his skin
my poor Uncle Johnny,
he chasing the dragon again
and that evening this is what happened to him
he shot up
he dropped
to his knees
his muscles seized up
his heart gave up
he never got up

he a byproduct of his father's disease
and by now
under his skin,
his blood starts to chill
in sets the rigor mortis
my uncle,
he a picture,
a ghetto still portrait
titled:
"Overdose in mom's kitchen"
my grandma
she comes home tired from work
not knowing his condition
not knowing that her worst nightmare has just
come to fruition
it's dark inside the home
the light switch is on the other side of the room
she feels an emptiness in her womb
as she passes a cold stump
she calls out for Johnny
there's no answer
he's not responding
she turns the light on
and sees her son's body hunched over
with his life gone
and that night
my mom
felt the same pain so many miles away
a little more than a year later
I join the family
And I'm the first after Johnny
and somehow because of this madness
I know our bodies are
oddly connected
but John Oliver Sr. still just as reckless,
still drinking
still turning from a man into a demon
still scheming on women

but one evening
it all began to catch up
payback for all them times
and all them lives
he done messed up
and for real
it's hard to feel any remorse or sadness
I still don't know all the details
but a woman who grew tired of his madness
took him off this planet for good
should I feel this way
truthfully y'all
I don't even know
all I know is that
this is a true tale
some of that ghetto non-fiction
of what happened to my family
and all because of addiction
addiction, y'all
this is my family tree

Reflections of a Black Boy

The rearing of a black family, let alone a healthy black family in America is a revolutionary act.

Our babies are born into a world intoxicated with the hatred for their kind.

Since the times of indentured servitude, slavery, Jim Crow, civil rights to the new era of Jim Crow, the black family has been under attack. And at every phase America has found a way to profit from the pain of black families.

Walk the streets of black America and you'll see multiple versions of John and Jane Olivers. They are our mothers, fathers, brothers, sisters, aunts, uncles, cousins, and friends. Born with the hopes and dreams of new life but had their birthright snuffed out by the social, political and chemical weapons constantly targeting the black life.

We self-medicate with alcohol and drugs in an attempt to inoculate ourselves against the pain caused by the world we live in. The side effects are often death and generational harm.

What breaks inside a human being making them capable of destroying themselves and their family? What testimony is that for the society that creates this phenomenon?

I never knew John Oliver. I never met him. My mother was raised with him as her "biological" father, even though he was not. He was the father of my aunt and two uncles, so his presence dominates the early history of my family, but I never experienced him firsthand. Still, his figure loomed large in my family. Since I never met him, I always felt like I never really had a grandfather on that side of the family. All I knew of him were these stories that were passed on to me. So much of those stories involved John Oliver in the role of what I described in the poem, "domestic terrorist." I don't want to be unfair to John Oliver; I tried to sketch the complexity of his personality. He was a good man but flawed like all of us humans are. We are not a perfect breed. All of us have imperfections, and character defects, and they can be exaggerated by time, place, and circumstance. I have heard great stories of John Oliver, but they get mixed in between what was more readily transmitted to me of the pain and sorrow of those who experienced him. That is what I know of him well. I know the impact that he had on my family. His addiction was dangerous for his family and himself; upon reaching critical mass he left a ground zero of collateral damage and unintended casualties. I was born in the days after the blast. I inherited the post-apocalyptic world of hollowed out frames needing to be rebuilt, burns and scorch marks upon the Earth. I played in the rubble of my family, vowing to never let this level of destruction visit us again. In some respects, John Oliver was like the ocean to my family. He was calm and still at times. He provided sustenance and on great days was the best place to be, but when the moon was high and full he amassed a wave that rose and fell, crashing upon the shores of my family. I was to receive all the stories secondhand via messages in a bottle scribbled by the survivors.

I have become the post-apocalyptic grandson without a grandfather. The years of stories and study of the aftermath makes me curious about the man responsible for the events that forever transformed my family. I know the impact of the mistakes that were made and I've been raised to never repeat them. I safeguard that training daily, it has allowed me to become a man who hasn't succumbed to what wrought havoc a generation before. I feel I'm ready to confront John Oliver and ask him why. As I search for him in my mind he appears to me in a field in Mississippi toiling the land. From afar as I approach I can tell he's a broken and withered man. I do not claim some self-righteous "better than thou" posture when seeing him in this light, but I can't help but notice the evidence of his various battles on his body. The weight of what has befallen him and his family coalesces around his shoulders, collapsing down on his frame. He's slightly hunched over as if looking for something on the floor. When he looks at me he knows me, but he doesn't really know me. He's aware that I'm there for him and that I know what happened. My words sound alien to him because they are wrapped in hindsight and a spirit of conquest over the demons that destroyed the men that came before me. He pauses his work, slightly turns his body to see me and in this place we hold conversation.

Without any words exchanged what becomes clear to both of us is that John Oliver created a situation in his family that forced all of us to evolve. I was born shortly after the untimely death of my Uncle Johnny. I wrote in the poem that my Uncle Johnny was "destined to be a causality of this chemical warfare," and if that was Uncle Johnny's destiny, then my destiny was to practice strict abstinence with drugs and alcohol. I've never touched anything in my entire life and don't plan on using any drugs or alcohol for as long as I live. I'm such a natural extremist that I completely avoid caffeine and, most days, bad sugars. I don't like any addictive behaviors that I become aware of, and at times for a challenge I'll choose a habit I know I've developed and begin breaking it to not be too dependent upon anything.

If John Oliver were a sculpture, he would be erected with pieces missing, leaving you to wonder what happened, how it happened, and why. I don't know the type of man he was morally and ethically. I've heard stories of how he treated people well when he wasn't under his addiction. What has been translated to me the loudest is what he did under his addiction to the people he loved. As I've matured and found numerous faults within myself, I've begun to see him through my own lens. I've now been blessed to experience more than three decades of life, which is enough time to live and author my own list of mistakes as a man, son, friend, husband, boyfriend, and partner. Lessons I didn't learn well enough the first time, life has found ways to teach over and over again. What I've gained from my numerous mistakes and failures is that because you don't know the full extent of a person's struggle, it's best not to judge. It's one thing to be angered with an action of a person; it's another thing to condemn an entire life. The usage of the term "domestic terrorist" is rooted in criticizing actions and not the man.

I never knew John Oliver; I'm not attempting to judge him as a human being. I have no authority to do so. I didn't know what made him tick. I don't know what drove him to drink and abuse. Any cursory reading of psychology would tell you that those who were abused most often become abusers. If that's the case, then a certain degree of fault is not on his shoulders. I don't have any evidence to show me that about him, so it's all speculation, but what I do know is that John Oliver was born into a world that placed little to no value on the black life, especially that of a black man in Mississippi.

There are many places that you don't want to be black in, at the top of that list you'd find Mississippi. Especially Mississippi in the early 20th century. In an attempt to approach an understanding of what may have impacted John Oliver we have to ask a few questions. How does one cope and what does one do to survive when the world they live in is constantly attempting to limit their potential? What do you do when your world's best options for you are incarceration or early death? I don't know what it must've been like for him to live during that time in America. We do not all survive the mental, spiritual, and physical beating that America puts us through. Our bodies might be above ground, but that doesn't mean we haven't been broken and are now walking spiritually and/or mentally dead. It's possible that John Oliver was fractured by America by way of Mississippi, his breaking like a slow-motion domino effect that reverberated louder and louder through his family until the last domino fell. It is possible that bearing the brunt of abuse from a society for so long caused him to internalize and manifest the same abusive behavior from the outside world upon those he loved most.

This is part of the tragedy of Black America. American society was never meant for black people and families to survive. Mankind is a fragile species, and everybody has a breaking point. Being confronted with constant obstacles, terror, and pressure will eventually force the strongest of the strong to their brink. Once reaching that edge, it is possible that some are equipped with a more healthy coping mechanism while others resort to self-destructive habits, which not only impact us but our loved ones as well. John Oliver's issues were played out in a theater that gave his family a front-row view. All are impacted in their own ways and are forced to find their own path if they want to survive.

I'm stepping away from John Oliver as a man briefly in order to look at him as a symbolic figure in the American context. According to America we are all "black serfs, slave, lumpenproletariat, and peasants" and our genetic marker relegates us to a class and caste that we cannot cast off. We are the ones to whom "transracial" does not apply; we are simply designated by this society as the unwanted other. Only people in seats of privilege can concoct such a ridiculous notion as "transracial," their privilege allowing them the power, opportunity, and agency to claim they can belong to another experience by opting in. John Oliver was not born in a seat of power. He was not born with privilege. Had he the opportunity to opt out to make things better for him and his family, I'm sure he would've taken that route. His blackness stained him and prevented him from anything other than what his society thrust upon his black shoulders.

The poem and this section is about John Oliver, who was sentenced to a life of cold black peasantry by America. He tried to run away from this status by attempting to leave the South. Born and raised in Mississippi, he sought the armed services as a way out. That was a common path for many black men during that time and still is. Black men and women have been fighting in, against, and for America since our day one in 1619. He had hoped his service would lead to a new path for him and his new bride and a child who was not his blood whom he decided to raise as his own. Making the decision to raise a child who is not your own is truly admirable, and it was because of this that my mother had a father figure. I am appreciative of that. I do not know much about his experience in the service, but his abuse and alcoholism paralleled that timeline. The beatings and alcohol abuse only intensified as he got older. His wife was his primary target, but all of his children witnessed his actions and were traumatized in the aftermath of his violent episodes. I want to state emphatically that it is never cool for a husband to hit a wife or wife to hit a husband or, depending on the makeup of your relationship, a partner to hit a partner. It doesn't matter if it is a heterosexual or homosexual relationship. Domestic violence is always wrong.

As the poem mentions, all of John Oliver's offspring began to experiment with cigarettes and alcohol. My aunt and uncle both have had their struggles with sobriety, but for the most part they've been largely in control of what they inherited from their father. My Uncle Johnny is the brutal exception to that rule.

If John Oliver can represent a symbolic figure, then my Uncle Johnny is equally symbolic. He is the all-too-familiar reality for so many black families in America. He too, like his father, was born into a world that devalued the black life. In addition to that, Johnny witnessed the man he was named after losing himself and abusing his family. What does that do to a child? Seeing that type of abuse befall your mother has to affect you somehow. I love my grandma with every particle of love I have, and I'd do everything in my power to protect her from anyone who meant her harm. I've been told stories of how brutal the beatings were. Johnny, like his siblings, heard the beatings through the walls and at times witnessed them first hand. As a child, you have to find somewhere to put that experience. It's not something you just sit and watch and let it run off your back. Johnny, like his father, began to find escape in drinking and drugs.

Johnny battled to get clean but eventually fell casualty to the same formula that claimed so many before and after him. In the piece, I mention how he became forever immortalized as the "ghetto still portrait titled overdose in Mom's kitchen." His life and death is an indictment that falls on deaf ears that the American system is not fair. His ghost hovers huddled in the same spot where his life expired in my grandma's kitchen. I remember him every time I walk over to where he breathed his last breath alone on the floor in his mother's home. The same home that housed all the abuse he saw was now the place where he would die. There is no other way to describe it other than a tragedy. It is something that could've been avoided but the ones who are principally affected by American injustice are the ones the system does not care enough about to reverse course to accommodate their suffering and struggles.

John Oliver attempted to leave one oppressive structure (the South) by finding refuge in another equally oppressive structure (the white man's military), fighting for corporate interests which the American public is told means "freedoms and rights." Those corporate benefits, "freedoms, and rights" were not extended to people his color in his own country. He then relocated to another oppressive structure (the city) filled with limited opportunities and segregated housing. These are the facts that I believe he saw no release from despite his best efforts, and they broke him. One of the consequences of the black experience in America is its intergenerational trauma/brokenness. It gets passed down like a cursed family heirloom. Broken families produce broken children who will eventually create more broken families. John Oliver may have inherited brokenness from those before him; I don't know; I don't know what he was given. I know he tried to overcome it, and his failure spilled over onto the futures of his children. Everyone tried to adapt, but not all were able to regain their footing, and we lost one in the process. My family wears the badge of mourning across our chests daily. Every family gathering, Johnny is a one-dimensional smiling picture on a wall instead of a living and breathing, laughing and joking son, brother, and uncle. We will never be the same as a result of our trauma and losses, but we must carry on. America hasn't stopped attempting to crush us, so we have to wake up, for the next morrow soon comes.

This is all I'm able to share with John Oliver as we talk. His response is an unyielding silence. No words pass his lips, but the tears in his eyes speak a language clear enough for both of us to understand. Once I realize there is nothing more to be said between us, I turn silently, and he slowly begins to resume his work. I walk away back to my world, back to my family, and we get back to carrying on.

Postscript

I feel the power that resides in this poem is born out of the cold reality that addiction and its consequences are present in every group of human beings regardless of demographic designation. This is not just a black thing. It's a human thing, and if you look deeply enough you can possibly substitute your family members for mine and then it becomes your story. Many of us have watched bouts of addiction play out in our families. Some of us are dealing with addiction issues amongst our families, friends, and loved ones right now. The consequences of addiction are raw, naked, and unforgiving.

I love hip-hop music/culture. I've benefitted a great deal from hip-hop. However, both mainstream and underground hip-hop have grown to glorify behaviors that can lead to addictions mentioned in the poem. In songs and videos, artists make alcohol and drugs sound and look appealing, but the real consequences of becoming addicted and the impact of that addiction on self and family are not glamorous. What my family experienced is what it looks like after the cameras are shut off and the actors and actresses go home. There was no director yelling, "cut"; there was no director of photography shooting multiple takes from various angles to get the look and feel just right. It was uncut human drama written by alcoholism that led to spousal abuse and drug addiction, culminating in death.

I'm not a censor; I have no desire to tell anyone to stop rapping about what their truth is, but I won't hold my tongue and not be critical when real critique is needed. We can't smoke, drink, snort, sip, pop, drop, and shoot up all the time and expect no consequences. Those consequences are not confined to the individual. They will also have an impact on the close relations of that person. The piece that really gets me about this entire thing is when you analyze it from a macro perspective, alcohol and most drugs, aside from marijuana, were strategically placed in our communities for the purposes of control and suppression. It is much easier to control a chemically dependent population and allow the negative effects of those chemicals to plague their families and communities. Today, mainstream and underground hip-hop culture sings songs celebrating the drugs and alcohol sent to destroy our communities. Facts. Purchasing those drugs and alcohol puts more money in the hands of families and companies who own Coors, Hennessey, Anheuser-Busch, and many others who have no vested interest in the liberation of black folks.

Using my family as an example, my grandfather purchased alcohol to satisfy his habit. That same alcohol forced him to morph into the monster that was terrorizing his own home. My Uncle Johnny bought heroin that was probably brought into this country via the Golden Triangle with some government/CIA/mafia connections. Most of these drugs ended up in urban America. Both my grandfather and uncle spent their own money on things that would damage them and eventually lead to their deaths. In essence, we voluntarily give money to our oppressors in exchange for the privilege of destroying ourselves and our communities. This idea essentially guarantees that we'll have more offspring who are "destined to be casualties of this chemical warfare." Our beautiful black family trees deserve a more fertile soil.

Under a Different Light (2001)

One day,
I was sitting at the dock of the bay
this cat walked up listening to Dr. Dre
and I thought about walking away
but he caught me in an awkward way
it's hard to explain
so I decided to engage
this man in a conversation
his hair was braided into some cornrows
he wore a jacket for the cold
with a cubic zirconia on his left earlobe
and he strolled like a gangster
with the infamous
hop in his step
face contorted by anger
my hypothesis
was a relationship
or his pockets weren't looking right
he sat without acknowledging me
but it didn't bother me
because it was obvious to see
he was preoccupied by thoughts running through his mind
we're all captives in this ball of confusion
for a period of time
trying to find solutions
invisible to the human eye
I kept one eye on his body language
but stayed focused on the most beautiful skyline the creator ever
painted
contemplating
the beauties of this world
but I still noticed when he
inhaled deep
He startled me

once he started to speak
under his breath saying,
"Something's gotta change, this madness gotta end, I can't do this
no more."
He caught my attention
because I know desperation when I hear it from prior experience
so I joined his conversation
and gave him a salutation,
Peace be unto you
I had seemed to
catch him off guard
but he regained his composure quickly
and said specifically
"What does that mean"
I replied, "truthfully,
the most important thing
because we all need peace to survive
and even though I don't know you personally
I still wish for peace in your life
and that's the first thing
that I say instead of saying hi.
He was like, "Yeah, I dig that,
but you one of them weird cats,
who be sitting on prayer mats
meditating all day.
I wish I was like that
but I lost my way some time ago and ain't found it every since."
I was like,
"There ain't no difference between me and you.
It's true I may hold another view
but we the same breed,
brother, we bleed the same things
and have the same needs.
Ain't none of us strong enough
to walk this path all alone.
And even the greatest of super heroes needs some saving at
times.

Well at this time,
I could care less whether I live or die
matter of fact I'm leaning more towards death.
I got no job, a baby on the way
and I'm facing my 3rd F,
25 with an L.
I might as well end it here.
My only fears be incarceration and failure.
I don't want my child to grow up with that psychological
fatherless paraphernalia.
It happened to me.
I never knew my pops
he'd been locked down my entire life.
I figured all non-whites was indigenous to cell blocks
my moms struggled to keep us well stocked
I had to hustle to get my first pair of shell tops
became a minimum wage slave as a bell hop
worked at the local Marriott
I had to cater to the demands of old rich white people
who thought they were greater than me
on some white supremacy
superiority complex
saying, Nigga, do that!
Boy, grab this!
Got me vexed
and one day I flexed on this old white dude
it wasn't my fault
I got hit with armed robbery and aggravated assault
when I never touched him
I was completely innocent
still all my freedoms were suspended
I got released after two years
without no incidents on the inside
but once on the outside
that F on my record
stood out like a scarlet letter on my chest
no one would hire me
because I was a potential liability

unemployment
I violated my probation
got locked up again
another disappointment
can you see this vicious cycle that's my life?
and I worked hard to do right
to do things that legal way
once again I got probation
and got a job as a mason
when I replied no felonies on my application
but it was only a matter of time
before they found out
background check
got released
but they said they wouldn't tell the police that I lied
and for months I tried everything
but playa, there were no opportunities
let down my lady
who was the only one to ever be true to me
and with a baby on the way
the only feasible way for me to get paid
is to slang D,
but killing my own people to make money don't make no sense
to me.
I guess I got a conscience, right?
I would move but I ain't got no funds
so I'm forced to rot here
under this California sun
and when I was young
I was told the streets here were paved in gold
and the sky is the limit
but now I'm looking to end it in this frigid pacific ocean
here's my white flag I surrender
tell the white man he's the victor again
and I apologize to my sisters, my family and my friends
especially to my lady and my unborn child.

And then he paused a while

I let it sink in
and started thinking
what would I do if I was him.
If things had gone contrary to what I expected
instead of driving by,
if that cop stopped, beat me down and had me arrested
if one of my parents died
or if I was denied a chance to go to school
would I be who I am now?
And before I could answer that
he told me something that I would never forget
as long as I live

man, I figured by now that you'd be able to tell,
but I guess I overestimated you
expected you to understand this tale that's my life
but can't you tell, that I'm just you under a different light.
And if they ask you who it was that died here tonight
please, make sure that they say my name right,
you know it's pronounced Ty-son.

Ty-son, what you saying you me
Ty-son, nah, homie you can't be

Who would you be if things in your life had gone differently
if life dealt you a hand that you couldn't handle
went from rags to riches
from fame to struggling
this life is precious but what are you really coveting
take a walk in someone else's shoes and experience their life
who would you be under a different light?
Who would you be under a different light?
Who would you be under a different light?

Reflections of a Black Boy

At all times in America, I as a black man am always mere inches or seconds away from jail, prison or death; either by state agents or traps of the street.

Your address can be 1600 Pennsylvania Avenue or somewhere in the lower bottoms in West Oakland, you're still black. This means you are destined to live a second to third class existence. No amount of fame, money, stardom, or prestige removes the black from your skin that America hates so much.

In a first encounter the truth is before I am to be known as Tyson Amir, I will first be known as all the noise and stereotypes associated with black life. In America I am forever stereotypically black   before   human.

_____

It is definitely important to acknowledge agency when discussing what is possible for men and women in our society. This body of work is not about scapegoating to escape accountability when it comes to matters that one can control. The system and the white power structure are not to blame for every misstep in a person's life. That system is at fault for myriad things; however, there are still areas where individuals can exercise control within the limited framework they possess, and it is essential that one seizes responsibility in those areas and makes the best out of what they have. All of us have responsibility when it comes to our lives, and we mustn't neglect that very real responsibility. That statement does not exonerate the inequity, the systemic preferential treatment directed toward white people in our society that allows them greater access to success.

I have experienced some tremendous successes in my life, and I am thankful and honored by the opportunities that I have received. I have not done any of this on my own; I was blessed with two parents who struggled hard to make things easier for their children. I owe a huge debt to my family and friends and those who came before me as standard bearers to make my path clearer. Yet and still, I could've easily found myself down a completely different path. It is possible that I may still find myself a victim of one of the clichéd tragic ends to black lives in America. I've safely made it into my third decade, but that doesn't mean the coast is clear for me now. Martin Luther King Jr., who is now celebrated by the American mainstream as one of the best examples of blackness in America, was killed at the age of thirty-nine, as was our dear brother Malcolm X. Both were killed because they stood up for basic rights that should've been freely given to black people, people of color, and poor folks. When you are black, there is no "get out of American racist persecution free" card. No age is safe. No amount of achievements and accolades prevent you from experiencing the "terrors" that befall blacks in America. Nothing. And this realization is a cold bitter fact of black life.

The point in all of this is to say that if you are born black in America, you are not given the same opportunities to live the life you want to lead. So much time and energy is dedicated to surviving this society that you aren't able to fully focus on self-growth and development. Imagine if great minds like Dr. King or Malcolm X could've dedicated the time they spent on liberation struggles to their own personal studies or on developing a talent or on their families. What might have been their fates? What might they have gifted to the world? We will never know. There are so many others who we can ponder over as well. What would have been the destinies of the millions who were unjustly enslaved here in America had they not been stolen from their homes to enrich the economies of the white world? We can ask the same question of what might have been for millions fed to the PIC, or the thousands terrorized, brutalized or lynched in these American killing fields, or swallowed by the traps of the streets. There are far too many to count. Almost nightly we learn of more lost lives about whom we're forced to ask what could've or should've been.

Those are all very tangible consequences of the racial apparatus at work. What we know well are the losses we can easily see and feel. Not every consequence is as evident as the "strange fruit" in southern trees or the millions of bodies locked up in jails and prisons. There are some consequences that are just as pernicious but they exist below the surface. They manifest in other physical, mental, spiritual, and psychological ways.

The business of attempting to survive in this world robs a person of essential time and energy they could be using to thrive and self-actualize. It also confronts one with the challenge of minimizing the harm caused by all the negative associations with the black life in American society. Those words, stereotypes, and images are all negative energies that are directed at the hearts, minds, and souls of black people here in America. It takes time and energy to survive this world as a black person. White people and others who benefit from white privilege have more time and energy afforded to them by this society because of their skin color. That extra time and energy they save due to white privilege is a very valuable asset that will never be in our hands here in America.

How does one begin to find out who they are when false stereotypes blind you and the outside world to your truth? The path to finding ourselves forces us to unlearn much of what we were taught about black people. Our system has no desire in providing the space for black people to learn about their beautiful black selves. That's a very real and very cold fact of black life. It is imperative for any people to know who they are. Our entire existence within the "wilderness of North America" has been totally controlled by white society. This society has no interest in providing a means for us to know ourselves. We've been prevented from practicing our native religions, languages, and cultures, systematically prevented from going to schools or segregated in inferior schools, all the while the larger society has lampooned black people with malicious false descriptions of what black, or the Negro, is. You cannot survive America without knowing yourself, and we cannot win against America without a knowledge of self. Minds that are far better than mine have spoken to this exact point.

Carter G. Woodson in his masterful work *The Mis-Education of the Negro* said:

"… if the Negro is to be elevated he must be educated in the sense of being developed from what he is, and the public must be so enlightened as to think of the Negro as a man. Furthermore, no one can be thoroughly educated until he learns as much about the Negro as he knows about other people."

In this statement, he is stressing education as the path to extricating yourself from your constraints, but it must be coupled with learning about yourself and your people. Black folks are taught more about white folks and white culture and all other types of white Eurocentric information and only know Dr. King. That's all America deems as important for us to know. Black history becomes the "I Have a Dream" speech and "y'all was slaves, but now y'all free because white people were kind enough to free you."

We must acquire what the Honorable Elijah Muhammad referred to as "knowledge of self." In *Message to the Blackman in America* he states:

"There is much misunderstanding among us because of our inferior knowledge of self. We have been to the schools where they do not teach us the knowledge of self. We have been to the schools of our slave-master children ... The lack of knowledge of self is one of our main handicaps. It blocks us throughout the world ... If we, the so-called Negroes, do not know our own selves, how can we be accepted by a people who have a knowledge of self?"

This society has not, cannot, and will not teach black people about themselves; this society is and will continue to exert pressure on the black life, exploiting the black life for purposes that are beneficial to the white society. This pressure and exploitation saps energy and time from black folks because they are so busy just trying to survive White America.

Here's a scenario to try to give some context to some of the intangible costs of surviving racism and how it literally takes away from a person's ability to be their fullest self. In their text, *Living with Racism*, Joe Feagin and Melvin Sikes, a sociologist and a psychologist respectively, quote a retired black psychologist who suggested what surviving racism is like: "... each human being has one hundred ergs of energy to live out their lives. The average man uses 50 percent of his energy dealing with the everyday problems of the world ... then he has 50 percent more to do creative kinds of things that he wants to do. Now that's a white person. Now a black person also has 100 ergs; he uses 50 percent the same way a white man does, dealing with what the white man has [to deal with], so he has 50 percent left. But he uses 25 percent fighting being black, [with] all the problems being black and what it means."

If you find any meaning in this analogy, then you can begin to see how black folks have a much more dangerous battle to wage with far less energy and artillery on a daily basis just to survive. The impact of the battle takes its toll on the body. The stress and pain accumulates and eventually attacks the body from within. Medical research correlates high levels of stress with certain physical, psychological, and neurological ailments. Cardiovascular issues, high blood pressure, and hypertension can be linked to increased stress levels. What the presence of this stress can also do is destroy much vital human energy that could have been used in building better individuals and societies. These are the very real economic, emotional, spiritual, mental, and physiological costs that black people have to pay as a result of surviving racism. A major costs of this reality is the price of not really being able to explore one's self to the fullest extent. The converse to this is, while we are not able to fully develop ourselves unencumbered by the American racial apparatus, America at every turn is constantly telling us who we are or what roles are acceptable for us to play. This brainwashing requires even more time and energy to deprogram in order to find our true selves.

"Under a Different Light" is me delving into the context of different life chances for an individual. I was inspired by the sci-fi black afro-futuristic writings of Octavia Butler and thought that a semi sci-fi poem would be an interesting lens for discussing divergent life possibilities for a black body. I've used the motif of meeting an alternate version of myself before in a piece but never on a scale like this. "Under a Different Light" is a very real piece for me because I know in my heart and soul that I am no different from any black man or woman in America, especially those who end up falling victim to the streets, jails, or prisons.

The version of myself that I meet in the poem very well could've been me. I've been in a great number of situations because of the reality of black living that could've ended up in any one of those occurrences that I described happening to my other self in that piece. The line between Tyson one and Tyson two is virtually imperceptible. The poem ends with my other version deciding that taking his life is his best alternative. Research shows that prior to the 1960s, blacks never charted high on the scale of suicide, but after the turbulent times of the '60s, suicide became a regular life event in the black community. Whites always charted higher in the category of suicide, but in the early 2000s black youth began to outpace their white counterparts in suicide deaths. Death visits us in many ways as a result of the conditions we are forced to live under.

Just recently I experienced two deaths that really broke me. I have been connected to so much death and loss that it is next to impossible to really quantify the level of hurt I've experienced. The grieving leads to immediately bottling up emotions and feelings because you have to face the world again in your black uniform. Both men were murdered; one was a near and dear friend, Basim Callens, and the other was a former student of mine, Mario Woods.

Basim was the victim of a carjacking in Atlanta, Georgia. Without attempting to sound clichéd, Basim was a really good dude. Like if I was a father I would've loved for him to have become my son-in-law. He was a good dude for the sake of being good. He had no ulterior motives; he was raised well and reflected the love and guidance he received in his daily life. His good deeds read like the good dude's All-Stars resume. Basim was all about his family and did all he could to take care of his mother and his younger siblings. The brother was a figure in the community, always promoting something positive. Basim was super educated; he learned Arabic and was fluent in it. Basim was about health and fitness, and was extremely humble, really working for the betterment of his people. From afar it would appear as if the life he lived was a formula for never falling victim to the traps of the streets. Yet and still, the poverty, systematic oppression, and limited opportunities of Black America led some young misguided kids to attempt to take something from him and in the process put multiple shots into my friend, terminating his life.

I'm from a spiritual path which has a tradition that says, "Whoever kills a soul it is as if he had slain mankind entirely. And whoever saves one - it is as if he had saved mankind entirely." As the saying states, any taking of a life is a tragedy similar to the slaying of all mankind. This is exactly what I felt in learning about the death of my brother Basim. To us, Basim was a nation of new possibility, and all it took was black poverty, bad decisions, desperation, fear, and a gun to completely kill off a nation. I learned about Basim's murder through social media, just like I learned about Mario's. At first I tried to deny it, hoping it was a terrible joke, that somebody was playing a ridiculous game or made some horrible mistake. But it was all true. Basim was dead, and so were the hopes of his family and of his people that he was filled with. If there was a way to survive the madness and transcend into something beautiful despite all the attempts to crush our dreams, then he was fashioned from that blueprint. His senseless murder was as if the hope for our new nation was completely wiped out. In that moment, I was once again violently reminded of my fragility and mortality. I just as easily could've been Basim, driving to work early one morning and not knowing I was driving towards my last breath.

The other death was a former student of mine, Mario Woods. His murder was captured in dramatic fashion and sent around multiple social media sites and evening news channels. He was murdered by the San Francisco Police Department in cold blood like so many other black men and women before him. SFPD claimed he made a threatening gesture, as if that justifies firing a volley of more than twenty shots at him. The autopsy report stated he was hit twenty-one times, and seventeen of those shots had a back to front trajectory, meaning he was shot in the back as he was moving away from officers. Mario who had recently received his high school diploma, fulfilling a promise he made with his mother, lay dead in the street. Going to jail is not a definitive statement of the character of a person. So many of our best and brightest have done time in jails and prisons or some might say, the concentration camps of North America. Having once been incarcerated in America is not proof of bad character. Mario had run into some "trouble" in his life, but he was making the necessary changes to honor his mother and himself. Sadly, SFPD does not take those steps toward change into consideration when they feel "threatened" by a man who makes no visible gesture of violence toward multiple armed law enforcement agents.

I attended Mario's wake and looked down into the face of the young boy I used to see smiling and full of life in my classroom. While I was looking at his body, I couldn't help but see myself in that same casket, in a similar suit with makeup applied to my face trying to make it appear as if I was still amongst the living. There is no way to protect yourself emotionally from everything you will feel when you're looking death right in the face. We will all die, but in America, Basim, Mario, and I live under the shadow of the sickle of death as it swings back and forth to reap the black seeds that have been sown in the soil of America.

I stated earlier in this section that I cannot count how many young black and brown men and women I've known who have been killed either by police or by the limited chances of street life. Traveling the country and seeing black life from the South, East, Midwest, and West Coast and doing work in jails and prisons in California has afforded me the opportunity to view my people from a variety of angles. What I see when I look in their eyes is me. It doesn't matter if they are wearing a suit and tie, jeans and a hoodie, county issue or California Department of Corrections and Rehabilitation uniforms, we are all subjected to the same racist reality. Some may have received a few more advantages than others and accomplished more things, but America isn't interested in your resume. America's first preoccupation is your skin color and the false stereotypes attached to it. I am Basim and Mario and the brothers and sisters locked up behind bars. They are me under any type of light in America that shines bright enough to show the blackness of our skin. That is precisely the reason why none of us will truly be free until we strive together to manifest our freedom and liberation.

Dream Revisited (2001)

You want to know my dreams?
I sleep to the sounds of M-16s
Because mostly blacks and browns died on the front-lines of
Viet-Nam.
Inhale aromas of
napalm
and carpet bombs
through my lungs
and exhale screams of Viet-Cong
in a language foreign to my native tongue.
Agent Orange burns
my chromosomes like
Gulf War syndrome
putting holes in my girl's ovaries
babies born deformed
my words form this ghetto poetry
and many nights I was torn from rest
like those police dogs who tore my flesh.
muscle from bone.

For freedom,
we marched determined
but Bull Connors and Mark Fuhrmans
turn on little innocent children
a powerful firehose.
Now my dreams consist of building named
Audubon
where bullets rip through my torso
like El Hajj Malik El Shabazz,
Malcolm X.
With stretch marks on my neck,
lynched, hung.
Under a southern sun

they cut my penis off
because they into those phallic symbols
and I sweat profusely in my sleep
because even in my dreams
I have to stay on my toes
nimble like
Bo Jangles,
Bo Jackson
So now we
shuffle
shuck
jive
to stay alive in black cleats
as athletes
or in black face
with buck teeth
like buckwheat
you see these types be stereo
so they surround me like sound
y'all we victims of these terrible scenarios
and some of us lose faith
which is one of the signs of this crazy world
where we don't go to the mosque
or to the church no more
because that's where they blew up
4 little girls
and many nights I had to make the street my pillow
it's where I dream dreams of poverty and skin disease
because eczema
covers my epidermis
from shooting smack in HIV infected
hypodermic needles
convulsions in a fetal position
in the back of a dark alley
as the poison kills parts of my cerebral cortex
because we already dead to them more or less.
So in my dreams
my children play with death,

some smoke sess and
others drink liquid death and
pack weapons of death on their waistlines
capable of causing an instant flatline
them tech-9s and latest designs
of high powered weaponry
I think you can see
these dreams
ain't no friend of mine,
Because in most dreams I'm claustrophobic
chained in the belly of slave ships
with my brothers and sisters
or confined by walls,
cells
6X9
doing time
25 to life
because my third strike
was theft of a slice of pizza
Ay, yo, Judge
I was hoping you could see I'm just a hungry child on welfare
with these crazy dreams of being a fresh prince of Bel Air
now I'm the prince of a cell with mildew and stale air
where a white guard will come escort me to a court yard
where I get to see the sun
for only 1 hour a day
and then back to lock up.
But you see this brother named Nas
he told me with words like this
"I never sleep because sleep is the cousin of death."
I'm trying to take that advice because this sleep ain't nothing
nice,
because in my dream sleep
is where zombies of fiends speak,
and I walk with bodies riddled by bullets because of these mean
streets.
Where the demon police
will leave you bleeding for speeding in a white Hyundai

and on the wrong day
if you dreaming in your car
and they wake you up with guns drawn
and you respond the wrong way,
it's bombs away,
bullet holes in driver side windows and doors
but the thing be
is these dreams are metaphors
reflections
of what I see in my 24-7.
The suffering
the oppression
the poverty
the depression
the hustling
without resting
these are my realities without question
and when I rest my head at night
you see my dreams
manifest them.

Reflections of a Black Boy:

I once saw a sign in the hands of a white supremacist which depicted Dr. King in cross hairs and the text read, "our dream came true."

Dr. King once criticized the Christian community of the United States for its racist and segregationist practices. In the 21st century segregation is technically illegal. Integration is the law of the land. In 21st century "integrated" America some of the most segregated places in America are found in American public schools Monday through Friday, every day of the year.

What does it mean to integrate when the system you're to integrate into is founded upon and still fueled by centuries of racial hatred and systemic discrimination for your kind?

Black people in integrated America are: the poorest of the poor, the most unemployed, the most negatively impacted by the medical system, the most incarcerated, the most likely to be killed by police or security personnel, the most housed in inadequate accommodations, the most pushed/kicked out of school, the most likely to die on a daily basis. All of this is sponsored by 21st century integrated America.

In my poem, "The Dream Revisited," I take more of a macro approach to happenings in America since Dr. King's famous "I Have a Dream" speech. The civil rights, black rights, and black liberation/empowerment movements of the '50s, '60s, and '70s marked an important time in Black America and in America overall. King envisioned a world where integration was a solution to many of the problems that black people had experienced as the outcasted other since 1619. Blacks have been constantly placed on the periphery of the American experience, even though America would not be possible without their labor and sacrifice since its inception. We are an organic part of this American social experiment. There is no America without the black contribution; the foundation of this society was thoroughly laid by black bodies.

If you want to examine it from a temporal lens, Jamestown was founded in 1607, and the first blacks were brought to Jamestown as indentured servants/slave in 1619. Twelve years into what would become the American experiment, black folks were here on this land being exploited for their labor to build up America.

Black people have literally put blood, sweat, and tears into establishing America for nearly 400 years, and, rightfully so, they want to reap some of the benefits that should be afforded to them on account of their work. When they begin to follow this natural inclination, they are punished, and what makes the sting worse is the fact that the very America we've built is one of the most resource wealthy societies on the planet. We have a front row seat to the milk and honey of the American dream, but we are forced to watch with faces pressed to glass as whites happily reap all the benefits.

The path to the civil rights movement was long and tumultuous. The fight since 1619 for the overwhelming majority of blacks in America has been for freedom and equality. This struggle culminated in a historic moment where parts of America began acknowledging the institutionally brutal treatment towards blacks. In 1954 the Supreme Court issued a landmark decision in Brown v, Board of Education of Topeka, Kansas. The Supreme Court stated regarding public schools that, "Separate educational facilities are inherently unequal." This decision made segregation in public education unconstitutional, and by analogy it made segregation in all public accommodations unconstitutional. However, it took another Brown v. Board decision the following year to actually "encourage" states to end their segregationist practices "with all deliberate speed." But ultimately, the Supreme Court does not have any enforcement authority so any decision it renders will not carry the weight of the paper it is inscribed upon unless other parts of the government and greater American society enforce the decision. Still, these decisions empowered the civil rights movement, and the push for full inclusion and integration was on.

Some of our leadership at the time thought that our being an "organic" part of the American experience would result in us being allowed a place at the table under integration once the policies of "separate but equal" were overturned. This is one of those places where theory is much different from reality. We as a people had never encountered this place before because America had never fully embraced inclusion of blacks at any time in the history of this land. The closest parallel would be the brief years of reconstruction immediately following the Civil War, but that was quickly replaced by the first iteration of Jim Crow.

In an attempt to be fair and truly understand Dr. King and the civil rights movement, it's important to note that black people in the '50s and '60s had reached a watershed moment that had never been witnessed before in their existence in America. From 1619 to 1865, chattel slavery was legal in America and the majority of black people in America were under that system. From 1865 to 1955, legal segregation in many parts of the union was law of the land, as well as "slavery by another name" i.e., convict leasing, debt peonage, sharecropping, and tenant farming. Millions of black people languished under this free but not really free status conferred to them. In response to this, millions of blacks fled the

South in search of new opportunities, but they inevitably found racism and institutional discrimination everywhere they went.

Blacks have always resisted the unfair treatment they've experienced in America. The mid-twentieth century provided blacks with a perfect storm for effecting change. What was it exactly that made the movements of the 1950s and '60s different? This is my rough approximation of those reasons. The difference can be attributed to myriad factors; one is the existence of an educated black mass that had been strengthened by years of political, social, and cultural struggle from previous generations. The NAACP was formed in 1909 and had a major impact on race-related issues. This strengthened those who would take part in the civil rights movement. The 1920s saw the rise of Marcus Garvey's UNIA and Noble Drew Ali's Moorish Science Temple and many other groups focused on rights and empowerment of blacks in America. We saw the emergence of new leaders both male and female. Voices like W.E.B. Du Bois, Ida B. Wells, and Paul Robeson, to name a few. The early twentieth century also saw the birth of a flourishing black arts culture. The Harlem Renaissance began to deliver new messages to black men and women throughout America. Black people had black icons to look up to that provided symbols of power and racial pride. The early 1900s gave black folks heroes like Jack Johnson, Joe Louis, and Jesse Owens. Each were the best in their respective fields for their moment in the sun. Imagine the feeling in the breasts of black folks who only decades before were just stepping off plantations and now were able to say a black man was the heavyweight champion or the fastest man in the world, able to legally beat all them white boys with ease.

The black community also started to capitalize on industrial dollars. Detroit had the largest black middle class ever seen in America because of the automotive industry. This money was invested in black businesses and black children, children who eventually went on to obtain diplomas, certifications, and degrees. Many historians will cite the return of black soldiers from World War II as a potential starting point for the civil rights movement. Black soldiers adorned themselves in the government-issued uniforms of the US of A, and they bravely fought and died for "liberty, freedom, justice, and equality" in America, but upon return they were greeted with the cold shoulder of state sponsored Jim Crow. In that moment, so many of them realized that in the eyes of America, Black Lives did not matter. We mattered enough to populate the military and fight and die at Uncle Sam's behest, but Uncle Sam and all of America's self-righteous rhetoric of justice, freedom, and equality for all was nowhere to be found when black people needed it.

These men also returned with tales of their experiences as black men in foreign lands. The message began to spread throughout parts of the black community that a black man could be treated as a man in parts of Europe. All of these elements coalesced and formed a strong current that began surging through Black America. This wasn't the black community that experienced the end of slavery via the Thirteenth Amendment. This was an entirely different black community, a new Negro. This was a black community that had heard America promise them freedom, liberty, and justice for all but saw the hollow emptiness of those promises. This was also a black community that had enriched itself with knowledge, courage, faith, cultural pride, and dignity to do something about America's all too familiar deaf ears.

This is the world that King emerged from. Armed with his belief in God, his people, and mankind, he marched forward to play his role in the struggle. On that momentous day in 1963, King approached the podium under the shadows of the Lincoln Memorial, overlooking the Washington Monument and the Reflecting Pool, and told the world about his dream.

The dream of being fully integrated and incorporated into a society is understandable, but how does one reach that when the hatred for your kind is deeply embedded in the soul of the country? What type of life is a person capable of in the face of that reality? Dreamers dream; it's what must be done. For a dreamer, the dream is necessary, like breathing is necessary for survival. Sadly, some of us dream dreams that are not made for our time and place. The dream of King on those steps that day is right; it's just; it's moral. It is what America should be, but hate and greed are irrational and very powerful. They can look at what is right and moral and ignore it to preserve self, especially when it is a hatred and greed woven deep inside the core of a society. America's greatness depends on the degradation of black lives. You can't deify the "Founding Fathers" if you are honest about their racism, sexism, rapist behavior, xenophobia, and hatred for the indigenous peoples of these lands. You can't celebrate achievements of industrial America when, once you brush the dust off the surface, you begin to find that it was built with coerced slave labor and the state-sponsored eradication of indigenous populations.

When I was younger, I was caught up in some imagined beef between Malcolm and Martin. It was like the '90s East Coast-West Coast hip-hop beef. I was in the camp of Malcolm. I'm still in the camp of Malcolm, but I love, respect, and benefit from King as well. It took me a while to fully appreciate the genius and commitment of King. That doesn't mean that I do not have a critique of some of his stances, but he was truly a man who lived and died for his people. He was sincere in his effort, and I love him for that. I am in awe of his commitment to non-violence in the face of such a brutal and inhumane system. I respect his vision of a dream for his people and America.

In an honest moment, I don't think there is anyone who cannot sympathize with his dream for black people in America. Who wouldn't regardless of color want to be judged for their character instead of some naturally occurring genetic marker? Who wants to live in a land where a complete false narrative sentences you to a lower quality of life because of the color of your skin or some other arbitrary descriptor? People want a society that respects them and their children, and allows them to be successful and pursue happiness. If you subtract out all the politics, religious debates, and economic theories you're left with the basic essence of what any social solution looks like. King had the audacity to say that in a racially charged America. He proclaimed a great dream, but as the poem details, we've witnessed the continuation of the long dark nightmare that America has given to blacks.

I'm a by-product of America's horrendous appropriation and clumsy application of King's dream. I technically live in an integrated society. King in his speech believed that complete integration is where white and black America needed to go to help answer the problems blacks faced. King was incredibly intelligent;

I don't believe he was shortsighted or ill-prepared for the dilemma black people faced in America. I know he knew America could still find a way around enforcing policies of justice and equality. He lived through Brown v. Board of Education. The decisions were passed down in 1954 and 1955; he was still fighting to desegregate public accommodations well into the 1960s. Integration has not brought America any closer to our beloved Dr. King's dream. Our society is still broken along the poisonous fault lines of "race." We are nowhere closer to resolving this issue. It is my opinion that America is not interested in full equality and inclusion of black people and other minority groups. My reason for thinking that is the fact that the dominant paradigm of America is at stake, and as King stated, " We know through painful experience that freedom is never voluntarily given by the oppressor; it must be demanded by the oppressed." The power structure in America has no interest in sharing what they have with anyone else. And at this point in time, they have no reason to, either.

Power will not concede power without force. We can demand it all we want, but America is unwilling to give in. If the power concedes, then what does it become? That answer is what America is fighting tooth and nail to avoid. Being integrated does nothing to erode the foundation of the white power structure in America. Being allowed to sit in the school, bus, or restaurant is something, but the power is in owning the restaurant, building, block, streets, and everything else. That is where the true power lies. We got our vote, desegregated schools, and public accommodations, but white America still owns every aspect of the world we live in. They will not give up that power. This is where the dream is deficient. The dream is rational and moral; it does not account for the greed and hatred in the hearts of men and women who want to protect their wealth and power. The hate in the response to the dream is the fuel to maintain the racial apparatus of power and domination. The hate is necessary, and as long as it is present, there is no equality through integration. They will use the hate to ignore, discard, or change the rules whenever they want to. The dreamers want peace, freedom, and equality, while those in power want to maintain power and control of wealth at all costs.

This poem was written in 2001 approaching the fortieth anniversary of the "I Have a Dream" speech. The "I Have a Dream" speech has become synonymous with the "success" of the civil rights movement and is used by white society as the calendric beginning of a post-racial America. They freeze King in that moment as if starting the following day, blacks and whites lived happily ever after. This was not the case. In fact, a little more than two weeks after the march on Washington, the 16th Street Baptist Church was bombed by white supremacist terrorists in Birmingham, Alabama, killing four little girls: Addie Mae Collins, Cynthia Wesley, Carole Robertson, and Carol Denise McNair.

In my opinion, the "I Have a Dream" speech is a great piece of revolutionary oratory. King was blessed with that, and you have to respect the courage he had to speak his truth to power. What I attempted to capture in my poem was some of what had transpired in America since his famous speech. I wrote it to update King on what our people have been going through since that moment in August of 1963. I reference many historical events that took place right after the march up until the present. The poetic attempt was made to show the fight for civil rights and the fight for racial equality has not gone in our favor. In some respects, we might be worse off than in 1963. That point is debatable; I have no intention of trying to convince anyone of either perspective, but the point remains the "struggle" is far from over. Our existence is still very dangerous, deadly, and painful, and "integration" into the American mainstream has not netted the result many of us had hoped for.

W. E. B Du Bois' famous work, *The Souls of Black Folks*, begins with the prophetic warning that, "The problem of the 20th century will be that of the color line." Du Bois knew that the racial hatred in America would be the seminal obstacle continuing to bar blacks from society. Du Bois was writing in the late 1890s but his words were certainly true for the twentieth century, as well as for what we've witnessed here in the twenty-first century. We can still dream the dream, but now that we've lived through four centuries of this land, we need to update that dream to truly fit our time and place. The color line is not going away any time soon. The hatred, greed, injustice, and racism are just as real and vicious. Our people need help, and America is not interested in helping. Integration has not been the solution to our problems. We have to go back to the drawing board and dream a new dream and then feverishly work to establish it here for our sake and that of our posterity.

Between Huey and Malcolm (2015)

Dr. Huey P. Newton had an epiphany when he once said, "I do not expect the white media to create positive black male images."

He wouldn't be surprised to see how
Evening networks
accumulate their net worth
of billions
off assassinating the character of our children.
They objectively report the news about black lives
matter
of factly
they spin white lies
that evolve into black lies
about black lives
because we don't matter to them
only in terms of
their bottom line.

Our worth in their eyes
is somewhere between
feline and pigeon.
Y'all we still less than k-9
because ninjas remember how they sent that boy Mike Vick to
prison
but be the color of George Zimmerman
a private citizen
and you can legally murder a nigga
and walk off Scott free,
but Walter Scott can't flee
and Eric garner can't breathe,
and Tyisha Miller can't sleep
and Oscar Grant can't see his daughter no more.
This ain't folklore.

Oh no, there's so much more
Four score and 7 years ago
nah, before that
1619
the first time these white beings
brought us to these shores
and since then it's been
all out war.
Their strategies and tactics have adapted,
They went from *de jure* to *de facto,*
ipso facto
they've tormented and attacked us
to extinguish the light of black souls.
Theirs is a pathological praxis
rooted in a xenophobic,
schizophrenic,
racially insecure
culturally immature social apparatus
forcing them to concoct a reality
that confers to them an unearned status
of unmerited advantage
to make them feel adequate.
In turn
we are termed
the thugs and the savages.
The whole deck stacked against us
we victims of bell curves
intelligent quotient averages,
recipients of jail terms
residents of a ghetto pan's labyrinth.
Very few can survive the madness.
And for those that do
government issued bullets
fly faster than light travels from the sun to our planet.
That 3rd rock from the sun.
Got me Malcolm in the middle,
nah, I'm Malcolm in the window
on third watch

watching over our daughters and sons.
Kalashnikov 47 cocked for them when they come
and we know
they will come
because for us
this land is a Robert Kirkman graphic novel
for it feeds off the blood of our young

We

are

the walking dead.
Just channeling our inner Tyrese
Because we're not destined to make it past
the first few letter boxes of the first few sheets

We

are

akin to proteins and fatty lipids in the belly of the beast.
Our appendages
are the meat of fleshy mangoes stuck in teeth
to be plucked and sucked in
moments after the feast
now let that digest

I know these words hit hard to the gut like dysentery
or hard to the brain
like religious missionaries colonizing souls and minds
no matter how you reduce it,
pain is the protocol
you either die or revoke your past
and try to pass for something you're not
on that Rachel Dolezal
but y'all
we can't opt out,

can't drop out,
especially when them cops is out
index itchy when them guns come out
we go to sleep dreaming at night wishing it would all run out
and be replaced by something different when the sun comes out.
But day breaks
and the morning is here
and we find ourselves
in mourning again
and I don't want to see
any more mornings
where we mourning kith and kin
So I guess it means
that we back on that Malcolm again

In essence it only means we want one thing.
We declare our right on this earth to be a man,
to be a human being,
to be respected as a human being,
to be given the rights of a human being
in this society,
on this earth,
in this day,
which we intend to bring
into existence by any means necessary!

Reflections of a Black Boy:

"I will fight until I die, however that may come. But whether I'm around or not to see it happen, I know that the transformation of society inevitably will manifest the true meaning of 'all power to the people.'" - Dr. Huey P. Newton

---

This poem right here was my poetic attempt at destroying the racist white supremacist power structure that is killing off this planet with one pen stroke. I tried to channel the spirit of all the ancestors and hurl their energy at the world because there is no telling how much time I have left. In whatever time I have remaining I want to create the purest and most quality work I can produce for the sake of my people's liberation. I know poetry alone cannot destroy this racist power structure but it can be a powerful tool in communicating a correct understanding of our condition and need to fight. That is the raw force behind "Between Huey and Malcolm."

What must become clear to us all is the fact that the hopes and dreams of white America are superficial in nature and are only possible because they are falsely propped up by the "American Way," which is undergirded with the very real application of systemic racism, discrimination, and exploitation. There is no American dream without the rape and pillage of black bodies for centuries. There is no American dream without the barbaric annihilation of indigenous populations of this land. There is no America without any of that. And for those who might be confused, there is no black liberation in America or the liberation of any people throughout the world without the dismantling of that entire system.

Instead of embracing all of those ugly truths about who and what they are, America as an institution and white Americans as a people mass-produce an artificial narrative to put themselves at ease. They become a little liberal with the story, too. They are quite adept at presenting their view of historical fiction as fact. Their idea seems to be a hint of historical embellishment makes the evil not taste so bitter. The problem with all of this lying is that once the lie starts they have to continuously lie to themselves about how righteous and honorable they are in acquiring and maintaining their empire.

White folks today try to recuse themselves from the horrors of the past and present by claiming they didn't do it. They weren't the slave owners or architects of the racist apparatus. However, they gladly reap the benefits of white privilege and supremacy. So much so that the median net worth of a white household headed by a person who did not, I repeat, did not complete high school is one-third higher than the median net worth of a black household headed by someone with a college degree. If we were to examine income inequality further, we would see more evidence of how the people who claim "they didn't do it" or they "didn't own any slaves," profit heavily from the system that they also claim to not perpetuate, while black people and other people of color still struggle. Being white in America means it doesn't matter if you're a high school dropout or highly educated; your privilege will guarantee that you will always fair better than your black counterpart or black superior. It's their game and they crafted it so they'll always win. How do you ignore such glaring discrepancies? What does a person, culture, or society have to do to act as if this blatant inequity is okay? The answer is constantly on display outside American windows. White society has erected a social culture filled with trivial pursuits and blinding distractions to occupy their minds instead of objectively analyzing the American experience. Because if they didn't, then they would see that they are not innocent. For the sake of white society that cannot be tolerated. They would crumble under the weight of their guilt if they truly acknowledge the evil they've manufactured for their little heads to rest comfortably at night. The famous slave owning and slave raping president Thomas Jefferson once said in his thoughts on America and its practice of slavery that, "I tremble for my country when I reflect that God is Just; that his justice cannot sleep forever." Thomas Jefferson knew he and this country were guilty, and it's that guilt that America works so hard to hide from its guilt.

If we personify America, I believe the experience of realizing its wrongs would trigger a psychotic episode. The mind of America would literally break. The body of America would be relegated to a vegetative state. America would lie comatose under the weight of understanding his/her role in the creation of this country at the expense of indigenous natives, blacks, other immigrant minority populations, and the environment. The guilt would be of epic proportions, causing America to choke on the guilt of what it has done. This is why America cannot afford to allow this to happen. Everything that is America and by extension Western civilization is at stake if a true accounting of history were to ever take place.

What would America and Western civilization be if they truly apologized and paid reparations for their crimes? What would happen if they compensated the native peoples for the lands they stole? If true compensation were to take place for the exploitation of resources (bodies, lands, minerals, agriculture, and labor), they would quite possibly be no more. America wouldn't be able to prop up its military-industrial complex, which it believes keeps it safe. It would not be able to support its parasitic capitalist economic system because it would no longer be able to strong arm for cheap resources and production. Its political institutions would implode because the weapons of control would no longer be present. The entire system would collapse upon itself. It is important to understand that and maybe I'm off in my prediction of possible ramifications of America's accounting but offsetting any of these potentials sheds light on very real reason why America and western civilization will fight with every ounce of its being to keep the game how it is.

When analyzing law and crime, investigators give attention to motive, the reason why an act was committed. The motive behind the rape and pillage of blacks and indigenous people is fairly clear. By doing so, America became the most powerful and profitable country on the planet. What would the motive be for not holding itself accountable for the various malicious crimes it has committed against the black and indigenous communities, as well as other communities? Simple. Money and power. In 2015 Professor Thomas Craemer of the University of Connecticut published an article in the Social Science Quarterly entitled, Estimating Slavery Reparations: Present Value Comparisons of Historical Multigenerational Reparations Policies, in which he put a price tag between 5.9 and 14.2 trillion dollars on reparations for blacks.

His formula for arriving at these numbers was as follows.

Craemer came up with these numbers by adding up the total hours worked by all slaves, men women, and children during the period of 1776 until 1865. This 89-year period was used because according to Craemer, "this is the time the United States could have abolished slavery but failed to do so." Focusing on slavery in that period Craemer multiplied the average wage prices of the day by the total amount of hours slaves worked. To give the amount a modern valuation he compounded an interest rate of 3% per year.

Professor Craemer's work is extremely important. In his research he also compared and contrasted instances when the

United States participated in the payment of reparations to other parties to further establish a context for reparations. Craemer developed two different scenarios to account for reparations owed, and based on his finding, "If the number of slave descendants is estimated based on the number of people who identify as African American or Black in the U.S. Census of 2006–2008 (37,131,771 individuals), per capita reparations would amount to $159,737.50 in Scenario 1 and $383,497.32 in Scenario 2."

Keep in mind that payout is only for 89 years of slavery. Professor Craemer made the decision to analyze that era of slavery because it was sanctioned under United States law.

If we were to truly attempt to calculate a total reparations payout we'd have to include the 150 plus years of slavery and indentured servitude that preceded this era in British colonial America. We also could not ignore calculating costs for black bodies killed, raped, brutalized; nor the cost of families forcefully separated by the institution of slavery. Although privatized chattel slavery came to an end in 1865 we'd have to include the hundreds of thousands of blacks who were victims of convict leasing, share cropping, tenant farming, and debt peonage. These were black men, women, and children who were re-enslaved legally in post 13th Amendment America. We'd also have to include black property that was stolen or destroyed by white society or agents of the government. We'd also have to account for the black bodies lynched in 19th and 20th century America.

This is not to belittle Craemer's research at all. His work establishes an important baseline for thoroughly analyzing the cost of reparations. His work is an important first step. The second, third, and subsequent steps would have to account for all the other harms to blacks in America that didn't occur specifically under the umbrella of chattel slavery. If we were to do all of that, then we'd be looking at the very real cost of black reparations. We haven't even began to attempt to calculate what reparations might look like for indigenous populations.

Still, the numbers Craemer provides gives you an idea of what is owed and also sheds light on why America would not be interested in reparations. Who is willing to pay out 14 trillion dollars? That number could possibly double or triple if we included some of the other historical injuries the American society has inflicted upon blacks. Fourteen trillion would be a bargain. The monetary loss would be astronomical but that wouldn't be the only loss, America would also suffer from a loss of prestige and power that it has accrued by showing a self-righteous face to the world while systematically controlling, enslaving, and exterminating its own people on the home front.

This is why the lie is so important for America to maintain. It has to keep the lie alive in order to sustain itself. The lie has evolved to the point where it has produced related lies that serve as "reasons" and "justifications" for why the theft, murder, and torture were necessary. This type of logic and reasoning is representative of what Dr. Joy DeGruy would identify as "cognitive dissonance." Keeping it to the American context, how do they explain away the slaughter and violent removal of indigenous natives? The cognitive dissonance response is, "Manifest Destiny," meaning that it was ordained by God that America destroy the various native civilizations. Why was slavery legal in early American history? "Founding Fathers" drafted Article I Section II, the 3/5 compromise, and later in the Dred Scott case Chief Justice Roger B. Taney elucidated, "The black man has no rights that the white man is bound to respect." More cognitive dissonance. Then when America appears to possibly change with some sincerity during reconstruction, America returns to form with various black codes and eventually legalizes segregation and Jim Crow via Plessy v. Ferguson, in which the cognitive dissonance again shines bright.

Justice Henry Brown, who wrote the summary decision, said:

"We consider the underlying fallacy of the plaintiff's argument to consist in the assumption that the enforced separation of the two races stamps the colored race with a badge of inferiority. If this be so, it is not by reason of anything found in the act, but solely because the colored race chooses to put that construction upon it."

It was a 7-1 decision against Homer Plessy who was classified in society as "black" but was so light that he could almost pass for white. And the "Justice" had the audacity to claim that it was the "construction" of black people that separate public accommodations marked blacks with a badge of inferiority. The sheer genius of that cognitive dissonance is expert level. Seriously, sometimes you have to sit back and admire the dedication and innovativeness with which they masterfully deflect personal accountability. It's events like this that give credit to oft repeated refrain in the black community, that white people are crazy. This man was saying it's not the society but the blacks themselves who made up this badge of inferiority stuff so they are claiming a phantom injury. I hate using the example of rape but this Supreme Court opinion is the equivalent of a man who rapes a woman and then is able to legally blame his rape on her because she asked to be raped by dressing or acting a certain way. It's completely her fault that she was raped, and according to Brown it was the fault of blacks that they felt some kind of way about being segregated. That's so wrong, and so hideous, but it's the American way.

The Purpose of "Between Huey and Malcolm"

I love this poem for the simple fact that I know that if I never have the chance to write or recite another poem, at least I was able to give this one to the world. Thinking of "Between Huey and Malcolm" and the larger body of work, *Black Boy Poems,* has created in me an even more peculiar feeling. None of us know when our time is up. Our physical life is a finite mysterious experience that we witness through emotions, thoughts, and senses. I'm fully aware of the consequences of the message of my work. I never anticipated a long life and fairly early on I tried to rid myself of the fear of death. This mindset made me appreciate the time I had to use it for the benefit of my people. In conversations I've had with my hero and mentor Elaine Brown, former chairperson of the Black Panther Party for Self Defense, she's reflected on the totality of her life and has said if she were to pass, she'd know she gave all she could for her people and would be at ease with that. Sista Elaine is a legend and I'm honored and humbled every time I have the blessing of an audience with her. She is unmatched in revolutionary authenticity and still wakes up every day to carry on the fight. I have done nothing that approaches a fraction of a percent of her contributions but completing "Between Huey and

Malcolm" and *Black Boy Poems* was the first time I felt that if I were to die, that I was able to leave something of value behind to help support my people in their fight for freedom and liberation.

I rarely write poetry anymore. I joke with a close friend of mine Amir Sulaiman, who I believe to be one of the best poets on the planet, that he ended my poetry career. I don't even think I am the best poet in my family. That honor goes to my cousin Prentice Powell. Even before I met Amir and before my cousin took up poetry, the best poet I had heard was my dear friend and brother, Ise Lyfe. I had focused primarily on writing music, but you cannot stop creativity when it is swelling up and forcing itself to the surface.

I don't know exactly how I conjured it, but it appeared. It thrust itself onto pages. I was in Rome, Italy, asleep in my hotel when I dreamt the first lines of the poem. I woke up and found the first piece of paper I could write on and began to jot down the lines from the dream. It is possible that the physical distance from the borders of America gave me a mental reprieve, which allowed me to access all of the emotions, pain, and hurt of the past few years and hurl it at the page. I don't know what the catalyst was; inspiration is its own universe and I was thankful that I was once again within its gravitational pull and I threw those words at that page as hard as I could.

If we trace the arc of the #BlackLivesMatter movement, we have to go back to Trayvon Martin and then to the deaths of Mike Brown and Eric Garner. That brings us from 2012 to the summer of 2014. These deaths and many similar executions of black bodies by law enforcement agents became more commonly displayed on social media and news networks over the following months. There's never an easy day to be Black in America and this past year and a half has been especially challenging. I personally know two men and a woman who were killed by law enforcement agents in 2015-16. All were students of mine, Alvin Haynes, Mario Woods, and Jessica Williams. There is no place to turn when you know that you and your people are devalued and deemed expendable in your society. That lesson has been ever present in America since 1619, but reinforced in multiple gruesome jarring ways over the past eighteen months. About a year after the murder of Mike Brown, in my hotel room in Rome, the floodgates broke open. My soul yearned to yell back at the chaos my people are living and dying in.

From the very beginning, I knew this piece was going to be a major statement. It didn't all come to me linearly though. I received bits and pieces that found their place toward the end of the poem and others that found a home in the middle of the poem. Sometimes my writing is more linear and sequential, and other times what needs to come out comes out and its proper position reveals itself over time. The two minds I've probably benefitted the most from on a "revolutionary" thought level are Dr. Huey P. Newton and Malcolm X. As I was writing the piece, words from both Huey and Malcolm called to me. I knew parts of their message needed to be present in the piece, but I didn't know where. Ultimately the idea of making their statements bookends to the piece seemed the most appropriate. To allow their words to stand alone and let my writing be the meat of the sandwich between their wisdom.

"Between Huey and Malcolm" is emphatic and powerful, but it is filled with tragedy. Our existence in America is tragic for the simple fact that black survival constantly puts you at odds with the system. The system cannot afford to include us properly. Every attempt at inclusion has been token in nature or so short-lived that we can only theorize about the historicity of it. America chooses cannibalism of its black inhabitants instead of granting them their rightful place. This is why I used so much symbolism of cannibalism in the piece. I reference *The Walking Dead* and the "meat of fleshy mangoes stuck in teeth." America is fine with eating us alive and is getting fat off of our pain and suffering.

Fighting for America to place value on the black life is outside of the paradigm of what America is capable of. The die is cast; we will always keep fighting for our worth, which will elicit the system's response of upholding its power by any means necessary. America and my people are locked in a never-ending struggle for power and position in society. It's a position we demand, and a position that America cannot afford to assign us. So we fight today, tomorrow, and all other days we will have on this planet. We will not lose. You will not win. This is why the poem ends with Malcolm who said it so clearly:

"In essence it only means we want one thing.
We declare our right on this earth to be a man,
to be a human being,
to be respected as a human being,
to be given the rights of a human being
in this society,
on this earth,
in this day,
which we intend to bring
into existence by any means necessary!"

Out (2005)

He was born out of wedlock
In and out of the arms of his pop
Who was in and out of trouble until he got shot
His mom in- between jobs
She in and out of relationships
He starts sliding in and out of the house quick
At school lessons go in one ear out the other
outside his window he sits to watch the gangsters and hustlers
jump in and out of new cars and new shoes
cash go in and out of their pockets to keep em looking brand-
new.
He's just a youth
easily influenced
so he's intrigued
by these cats with no job
getting money without a degree
now he
starts cutting classes
drops out of school
Now his hands are in and out of his pockets with rocks like them
other dudes
He's a pawn in this game that's hard to break out
He hangs out on the block
as this new scene plays out
the decision's laid out
it's either you in or you out.
Without a doubt he jumps in
scene one fade out.

His moms is out of his life now
because she's living right now
she told him to stop hustling
that's the same path your pop went down.

He can't hear her he blocks it out
back on the block where the cops is out
staking him out because now he's got clout.
An undercover approaches to buy
he had a notion something was strange
but he ignored it because he's out of his mind
he's drunk and he's high
Product and paper exchange hands
PD jump out of three gray vans with guns drawn
he's told
hands out your pockets better keep them high
his mom's prophecy comes true ain't no escaping this time
he's now property of the state
and can't wait to get out but on the outside life doesn't wait
he finds out his woman is late
another born out of wedlock
away from the arms of his pop
who's going to spend the years of his son's life behind the doors
of a cellblock.
When will this nonsense stop?
Y'all got to tell me when will this nonsense stop?

His baby is getting older now
starting to crawl
you see youngster out on the yard playing basketball.
You see him out by the three-point line busting his J
with no thought of changing his life when he gets out someday.
He can't seem to think outside of the box
or outside of his block
he's preparing
to spend his life in jail
or outlined in chalk.
Because on them streets you're always outnumbered and
outgunned
prison and death are the only logical outcomes.
But he's way out of control
he's in and out of the hole
is he ever going to figure it out

and break out
this outlaw Scarface complex
Meanwhile his son is without a father
who lives without a conscience
Because it was underdeveloped
enveloped by these hellish streets
I just tell it how I see it
some of y'all claim these words sound bleak
I would prefer if these stories never came out my mouth
but I am going to speak to the madness until my folks break out
break out

Reflections of a Black Boy

When this society says and thinks black, what comes to its collective mind? What labels/terms are applied to black people? How many positive stereotypes for blacks can you come up with in mainstream American society?

In the Islamic tradition there's a famous narration attributed to the Prophet of Islam which states actions are according to intention. If we apply this idea to America in order to analyze its intentions and actions towards black people, we might learn something very interesting. From the beginning the intention for black lives in America has always been to be beast of burden, the exploited lesser. This intention is important to grasp because it evolves into actions that form the laws, policies, social and cultural "norms," and mores. All of these things together create the limited space black people are allotted in this society.

This limited space leads one to weigh options to try to pick paths that are less harmful instead of make choices that represent independence and self-determination. How can you fully know yourself when all you do is react in order to survive? This is added to the fact that we've already inherited the spiritual amputation of our culture and traditions from Africa. It's a cold game.

I am not blind to the privileges that exist in American society. Although my skin color has granted me a second class existence, that does not prevent me from seeing the fact that I do benefit from a number of privileges. Still, America has designed roles for us in this society. Initially, our role was to provide cheap and free labor for America's emerging agricultural economy. So much so, that by the start of the Civil War in 1861, the United States was responsible for two-thirds of the world's cotton production and that labor was supplied by black bodies. Once the Civil War ended, the need for cheap black labor didn't magically disappear. The southern economy simply morphed and created a new system which writer Douglas A. Blackmon called *Slavery by Another Name*. The end of slavery granted more mobility to some blacks, and as a result, we started to see mass migrations out of the South. The industrial movement was booming in America so some blacks were able to find work in factory towns and began to do better when compared with their life in the South. Regardless of the black life being lived in the North or the South, there were very specific roles carved in social granite that black men and women had to fulfill. Stay within these boundaries, and you were relatively safe; step outside of them, and you were risking life and limb.

In every evolutionary step the American social order has experienced, it has cast its roles for its black subjects in that social granite. The premise is always the same; we are to be a subjugated people, exploited to benefit the American machine. Post-1865, those roles have been teased by the appearance of equality and opportunity, but it always reduces to the same solution: We are a class or two stratum below. There is a quota for the outliers of black men and women who have been granted access to certain roles. Very few will be allowed proximity to the most coveted areas of white American society. Some will be able to lead a middle-class life where they can own, but most likely rent a home. Their children can be raised in fairly well-to-do areas with decent schools. Still, the reality of blackness cannot be forgotten, so these middle-class blacks still hope they and their children avoid any run-ins with the system or law that could result in a police officer accidentally taking another black life.

For most blacks in America, we are to exist under the poverty line. We are to be the most unemployed. We are to live in the worst neighborhoods, attend the worst schools, be perpetually involved in a game with the authorities that has gone by many names, the latest of which has been called stop and frisk. The other perennial favorite is hide and go seek, aka arrest and lock niggas away in jail and prison. From our schools, we are the most likely to be pushed out or drop out. As a result, we have the lowest graduation rates. Our children are to be raised in neighborhoods with limited opportunities for growth and development. Guns and drugs, two of this country's greatest tools of mass control and destruction, are always readily available.

Presently, this is the typecast role that America has written for us. We die more than any other group of Americans due to the slow suffocating hold America has on our communities. Some of us are able to perform magical feats to escape the limitations placed on black lives, albeit the escape for many is temporary. We can either out think, rap, dance, sing, dribble, shoot, run, throw, act, or create some new piece of culture that Americans will soon attempt to appropriate from us. The overwhelming majority of us fall into one of the non-extraordinary roles. It is difficult to assess exactly when and where it happens, but somehow somewhere there's a quick edit or cut scene which leads to a seamless transition from child with all hopes and dreams to lights, cameras and action, cue broken black faced child center stage stepping forth to play his or her part in the ongoing blockbuster "The Life and Times of the Tragic American Niggers."

That's what "Out" is. The piece is fairly old, but the content is forever relevant due to the treatment of the black life in America. I think at the time I had taught in San Francisco jails for a little more than three years. One of my mentor teachers had shared with me a very wise piece of advice; she said, "Teaching is about relationships." I endeavor to create strong relationships with all my students in order to foster a healthy learning environment, so I can better serve their needs. As a result, we would share some very real moments where students would open up about life. In conversations with my male students, I kept hearing the same stories over and over again. There were some minor differences, but the essence of the story was always the same. It might have started out with both parents being gone, or moms was lost in the streets or prison. Some stories began with being raised in group homes. Many of my students actually liked parts of school, but there always came a moment when the cost-benefit analysis didn't work out in schools' favor any longer. Armed with the power of their decision, they were out in the street trying to survive best they knew how.

It's always a trip to witness the moments when my students unintentionally break character. It's like a glitch in the matrix; they fall out their role and begin to think and act differently. It might happen as a result of solving a complex mathematics problem that they felt they could never conquer, or it might be when they realize how industrialism singlehandedly changed the course of human society culminating in the creation and marginalization of blacks and other peoples of color in urban ghettoes, or it might be when they learn in an economics class how to invest and make money off their practice stock portfolio. It can be anything, but in those moments I can witness the makeup come off. I see the actors out of wardrobe, off camera, and off stage. For a brief moment they realize they are not what America has told them they have to be. For a split-second, they begin to believe that they can be more, that there is more to them and for them. They begin to see that they are capable of something greater than the sad blaxploitation reruns that we have been conscripted to live.

America for the most part robs us from birth of the right to be our authentic selves. I think of two passages from the *Autobiography of Malcolm X* where Malcolm describes this very phenomenon. In one section he speaks about black folks who could've been scientists, innovators in the medical field, and made other great contributions to mankind but so many are denied those opportunities because of the color of their skin. In another section he makes commentary about his former numbers runner West Indian Archie. Malcolm believed Archie had the mind of a mathematician because of how he was able to work numbers. West Indian Archie's math genius should've been featured in another arena but because of his blackness he had to use it to survive on the street.

Both instances reference black men; the roles and restrictions are equally if not more restrictive for black women. And this is what I see in the stories that I hear from my students. This is what the piece is attempting to convey, the tragic figures that our society has forced us to play. The casting call is made for all black boys and girls to audition for. We arrive at that place in different ways, but the outcome is a forgone conclusion. Prison and death are the only logical outcomes. Some play the role with a little more flair; maybe they put their own spin on their interpretation of the character, and the crowd goes wild when they finally fulfill their character's doomed destiny. Backstage the money changes hands, some in attendance will stand and applaud, and like any great production the audience will come back for more.

The American script writers have done a remarkable job of creating multiple versions of the same sad black roles. As much as I'd love to ignore it I know that I too, play a role. In every age there are the agitators, the resisters, those that attempt to step outside of the confines of the underdeveloped roles and write our own script. I cannot accept what America has sentenced me and my brethren to. I reject it on every level. I will not wear your makeup or fit your wardrobe. I will not answer your casting call and audition for your parts. I will not stand on your stage in a bastardized rendition of a once great people. I am dreaming up something new and different that you can't appreciate the beauty of because your lens is too myopic. I could easily conform and seek out one of those comfortable middle-class quota positions. I know the path to "ease" and "comfort" in America. I've been groomed to walk and talk correctly to "make it" in America. Taking that path would mean I gave up on myself and my people for a few extra dollars, more comfortable shackles, and better slave accommodations. I cannot do that! I will not do that! I could also drown myself in drugs, alcohol, women, lust, streets, and any other distractions that suck the life force out of black men and women. It's so easy to do, but I reject that as well. So I'm left with one possible role: the outsider, the agitator, the angry black revolutionary who will always be involved in some form of fight against the system. This is not a role created for blacks by America; it is an independent production, but our role is a byproduct of the scandalous theater America has been running for the last 400 years. I am a freedom fighter, and I will fight for the freedom of my people by any means necessary. That is my purpose; that is my role. It is the only one that I am suited for. It is the only one that I can play with honor and dignity.

Blue Devil (2002)

Boxed in on all sides nowhere to run or to turn to
I box concrete walls until my hands turn blue
broken and swollen knuckles
skin torn and chapped
I find freedom in syntax that seeps through the cracks
in the walls
to reach them cats still on the outside
how many years have I been on the inside
I lost count
days become nights, weeks become years
planets revolve around the sun
I'm still stuck inside here
evolved into an animal
forgot what the world looked like.
Push-ups and sit-ups prepare me for fist fights
they move me through the prison population
cuffs fit my wrist tight
I'm at my wits end because my bid is life.
Can you imagine being locked in a cage
for the rest of your days plus some?
I'm surrounded by shadows and dark thoughts
of making my heart stop
with bad habits and odd customs.
Try to hang myself when the doors are locked
to make it stop
but more of us get locked up everyday
over 2 million and counting
from a bird's eye view I have flashbacks of old days
how they carried us away from our homes shackled in chains
deja vu because modern day prisoners are slaves.
Check your constitution I ain't the first one to say it
the prison industry is the new slave ship, slave ship.

Innocence a commodity that's bought and sold
but oddly escapes the possession of my black body
I manifest Rodney King dreams
when I hear license and registration
because reaching for my ID could be
justification for my homicide
the wrong color at the wrong time
you a fool if you believe justice is colorblind.
In the belly of the beast on streets I stand
with hands cuffed behind my back
and get beat with black wood objects
in Oklahoma City
or smashed on hoods of squad cars in Inglewood projects
already walking with chains around my neck
they just ain't found a crime to convict me of yet
but as I speak they framing crime scenes to confine me
so what I'm rhyming about be pertinent
because police interaction be beyond permanent.
Pigs becoming judge, jury, and executioner
majority of pigs are white
and this is why some might compare white folks to Lucifer.
For many this life be a living hell
so we rebel in these streets
screaming and yelling
product of environment so therefore I'm a son of rebellion.

Reflections of a Black Boy

"The birth and development of the American police can be traced to a multitude of historical, legal, and political-economic conditions. The institution of slavery and the control of minorities, however, were two of the more formidable historic features of American society shaping early policing. Slave patrols and Night Watches, which later became modern police departments, were both designed to control the behaviors of minorities ...

"Blacks have long been targets of abuse. The use of patrols to capture runaway slaves was one of the precursors of formal police forces, especially in the South. This disastrous legacy persisted as an element of the police role even after the passage of the Civil Rights Act of 1964." - Victor E. Kappeler, Ph.D.

The greatest fear I had as a child was going to jail or prison. I became aware of this fear very early on. I didn't fully understand the concept of jail and prison, but I knew it was a place that I didn't ever want to be. In my childhood days I heard a phrase over and over again that over time terrified me, "Elmwood." I did not know what Elmwood was. Nobody took the time to tell me that Elmwood was the largest jail in San Jose and is conveniently located on the border of San Jose and Milpitas right across from the Great Mall, auto dealerships, and multiple gated communities. One of my best friends and his family live in one of those gated communities now. It is possible that nobody took the time to explain that to me because they didn't think a child my age should have to worry about or be afraid of jail/prison. The reality of black childhood presents very different possibilities for parents and children alike to deal with. Not fully knowing what Elmwood was allowed for my imagination to do its thing. Elmwood became this horrible place in the woods where people disappeared to, and some never came back. In my mind it was always dark and draped in hecka foliage. There was a sinister fog mist present that made it cold and terrifying. I would hear, "so and so is at Elmwood," and immediately it conjured up an image something like the Bermuda Triangle where they would be lost forever. It got to a point for me where I didn't ever want to go to a forest or the woods. Skip camping. That was completely out of the question. In my mind there was no address for Elmwood, which meant that it could be anywhere. All I knew was that if somebody was at Elmwood, we weren't going to see them again for a long time. I did not want that to be me. As I got older, the pieces started to make more sense. Elmwood was a jail and police were the ones who took you to jail. So my fear of Elmwood eventually contributed to the development of a healthy fear of the police. I didn't want to be anywhere near them to give them a chance to take me to Elmwood.

Black folks have had these healthy fears of police and the state since day one, and rightfully so. As Dr. Kapeller points out, the oppressive institution of slave catching is the predecessor of what eventually became the American police system. This historical foundation is important because it provides a much needed contextual backdrop for understanding police practices and the development of the prison industrial complex. Another important fact to include is that many police departments in majority black areas throughout the country, and especially here in California, were populated with white officers from southern states. These are the departments that truly embodied the spirit of their slave catching DNA. That history makes the present reality of what my brother Tongo Eisen-Martin reported for the Malcolm X Grassroots Movement, that every twenty-eight hours in America, a black person is murdered by a security/law enforcement agent, more understandable. It doesn't matter what era of black life we examine the police, pigs or slave catchers all had the same goal "to control the behavior of minorities", specifically black folks, by any means. That is exactly why some of us experience those traumatic intergenerational flashbacks of our ancestors who were held as slaves when we encounter law enforcement agents. It is not just a cop talking to a black man, woman, or child. It's 400 years of slave catching/policing all present in that "request" for license and registration. Shackles and handcuffs are the same. Being confronted by a slave catcher a few miles from masta's plantation feels the same as having bright lights flashed in your eyes on the streets of West Oakland. There is no difference between those encounters. In understanding that all of these encounters are the same we also know that any interaction with police/slave catchers anywhere within the borders of the United States can mean injury, incarceration/enslavement, or death.

Let's take a step back and discuss the modern day systems of policing, the criminal justice system, and the prison industrial complex. The numbers are well substantiated, which should lead an objective mind to clearly see beyond any shadow of a doubt that the criminal justice system, which includes law enforcement, courts, jails and prisons, is racist. The misapplication of justice and the intentional overemphasis of policing in poor black and brown neighborhoods is also well documented. I know not all cops are bad, and the same goes for judges or employees of jails and prisons. I refuse to paint individuals with a broad-brush stroke. It's simply not right to do that, and it's not accurate. I don't like being falsely stereotyped, and I refuse to do that to other groups. However, what is right and what is accurate and supported by volumes of empirical data is that all these individuals belong to much larger institutions that operate with racism as founding and guiding tenets.

There are good individuals who seek to be just or change these institutions from the inside, which is commendable, but the institutional practices, as well as some individual practices of people who represent the Criminal Justice System (CJS), unequivocally demonstrate racial bias that largely affects the black community in America. I will not exhaust the reader with a long list of statistics, but there are some numbers that help to provide some context for my hatred and harsh criticism of the institutions of law enforcement and the CJS. This knowledge and experience is what drives the tone in the poem "Blue Devil."

If you are interested in a more comprehensive look at the CJS and its incarceration habits, then read Michelle Alexander's *The New Jim Crow*, and if you want to look at even more brutal incarceration history, then read Michael Blackmon's *Slavery by Another Name*, or *A Brief History of Slavery* by Dr. Victor Kappeler. Each have created works that shine bright lights on the CJS and PIC. Still, here are a few numbers and points that need to be discussed for the context of Blue Devil to make sense.

Demographic Data

Blacks are 12 percent to 13 percent of the American population.

Whites are about 78 percent of the American population.

Depending on how you define "black," you'll find blacks making up somewhere between 40 to 60 percent of the incarcerated population. This is according to the Bureau of Justice 2009 report.

People who identify as two "races" are not counted among the black population. Law enforcement agents, in their liberal use of "probable cause" to stop someone who they believe appears "suspicious," do not first conduct an authentic "black" test to determine whether they should stop the person. The stops are largely subjective assessments heavily influenced by the color of one's skin. This means you might be black enough to be stopped by police but not "black" enough to be counted as part of the black jail/prison population. That is one reason why the percentage shift is so dramatic. Forty percent of all inmates in jails and prisons today are solely identified as black. Depending on your definition of black, when you compare that with the population of blacks in the U.S., you can see that blacks are either 300 percent to 500 percent over-represented in incarcerated facilities. That breaks down to an average of six times more likely to be incarcerated than their white counterparts.

On the other side of the equation, whites constitute 78 percent of the American population but only comprise a little more than 30 percent of those incarcerated. Whereas, blacks are way over-represented in incarceration when contrasted with their total percentage of the American population, whites are under-represented to an incredible degree. What one would reasonably assume using scientific measurement as a standard in a just and fair society, is that incarceration numbers should correlate closely with the respective group's population percentages. Simple logic would dictate that if there are fewer blacks in America, then there should be fewer blacks in incarcerated populations. More whites in America should logically lead to incarceration rates closer to the total white percentage of population in America. But that is nowhere close to what we see when we analyze American incarceration data. This leads one to hypothesize that either blacks are inherently more prone to crime, which we know is false, or the system profiles a specific group of people as criminal. As the homies on the block who serve as street corner philosophers would say, "youngster, them numbers don't lie." I always liked that line, but we do know numbers can be manipulated. However, when it comes to who is incarcerated in America, those numbers are as true as can be.

Police Contact

This section details how people contact police. Most people arrested in the United States have been arrested for non-violent "crimes," mainly drug-related offenses. Empirical data tells us that all groups of people use drugs. No "ethnic" or "racial" group says no to drugs. Drugs can be found in any neighborhood, in every city or town in America. The actual group that statistically uses drugs more than any other group is whites. According to journalist Saki Knafo in an article citing findings from the Substance Abuse and Mental Health Services Administration, Human Rights Watch and the BJS:

"Nearly 20 percent of whites have used cocaine, compared with 10 percent of blacks and Latinos, according to a 2011 survey from the Substance Abuse and Mental Health Services Administration—the most recent data available.

Higher percentages of whites have also tried hallucinogens, marijuana, pain relievers like OxyContin, and stimulants like methamphetamine, according to the survey. Crack is more popular among blacks than whites, but not by much.

Still, blacks are arrested for drug possession more than three times as often as whites, according to a 2009 report from the advocacy group Human Rights Watch.

Of the 225,242 people who were serving time in state prisons for drug offenses in 2011, blacks made up 45 percent and whites comprised just 30 percent, according to the Bureau of Justice Statistics."

All that means the calculus is something like this: There are fewer blacks in America. Fact. There are blacks who use drugs. Fact. There are more whites in America than blacks and not just a little bit more; there are about 246 million white people in America. Fact. There's about 42 million blacks. Fact. Do the math. If you borrowed correctly, you'll see there are 204 million more white people than blacks in America. Fact. 200 million more whites. That's five times the number of whites than blacks. Understand that number. Whites constitute a greater percentage of America than blacks and are statistically speaking more likely to use drugs than blacks. Fact. But blacks, who are dwarfed in number by the population of whites, are more likely to be arrested and put in jail or prison for drugs than whites. Fact. That does not make any type of logical sense at all. The only way to attempt to make sense for these horrendous disparities is by accounting for the racist practices of the PIC and CJS.

Some folks are arrested for violent crimes too, but most folks are in jail and prison as a result of drugs or other related non-violent crimes. Since no community has a monopoly on drug use, why is it that some communities are policed more in regards to drugs? Since we know that white communities tend to have and use more drugs than other communities, why is it that we see fewer white folks incarcerated for drug sales and possession? These are essential questions a person with a conscience must answer.

A few things to consider

- Depending on what locale you're in, blacks are somewhere between six to thirty times more likely to be arrested than whites. There are some instances where more black people are arrested than actually live in a city or town. Dearborn, Michigan is one example of such ludicrous policing. Dearborn has a majority white and Arab population, current census numbers state there are around 4,000 blacks in Dearborn. According to arrest records submitted to the FBI in a two year span of 2011-2012 the Dearborn police reported more than 4,500 arrests of blacks. That's 500 more than actually live in the city. Let's break this down, Dearborn PD arrested so many black people in those two years that they could've arrested every black man, woman and child once, and some twice. This insane statistical reality means that blacks are 26 more times likely to be arrested than whites or Arabs. Black folks represent 4 to 5 percent of the total population in Dearborn but account for more than 50% of arrests. Sadly, this isn't the only extreme example in our nation.

- I'm from San Jose, California. Blacks make up 2 percent to 3 percent of the San Jose population today. Blacks are virtually invisible in San Jose, which is quite telling because of San Jose's importance to the tech industry and the future of America, but that's for another discussion. When I was a kid, blacks constituted a greater percentage (6 to 8 percent) of San Jose but not by much. My parents literally stitched together a black community for my sister and me to grow up in. Despite our relative invisibility, the San Jose Police Department seems to see blacks fairly well because we are 10 percent of all those arrested. You actually have to look hard to find black people in San Jose, but cops seem to find them and arrest them one out of ten times a person is arrested. Now statistically speaking when a group is overly represented in a category, this tends to suggest a correlation of some sort. The correlation that I'm asserting is policing is biased along the lines of race. San Jose is around 35 percent Latino, 30 percent white, and 32 percent Asian. Pardon the generic descriptors, but that's how it's broken down. Both whites and Asians are far underrepresented in their arrest numbers when compared to their population totals. Whites were 19 percent of total arrests, and Asians were 14 percent of arrests. The other over-represented group was Latinos, who were 52 percent of total arrests. This is just police contact. This doesn't even account for how the contact happens or if force was used.

- In Oakland, California, you have a greater concentration of blacks. Black folks make up about 28 percent to 30 percent of the population. Consequently, they are 62 percent of those stopped by police. Latinos were 17 percent of stops, whites 12 percent of stops, and Asians 6 percent. Total Oakland population: whites 35 percent, Asians 17 percent, and Latinos 25 percent. Every other group is under-represented regarding arrests according to race and their population numbers.

- San Francisco, CA. This language is taken directly from a San Francisco city-commissioned study by the Reentry Council in conjunction with the W. Haywood Burns Institute: "Black people are 7.1 times more likely to be arrested in the city than white people, 11 times more likely to be booked into jail, and 10.3 times more likely to be convicted. Those convicted spend more time on probation or behind bars." Data is based on records through 2013. Demographics of San Francisco: whites 50 percent, Asians 30 percent, blacks 6 percent, Latinos 14 percent.

- California is supposed to be a bastion of liberalism and inclusion. Even Berkeley, which is famous for its hippy culture and alternative politics, has similar statistical abnormalities, which are actually normalities in America. Blacks are 10 percent of Berkeley's population but account for 31 percent of people stopped by police. Whites are 60 percent of Berkeley's population but account for 36.7 percent of police stops. Of the two groups stopped, 66 percent of blacks were let go without being arrested or cited, and only 38.1 percent of whites were let go without being arrested or cited. So the Berkeley Police Department is telling me more blacks were stopped for no violation than whites. Sixty-six percent of all blacks stopped had to be let go because they had nothing on them or weren't doing anything they could be arrested for. While about 62 percent of the whites stopped were found to be in "violation" of some type of law necessitating arrest. Still, BPD wants to focus their efforts on a law-abiding black population and ignore a law-breaking majority white population. That is not "policing," that is targeting and hunting a specific group of people in hopes of making them look criminal.

- We can go on and on. In almost every locale where black people reside in America, you'll find these over-representations with police contacts. If you control for gender, you'll find similar data for black women when compared to white women and other groups of women.

Law enforcement agencies want to brush the data aside with various innovative uses of cognitive dissonance. They cite problems with interpreting data. They might say the statistics don't fully represent the picture. They'll use buzzwords like high crime areas to explain why they concentrate resources in certain places. People are mainly being arrested for drugs, not robberies, murders, rape, burglaries, or larceny. Drugs. Blacks aren't the only people with drugs; whites are the folks with more drugs than any other group, and there's 200 million more whites in America. Yet and still, we see "policing" of black and brown communities more than any other group of people.

Incarceration

- You have to have been contacted by the police somewhere to end up in jail or prison. Once that happens, you enter the criminal justice system, and the empirical data demonstrate once again that this institution is skewed heavily due to race. We'll refresh the numbers: Blacks are 12 percent to 13 percent of the nation's population, but, depending on how black is defined by "authorities," we are 40 percent to 60 percent of the incarcerated population. So basically four to six out of every ten people locked up in jails and prisons are black. In some areas, the numbers for all black men living within a jurisdiction who are incarcerated are one out of three black men in the total adult male population. In other places it is two out of five of the total adult male population. This means if you were to take all the black men in a city and line them up, one out of three or two out of five would be in department of corrections uniforms. In Washington, D.C., four out of five folks arrested are black even though they make up 47 percent of the population. Since blacks are the majority arrested, they are the overwhelming majority in D.C. jails. It is a statement of fact that D.C. jails are almost completely black.

- It is a statement of fact that there isn't one state in the Union where rates of incarceration for blacks are ever equal to or less than incarceration rates for whites. Nor is there a state where blacks are incarcerated equal to their percentage of the population. Hawaii is the state where black incarceration rates are the lowest in the country, but even in Hawaii blacks are more likely to be locked up than whites. According to census data, we are 2.5 times more likely to be in jail or prison than whites. This is the lowest rate in the country. The corresponding highest rate is found in Iowa, where we are eleven times more likely to be in jail and prisons than whites. And this is only one small piece of the puzzle. We can talk about sentencing and solitary confinement as well as death row. We can discuss parole and probation terms. All of it can be viewed through a color lens, and what you'll constantly see is that disparities emerge when you examine how black men and women are treated by the CJS.

"Blue Devil" is the justifiable angry response to America's criminal justice practices. For many blacks in America, law enforcement and the CJS have served as institutions of terror. Just recently, we've had a number of politicians come forward and apologize for the decisions they made to lock up more people for nonviolent offenses. Former President Bill Clinton has apologized for laws that he helped pass while he was president that led to more men and women in jails and prisons. Clinton admitted in a speech delivered at the 2015 NAACP annual meeting in Philadelphia that his signature on a crime bill made the problems worse. Clinton was referring to the Omnibus Crime Bill he signed that led to federal three-strikes laws that mandated life sentences for convictions after two or more prior convictions that could either be violent or nonviolent. The Reagan and Bush administrations before him passed laws that helped create the PIC as well. Clinton's apology is noteworthy but in his apology he still attempted to justify why he did it using his presidential cognitive dissonance. He blamed the necessity of the law on rising crime from the previous decade. At one moment he attempted to tell a story about rampant gang warfare and how little children were being killed in drive-bys. Clinton's apology is negated by his passionate pleas to justify why the law was needed at that time.

There is no doubt that crack changed the inner city, but crack and the high-powered weaponry that accompanied the drug trade didn't magically appear in the hood. Those things were imported into the hood with the aid of government agents. This is no conspiracy theory. The Contra conflict was funded by profits from cocaine sales throughout the West Coast in the '80s. The Central Intelligence Agency helped facilitate the sale of cocaine to inner cities largely populated by black and brown folks in exchange for millions of dollars to fight to overthrow a Communist regime that white business people and politicians didn't like in Nicaragua. Secretary of Defense John Kerry published a report in 1989 while he was a senator detailing the CIA's dealings with drug traffickers.

Drugs get sold in the neighborhood when people are depressed, poor, unemployed, and without viable options for a healthy and productive life. There wouldn't have been a need for the drug economy if jobs weren't taken out of the inner city and if schools and social services were well funded. Provide people with access to good jobs and education, and you minimize the chances of poverty-induced epidemics. Our politicians act as if they don't understand that logic because they do not care about our lives. Clinton's apology in the grand scheme is confirmation that the system has been exploiting us, but tangibly it hasn't overturned any of the laws on the books. His apology has not set anybody free or changed one law.

We've even had leaders of major police forces and jails and prisons call for major reforms. They have come together and formed an organization with an official website and everything. They call themselves The Law Enforcement Leaders to Reduce Crime and Incarceration. In their own words:

"We believe the country can reduce incarceration while keeping down crime. We believe unnecessary incarceration does not work to reduce crime, wastes taxpayer dollars, damages families, and divides communities. We aim to build a smarter, stronger, and fairer criminal justice system by replacing ineffective policies with new solutions that reduce both crime and incarceration."

Their Mission Statement

"As current and former leaders of the law enforcement community—police chiefs, sheriffs, district and state's attorneys, U.S. Attorneys, attorneys general, and other leaders—protecting public safety is a vital goal. From experience and through data-driven and innovative practices, we know the country can reduce crime while also reducing unnecessary arrests, prosecutions, and incarceration. We can also reduce recidivism and strengthen relationships with communities. With the goal of building a smarter, stronger, and fairer criminal justice system, we are joining together to urge a change in laws and practices to reduce incarceration while continuing to keep our communities safe."

This is an important move on the part of men and women who have played a role in perpetuating the system. They should be commended for speaking out against what they view as major wrongs. In short, the people that operate the system are saying it isn't fair. They are making my job that much easier. I am still definitely a very angry black man when it comes to the "justice system" in America. I wear that proudly on my shoulders but the system is justifying my anger by saying it is wrong. The architects of the system are saying it is unfair and it is destroying families. Black people have been in the know on that since 1619. That is the energy at the heart of Blue Devil. One of my lines is, "innocence is a commodity that's bought and sold but oddly escapes the possession of my black body, I manifest Rodney King dreams when I hear license and registration because reaching for my ID can be justification for my homicide, the wrong color at the wrong time, you're a fool if you believe justice is colorblind..."

The appeals and apologies made by the framers of this system are necessary, as well as their attempts at reform, but they are crocodile tears for the men and women who've encountered this misapplication of justice in America. No reform or apology will give years back, or lives back. And what about the blemished stigmatized existence many formerly incarcerated peoples deal with once they reenter society. Make no mistake, with no apology and no minced words, I hate the system. How could you love, respect or view in a moral light something that has been so grossly abusing lives for so long. This is what Blue Devil speaks to. It's the hate and contempt for a system that has wantonly terrorized black people for centuries and will continue to do so because the system is comfortable with how it operates. We will forever be at odds and therefore it will forever be the devil in our eyes.

Again, not all police officers are bad. Not all members of the CJS are evil and out to get black people, but the institutions as a whole all over the United States operate in a way that negatively impacts black people more than any other group. The disparate treatment is even more egregious when you compare and contrast the black and white experience with the system. It's wrong; my voice is not the only voice proclaiming how wrong it is. I hate it because I've lived through what it has done to people I love. It's unfair; it is unjust; it is apartheid. I'll end with this. For blacks in America, justice has never been the rule. It has always been the exception. For blacks in America injustice has always been the rule, no exception.

War Zones (2002)

I wrote this for my people.

We the types jumping out of street gutters
and man hole covers
I ran with brothers that came straight from the sewers
the type to give Freddy Kruger a nightmare.
Young folks of color without a care in the world
who ain't afraid to die.
From the Southside to the east
we war with the beast
police send in their calvary new battalions
while I'm freestyling rounds from under a broken street light
from a sniper's distance
with pinpoint accuracy
to cause confusion on the premises
to make sure that we safely retreat
but some of us won't make it back to the street
prisoners of war
held in detention camps with names like
Elmwood, San Quentin, Soledad Maximum Security Prison
I spit with conviction
until I get dizzy
stay camouflage by the foliage of the city
backtrack to the barracks
stay away from generic soldiers
turncoats, possible informants
young folks hollowed out by federal torments
reintroduced to the game
to prevent the gains
of the side they used to fight for
if you didn't know by now this life is war.
Whether you believe it or not

we squeeze shots to ease tension on the block
avoid lockdown
David versus Goliath.
We triumph with justified violence
fling rocks blessed by the Most High
from sling shots concealed in pockets of our baggy exterior
with name brands like Akademiks
because the mission is truth
salute my folks with the words of peace.
Not knowing if our eyes will meet again
just knowing that we fought for what was right in the end
the end
the end
war zones
war zones that we're forced to call home.

My pants sag when I walk to show ain't nothing you can tell me
every social institution you created has failed me
all they do is kill and jail me
to wipe out my chromosomes
so every block
I walk
filled with cops
is a war zone,
a war zone

Most likely seen running from cops in Reebok high tops
because they got high ankle support
got to get free
alive you ain't taking me
ain't trying to see the inside of a court
jury of my peers
even if innocent they'll make me serve 10 years
there goes the prime of my life time
when we hear them sirens
iron is flying
under the night stars and sky line.
Ain't trying to see a cell with iron bars

repel down the sides of building walls
with a camouflage
beaning around my noggin.
We move in secrecy like Bin Laden
communicate with young soldier
on chips in Motorolas and two-way Nextel
who accustomed to having they flesh swelled
by them demons, them devils with the letters PD on they lapel.
They get done up like Latrell Sprewell
so cold
because little Lakim got hit with a Radio Raheem chokehold
12 years old,
snot nosed
armed with a snow cone
they said it was a handgun,
they choked him until he coughed blood on his And 1's.
I'm told this is how they have fun
and one comrade named his magnum Adil
the arabic word for justice
the enemy tries to crush us
this oppression hugs us
don't question our actions
only God can judge us

Reflections of a Black Boy

"What, to the American slave, is your 4th of July? I answer; a day that reveals to him, more than all other days in the year, the gross injustice and cruelty to which he is the constant victim. To him, your celebration is a sham; your boasted liberty, an unholy license; your shouts of liberty and equality, hollow mockery; your prayers and hymns, your sermons and thanksgivings, with all your religious parade and solemnity, are, to Him, mere bombast, fraud, deception, impiety, and hypocrisy—a thin veil to cover up crimes which would disgrace a nation of savages. There is not a nation on the earth guilty of practices more shocking and bloody than are the people of the United States, at this very hour.

Go where you may, search where you will, roam through all the monarchies and despotisms of the Old World, travel through South America, search out every abuse, and when you have found the last, lay your facts by the side of the everyday practices of this nation, and you will say with me, that, for revolting barbarity and shameless hypocrisy, America reigns without a rival." (Frederick Douglas)

These words by Fredrick Douglas in 1852 in many ways sum up the tortured existence of black people in America. We live in a land that claims freedom, liberty, equality, justice, fraternity, and a path for pursuing happiness, for all. Those words ring hollow in the ears of America's despised and dispossessed black sons and daughters. We often hear about the greatness of this country; we are told about the amazing freedoms which are reserved for every man. What we know and in the event that we forget, America is quick to remind us with multiple examples that that "freedom" was not and will never be for us. This means that our fight for freedom continues while the others are well into their second century of victory celebration. I wasn't born to fight. I often describe myself as a lover and not a fighter. I am a lover who has been forced to learn the ways of a fighter. I wish I did not have to fight like I do. I wish with my entire being that my people didn't have to fight the way that we do. I wish that we didn't die so often in America like we do. All of this is because we are not free, and so we fight. For us the battlefield that we call America has been a dark night on an unforgiving mine-riddled terrain passed down to us like an unwanted hand me down. We're scratching and crawling to make it to the day, and we know that the day carries no guarantees that it will be any better. One of the greatest revolutionary/freedom fighter minds of the 20th century, Dr. Huey P. Newton commented on the reality of a revolutionary/freedom fighter.

Dr. Huey P. Newton quoted Bakunin, who said, "The first lesson a revolutionary must learn is that he is a doomed man. Unless he understands this, he does not grasp the essential meaning of his life." This is part of the reason Newton coined the term "Revolutionary Suicide"; this term reflects a knowledge of taking up a fight against the power structure that will more than likely result in death before victory. In his Manifesto section from his autobiography *Revolutionary Suicide*, Newton quotes Che Guevara, who said, "to a revolutionary death is the reality and victory the dream."

Newton went on later to say when explaining his theory of revolutionary suicide, "Yet when I think of individuals in the revolution, I cannot predict their survival. Revolutionaries must accept this fact, especially the Black revolutionaries in America, whose lives are in constant danger from the evils of a colonial society. Considering how we must live, it is not hard to accept the concept of revolutionary suicide."

Although I fight, the fact remains that I wasn't born to fight; I inherited this battle from my parents who received it from their parents who were simply passing on what was given to them. It's a generational fight, and when my number is called I have to assume my position in the battle. All those who answer the call to arms have become Arjuna in the "Bhagavad Gita." We are a princely warrior caste, and we must do our dharma, which is to fight because our home has declared war upon us due to the color of our skin. The black child is born into a war zone, where he/she is destined to live and die.

We remember the stories of our fallen daily. There is no day without a fight. We are perpetually engaged in a fight against the state. Every twenty-eight hours, a black person is killed by a law enforcement/security agent. About every four hours another one of our comrades dies. This means that in a twenty-four hour span, about six black bodies die every day, 365(6) days a year. When it comes to our casualties, we have dead above and below ground. Our men and women confined behind bars, cells 6 by 9, are our walking dead who have been buried alive. Those who have had their lives stolen are our physical dead. More black people are killed by police every year than casualties that America experiences in "real wars" in Iraq or Afghanistan. We are at war for our very survival in America. A few generations ago, black men and women were lynched almost daily. A few generations before that, slavery was still legal in the United States as a viable source of labor for America's agricultural economy. Black men and women have been fighting for their survival since the day they were first brought to these shores. There hasn't been a ceasefire. There is no stalemate. The war simply rages on. The shelling doesn't stop, so much so that we do not have the time to count how many we've lost. We can't predict how many will be lost in the days ahead. All we know is that this is war, and our survival as a people is at stake.

Our insurgency, our resistance is not one of choice. It's a matter of consequence. We are drafted into the fray. Our B-day is D-Day, and we're pushed from the womb into no-man's land. Raised in the trenches. Conscripted by birth, our uniforms are many shades, but the battle is the same. And the fight is not our doing. We did not start the fight, but we are so deeply involved in the core of the struggle that we know that we have to fight it to the finish. We know we are being slaughtered by the millions, yet we press on. Because we know to not fight means certain death. To fight at least allows us to remain hopeful that there might be some victory in the not-too-distant future. To fight means that we can at least look at ourselves in the mirror and be proud of that fact that we lived and died with dignity.

Our great poet Claude McKay said:

"If we must die, let it not be like hogs
Hunted and penned in an inglorious spot,
While round us bark the mad and hungry dogs,
Making their mock at our accursed lot.
If we must die, O let us nobly die
So that our precious blood may not be shed
In vain; then even the monsters we defy
Shall be constrained to honor us though dead!
O kinsmen! We must meet the common foe!
Though far outnumbered let us show us brave,
And for their thousand blows deal one death blow!
What though before us lies the open grave?
Like men we'll face the murderous, cowardly pack,
Pressed to the wall, dying, but fighting back!"

We could hope for a peaceful rest knowing we lived and died as strong men and women fighting for the cause that we believe in, which is our freedom and survival. The betterment of our world for our offspring. That we did not die in vain. This is why we are insurgents. It's the only way we can live and truly be proud of who we are in this war zone.

Minister of Defense Huey P. Newton:

"Thus it is better to oppose the forces that would drive me to self-murder than to endure them. Although I risk the likelihood of death, there is at least the possibility, if not the probability, of changing intolerable conditions. This possibility is important, because much in human existence is based upon hope without any real understanding of the odds. Indeed, we are all—Black and white alike—ill in the same way, mortally ill. But before we die, how shall we live? I say with hope and dignity; and if premature death is the result, that death has a meaning reactionary suicide can never have. It is the price of self-respect."

Daily reminders are seared into our brains to indicate that this land and this freedom is not for us. Although we've built up the foundation of America, we've built it up for another people to enjoy, and any time we try to enjoy a piece of what we think is rightfully ours and is rightfully ours, the system responds with all its various types of warfare. Be it total war, destroying our communities with guns, dope, and under-developing schools and social services. Every social institution geared to help is equipped with munitions that are directed at black lives. They've used operation redline to house us in ghettos that slowly suffocate the lives in our communities. We've seen their concentration camps like jails and prisons that house millions of our brothers and sisters in arms. We face espionage; the use of the media and other public outlets to attack and brand us as criminals and deviants.

One of the most recent and popular tactics has been counterterrorism, sending the police into our neighborhoods instead of other communities to "serve and protect." They preemptive strike with their stop and frisk policies and detain with no probable cause. We've also witnessed drone warfare; politicians and businesses making policy decisions from afar to limit opportunities. They sit comfortably in offices in remote locations and push buttons and pull strings that result in death and destruction on the ground. I would argue the most insidious method of all is their version of Cold War, the art of fighting without technically fighting. The United States has the Thirteenth, Fourteenth and Fifteenth amendments; we have various civil rights acts and voting rights acts. Brown v. Board of Education and MLK Jr. Day is a federal holiday. We have affirmative action and provide some government assistance and use politically correct speech. The forty-fourth president of the United States is half-white and half-African with a black wife from the South Side of Chicago and two black daughters. From the outside, it would appear that all is right and there is no reason to fight, but the fighting is cloak and dagger; it's covert and discrete. We don't see the attacks, but we feel the losses. Black unemployment is the highest of all populations; black incarceration is the highest. Black infant mortality is the highest; black education is the lowest. Black earnings from jobs are the lowest. We feel the force of the blows but the Cold War masks the attacks.

Those of us who recognize it all are able to see that we are in the depths of a hellish battle. Some of us don't even know we're in the middle of a war. Some of us drop out of the war, we attempt to conscientiously object to the fighting through distractions like gangs, drugs, liquor, sex, and other addictive behaviors. Some of us are shell-shocked and PTSD'd, so we can't fight any longer. You can see it all in the eyes of the rank and file. We are a people who did not choose war, but war is at our front door every day. We have our heroes, heroines, martyrs, and prisoners of war whose only crime was fighting for their people. We have our Nat Turners, Harriet Tubmans, David Walkers, Ida B. Wells, Kings, Malcolms, Medgar Evers, Marcus Garveys, Newtons, Fannie Lou Hamers, and Shirley Chisholms. They are our honored fallen who await us on the other side. As Prodigy from Mobb Deep once said, "There's a war going on outside no man is safe from. You can run but you can't hide forever." None of us are safe, and if you are black, you cannot hide. Every man and woman upon the Earth is destined to die; therefore, how will you live?

"The concept of revolutionary suicide is not defeatist or fatalistic. On the contrary, it conveys an awareness of reality in combination with the possibility of hope—reality because the revolutionary must always be prepared to face death, and hope because it symbolizes a resolute determination to bring about change. Above all, it demands that the revolutionary see his death and his life as one piece. Chairman Mao says that death comes to all of us, but it varies in its significance: to die for the reactionary is lighter than a feather; to die for the revolution is heavier than Mount Tai." - Huey P. Newton

My pants sag when I walk to show ain't nothing you can tell me
every social institution you created has failed me
all they do is kill and jail me to wipe out my chromosomes
so every block I walk filled with cops
is a war zone,
a war zone.

The Rose (2015)

I'll attempt to collect my thoughts to show you all what I've
been thinking through

A humble depiction of the conditions
some of these men and women I know on the brink have been
through

Word to the wise: don't hold your breath waiting for this society
to save you
because if you do, then you'll soon be blinking blue.

In the eyes of many, we belong to
a disease infested, decrepit stinking few.

Stranded in gentrified neighborhoods where it's hard to survive
levees breaking got us sinking too
call it (Katrina Redux)

Meanwhile constantly seeping through cracks
are noxious toxic chemicals
asthma and cancer are perennial visitors
to where we sleeping through

Now can y'all see me move,
what I speak can take you in and out of these streets
quicker than them policemen do.
That last line wasn't a swipe at the boys in blue,
what I'm speaking is deeper than that

This is defining everything outside in our environment set to
poison you

I heard from one of our elders by the name of Langston Hughes

A question of the deferred dream

It's sad when we even have to consider such an absurd thing

That for some boys and girls
that word means
something less tangible

That it's harder for them to grab a handful

So their hands stay closed

Just as schools close and homes foreclose

Yet it still seems so close.

Just like when you standing on the corner of Jones and Post
you can see the wealth of Union Square vivid and up close,
but it's oh so far

That Financial District might as well be another geographic
jurisdiction

The jurist in my district
don't understand that the blocks we from force conscription

Men and women are drafted from the womb
to be at war with the system

There are a few ways to make it out,
but everyday it gets harder to pick them

Our war is of attrition,
the fatigue bleeds deep into our bones

The fatigues we wear look like

white tees, jeans, air ones, fitted cap over the dome

But we soldiers of misfortune
who don't even know what we're fighting for

Is it for the hood or for the block,
is it for the good or for the guap,
for the dead homies
who just waiting for the next dead homie to drop.

We so confused,
we so traumatized and so abused.

But still in this midst of all this did y'all hear what Pac said,

Did you hear about the rose that grew?

From a crack in the concrete.
Yeah, we got crack up and down our concrete
but even through that trap the rose grew.
That rose is you.

Through underfunded schools,
the war on poverty,
the war on drugs,
the war on terror
the war on our young,
prison industrial complex,
bracero programs,
united farm workers,
civil rights,
jim crow,
forced migration to reservations,
Ellis and Angel island,
sharecropping and slavery,
we've survived it all.

We're made strong by the legacy of those that came before us, we triumphantly march into the greatness of our moment.

But don't be mistaken,
see the matrix is quick to shape-shift.
It'll try to take that faith you have in yourself
and make you an atheist

it'll try to get you to forget what this date is,
but we will never forget

on the 18th day of June
in the year two thousand and fifteen
a rose grew

in the face of all things attempting to stifle it,
it still bloomed

and its bloom yields all these incredible hues

strengthened by the struggle
found in our soil and roots

It doesn't matter what they do

Every day this is what we need from you

Stand tall,
greet the sun,
shine bright and bold

and give your beautiful brilliance to us all

That's what a rose will do

and that rose is you.

Reflections of a Black Boy

There is a significant degree of power in knowledge but the true power is in the practice an application of that knowledge.

From a physics standpoint acquiring knowledge is keeping it in a static state. It has value but the true force is felt when that knowledge becomes dynamic. It's put in motion.

Education of blacks was illegal in most slave holding colonies/states. In Mississippi laws were passed to force free blacks out of the state to prevent them from attempting to educate blacks who were still enslaved.

Our path to freedom and liberation is only possible through knowledge and a strict revolutionary application of what we will learn.

For too many of us, the path to true education is found somewhere outside of the "traditional" place of education in the American society. If we only depend on our school experience to provide us with a foundation for our futures, then we are doomed to the same tragic existence, if not worse, that black folks have experienced in America. Malcolm X was born in 1925. He was an incredibly smart student, but eventually was crushed by the ugly face of racism in his middle school years when a teacher told him that a nigger couldn't be a lawyer. It wasn't until Malcolm spent time in prison in his 20s that he began to "educate" himself again. This extracurricular education is what saved him. The same is true for so many others. Dr. Huey P. Newton spoke candidly about his experience in Oakland Public Schools. He said, "Throughout my life all real learning has taken place outside school. I was educated by my family, my friends, and the street. Later, I learned to love books and I read a lot, but that had nothing to do with school. Long before, I was getting educated in unorthodox ways." For both of these men it was their education outside of school that gave them hope and filled them with the courage to dream. Sadly, the experiences of both Malcolm and Huey are not isolated instances confined to the early part of the 20th century. Their experience is replicated millions of times a day all throughout the United States of America in the lives of black and brown students.

Scholar Carter G. Woodson said, "The chief difficulty with the education of the Negro is that it has been largely imitation, resulting in the enslavement of his mind." The "education" that supposedly has been provided to black people in America has been pitiful. It has not educated in the sense of empowering with relevant information. It has educated by instilling inferiority and making black people easy to control. The Dragon, George Jackson said, "I now know that the most damaging thing a people in a colonial situation can do is to allow their children to attend any educational facility organized by the dominant enemy culture." Fact, the educational system was created by the descendants of those who enslaved us. What type of "education" do you think your former enslavers and current oppressors are going to give to you?

I am an educator by trade, and I guess you might say by nature. I'm a third-generation educator on my father's side. What being an educator has taught me is that the American educational system is not made to educate and empower black minds. It has also taught me that education, knowledge acquisition and application, and knowledge of self are essential for any attempt at combating this fabricated but oh so real reality for black people in America. Knowledge and application is the key. It has to go further than knowledge/education or assimilating data; that knowledge has to manifest itself and become part of how a person lives.

I've always had an issue with the clichéd statement that knowledge is power. I disagree. I say knowledge is power when it is put into practice. We do not profit from storing volumes of information. It is great to be informed. It's admirable to be a storehouse of information, but what does it profit you if you cannot use the information to benefit yourself or your people? Knowledge becomes power when it is utilized. We are not attempting to become walking encyclopedias with random facts and figures; it needs to have praxis; it needs to be tangible and find a way into reality.

I teach incarcerated men and women in a charter high school in San Francisco. The numbers that attempt to explain how people end up incarcerated are very well established and consistent. They tell us most of the men and women are black and brown and are incarcerated due to drugs and other nonviolent offenses. They also tell us that the overwhelming majority of the men and women incarcerated have major deficiencies in their academic careers. Most never completed high school. A 2003 report published by the Bureau of Justice & Statistics titled 'Education and Correctional Populations' stated that 68 percent of the state prison population then had not received a high-school diploma."

The correlation between lack of education and jail and prison is thoroughly documented by more agencies than just the BJS. One of the more popular social/political buzzwords of the day is the school-to-prison pipeline. The American Civil Liberties Union states, "The 'school-to-prison pipeline' refers to the policies and practices that push our nation's schoolchildren, especially our most at-risk children, out of classrooms and into the juvenile and criminal justice systems. This pipeline reflects the prioritization of incarceration over education."

How do we arrive at the school to prison pipeline? The ACLU highlights multiple points; we'll look at a few. "For most students, the pipeline begins with inadequate resources in public schools. Overcrowded classrooms, a lack of qualified teachers, and insufficient funding for "extras" such as counselors, special education services, and even textbooks, lock students into second-rate educational environments. This failure to meet educational needs increases disengagement and dropouts, increasing the risk of later court involvement. Even worse, schools may actually encourage dropouts in response to pressures from test-based accountability regimes such as the No Child Left Behind Act, which create incentives to push out low-performing students to boost overall test scores."

Public schools are not providing the necessary educational resources to allow young people to be "successful." This is a result of choices being made by people who control the system of education to lessen the opportunities and access of young black and brown kids in favor of their white counterparts. Some may feel that is a loaded statement, but it's not. Once again, data clearly shows the bias in which kids receive what funding based solely on the color of their skin. Data scientist David Mosenkis, who was kind enough to allow me to use his research in this text, recently published research on 500 school districts in Pennsylvania. He examined their funding data based on racial composition of school districts, and what he found might be alarming to some but simply confirmation to others who already know the widespread institutional discriminatory practices of public schools. Mosenkis found:

"If you color code the districts based on their racial composition you see this very stark breakdown. At any given poverty level, districts that have a higher proportion of white students get substantially higher funding than districts that have more minority students." That means that no matter how rich or poor the district in question, funding gaps existed solely based on the racial composition of the school. Just the increased presence of minority students actually deflated a district's funding level. "The ones that have a few more students of color get lower funding than the ones that are 100 percent or 95 percent white," Mosenkis said. Pennsylvania is not an anomaly, much of what Mosenkis reported on schools in Pennsylvania can be found in other states throughout this nation. Most inmates have not obtained their high school degree, and that is not a direct result of bad decisions on the part of that individual. Who successfully completes school and who doesn't is a race-tainted algorithm of misallocation of resources and limited academic opportunities for certain students, while others receive more resources and opportunities. Another reality of this system is once you have been made part of the criminal aspect of it, it becomes extremely difficult to extricate yourself.

I have my little classroom, and when I look at my students, I see the evidence of the school to prison pipeline. Some might consider me fairly well educated. I am a product of American public schools, but my most important learning experiences did not happen in public schools. My father was a teacher, and he made sure that I would have access to information, whether or not it was taught to me in class. My parents formed what could be termed "black school" for my sister and me. We would take weekly classes at SJSU that were led by community members and learn black history. That was such an important extracurricular learning experience for me. I was fairly gifted as a student and didn't struggle too much with subjects. However, math started to be an obstacle for me around my sixth-grade year. I did well in class, but my father wanted me to master the material so he enrolled my sister and me in the Jose Valdes Math Institute. This was a program offered for free to black and brown students to help improve their math understanding because black and brown students were underrepresented in the higher level math courses. Jose Valdes was a passionate math instructor who took responsibility upon himself to create change for young kids of color because he knew the school district was not going to do it.

The other nontraditional transformative educational experience for me was hip-hop. I learned black history from my elders, but I can't describe the pride and intellectual stimulation I received when I saw young black men and women on TV spitting bars about Malcolm X, the Nation of Islam or Africa, or dropping some ill historical facts about black people. The hip-hop of the late '80s and early '90s taught me so much. I remember the RZA from Wu-Tang Clan on the album *Wu-Tang Forever* at the end of the track "Bells of War" saying:

"That's that Wu, that's that Wisdom
That's the Wisdom of the Universe
That's the truth, of Allah, for the Nation of the Gods
You know what I'm sayin ...
We got the medicine for your sickness
Out here, ya know what I mean
I was telling Shorty like
Yo Shorty, you don't even gotta go to summer school
Pick up the Wu-Tang double CD
And you'll get all the education you need this year
You know what I mean"

To a certain degree the RZA was right. I wouldn't recommend that a parent or a teacher allow a student to listen to hip-hop albums and think that will educate them enough to achieve a high school diploma and go onto higher education, but there was value, knowledge, and wisdom in much of what some artists put out at that time. There was a raw commentary that inspired thought and encouraged critique of your surroundings. That type of knowledge and wisdom was nowhere to be found in classrooms. There were many times when something I heard in a verse made me more interested in learning about the subject once it was brought up in class. This is why I say those teachings were very valuable. One particular song was better than any history lesson I ever had in a classroom setting. Ras Kass' "Nature of the Threat." What that man did with that song in my opinion is unparalleled. He was able to condense more than 2,000 years of history into an eight-minute song. Complete with analysis and Cress Welsing race theory, and much of what was said is historically and contextually accurate. It is written from a specific point of view, which colors the interpretation of the historical facts, but overall the piece is an exceptional work. I can't recall how many times I've been in a social science lecture when I heard something that triggered a memory from a line from Ras Kass' song.

If it wasn't for these nontraditional educational experiences, I really do not know what would've been my fate as a student. I learned to think and reason outside of school. I had pride in myself and my people due to courses I took outside of school. I had mastered what was my hardest academic challenge, mathematics, up to that time with hard work and dedication through the Jose Valdes Math Institute. And little by little, my favorite rappers kept dropping jewels on me that helped broaden my understanding of the world. As rap grew in influence and scope, so did my perspective with the music I was listening to. By the time I entered my ninth-grade year, I had confidence in my learning ability because I knew that if I focused enough, I could learn anything I put my mind to. I do not want to claim that my learning experience was an exception, but many students did not have the same extracurricular academic experiences I had. When I look at the students who I teach in my courses, most of them have never in their lives experienced anything remotely similar to what I went through. They learned primarily from school and whatever was around them. One of the first things that I try to do as a teacher is help them develop confidence in their ability to learn. I think this is one of the most important concepts when trying to teach. Your students have to feel affirmed in their own cognitive ability to be successful in acquiring knowledge; you can be the most gifted teacher on the planet, but if your students do not feel confident in their ability to learn they will still experience difficulty in acquiring the information. Once that is established, there really isn't any task that your student will not be able to complete because they understand that with time, patience, and hard work, they will eventually be able to master the concept, and they trust you enough to be their guide as they work through the subject matter.

Origin of 'The Rose'

I hate jail. I hate prison. I hate what it can do to men and women, to girls and boys. The concept of the institution is to completely strip away all humanity and dignity. A person is referred to as a prisoner or inmate. They are issued a number for identification purposes and given a common uniform to prevent uniqueness. Those are just a few of the signs of the dehumanization process men and women experience inside those walls. I seriously despise the entire institution of locking up human beings. The philosophy is socially immature and even more backwards when it is paired with a system of racism and widespread institutional discrimination for monetary gain. Jails and prisons in America have literally destroyed generations of people. Walking in and out of jails and prisons as an educator for years has its impact. Inmate, Officer/Deputy/CO, or civilian staff, it doesn't matter what your role is; all are affected by their time in those places.

You become saturated in the funk and stench of incarceration. It encroaches on every part of who you are. It's a dark and cold place that wields the hellish power of breaking a man or a woman down. You're locked up, in some instances without access to any piece of the outside world. No sunlight, no sky, no breathing in fresh air for days. Your entire existence takes place in an artificially scheduled world. Completely isolated from everything and everyone. If you're a parent, your children are hopefully being cared for by others, and if not, then they are constant worries in your heart and mind. You're most likely stressing out about your case or simply trying to do your time. There are so many things out of your control that stress you out because you wish you had some say in what the world was dictating to you. It's an experience that leaves you utterly helpless, and, as a result, some become hopeless. Some are able to adjust to "doing their time." They might create a program, routine, or regimen for themselves. Everyone who is in those facilities has to figure a way to survive it. What works for one might not work for the next. Some folks who work in those environments find outlets in addictive behaviors or extreme sport activities. Folks who live on the inside design multiple ways of coping with being locked up. Drugs, relationships, programming, fighting, working out, learning to be a better criminal, reading, writing, games, religion, clean living, prayer, or memorizing the program, schedule, and habits of those who work in the jail.

My school has become one of the ways that incarcerated men and women do their time. The educational programs are compulsory for all folks without a high school diploma. I don't agree with this policy at all. I understand where it comes from, but I don't think the best way to build an educational environment in a setting where every action is controlled by someone else is to tell people they have to go to school or face some punitive consequence. The very idea of the power and application of education is freedom, but folks are being forced to go to class. I think jail and prison environments would have a much greater impact on their population if they incentivized education. Grant folks a reduced sentence for achieving academic goals or some other perk that would inspire men and women to see education in a new light. That's my aside; now when folks go to class many become focused on lessons and learning, and in the process notice how quickly their time passes. This is the goal of almost all folks locked up. They want time to pass as fast as possible and get out. So anything that helps with making it seem as if time is passing more quickly is coveted.

I get men and women who come to my class ready to learn and or be entertained for a few hours. Some folks really begin to realize how important it is for them to educate themselves, I do my best to impress upon them the value of education. I don't sell wolf tickets though; I know and I tell them that becoming "educated' will not solve all of their problems. That is not the way our world works. There are many other steps to take, but becoming empowered through education is one of the steps that must be accomplished in order to move forward.

If you want to control a people, you keep them ignorant. A mind that does not receive the proper intellectual stimulation to grow and develop is a tool in the hands of those who seek to control and wield power. It is imperative that you educate yourself to become your own master; if you don't, then someone else will assume the position of your master. I also try to appeal to the men and women I have who are parents to empower themselves with education, so they can be there for their children to help them whenever they need help, at the very least to be an example of acquiring education and applying it to break the cycle of death and destruction that many of us are confined to. And, as we pointed out earlier, most of their children will be going to schools that are ill-equipped for providing them a solid academic foundation.

I realize that every time I step in my classroom that so much is at stake. I'm not responsible for the personal decisions that my students make, but I feel responsible for doing all that I can to deliver quality instruction and speak to them straight about the world that they live in. I owe that because that is part of my calling as a man. I was raised to do your part when it is your turn. I do receive a paycheck for my labor, but my connection to the work is bigger than my salary. I also have to keep a careful balance between responsibility and savior. It is easy to lose focus on the mission if you get the savior thing wrong. I cannot help save anyone, but I can support someone who is working on changing. It would be false for me to put that on my shoulders. However, I am driven and committed to helping my people to the extent my responsibility will allow by any means necessary. In those hours that I have my students, my means is education and whatever example I can give them to show that we are at war with ignorance and a discriminatory society. I try to demonstrate the knowledge that we can win enough battles in the fight to eventually win the war. The first battle that we must win is mastering our minds, souls, and bodies through education.

That's exactly what I tried to place at the heart of "The Rose." It's about my people, my students, these men and women who so often are fragmented, extra delicate but have the toughest exteriors.

External edifices cast in steel and bronze. On some Mac Dre, too hard for the radio. I know the secrets to their hardness. I've had to master it too. Once they recognize I know the language of protecting self through an impenetrable exterior, I am able to get them to take off their masks. This allows me to know them in moments when they let that guard down and reveal some of what the world has made them cover up with various facades. That's who I teach, and that's who I was attempting to remind was "The Rose" that Tupac Shakur spoke of. We are that rose. We are that thing that in the face of the most outrageous circumstances; we can still produce some of the most amazing beauty the world has seen. We are tough and thorny but our beauty is like nothing the eye has framed before.

I've never had a major fanboy connection with Tupac. His work that was "conscious" always caught my ear and really spoke to me. I wasn't able to fully embrace Pac because I didn't understand how a man who could make conscious material could turn around and make songs that celebrated thug life and denigrated women. I was young then. I was judgmental in my youth. I didn't fully recognize that Pac was killed when he was twenty-five; he was a young man who was afforded this incredible platform and had all this knowledge in him, but was still trying to find the wisdom in how he walked and applied it. He was searching for the balance between the fire in his heart, his gut, and the wisdom in his soul and mind. His heart and mind were for his people. While at times his gut had him acting a fool in the street. As history would have it, we didn't get a chance to see him mature and grow. Yet his work is still powerful and lives on. I wanted to channel some of Pac's genius in this piece for my students.

When I write, I first write for myself. My art is my way of coping with what I experience in this world. I rarely write for others. This poem was a complete opposite of that because I was writing for my students. I wanted them to see themselves for who they are. I also wanted to show them how amazing they appear in my eyes because they are able to overcome and survive some of the worst of what we have to go through on a daily basis because of the color of our skins and the reality of our birth.

The commencement celebration is the biggest event in our school year. We have one in January and one in June. I was asked by some of my supervisors to give an address at the event. I personally am not a fan of speeches. I prefer actions to words. I expressed my desire to do something else aside from speak, and we compromised on me reciting a poem. My school is aware of my music and poetry, and they were receptive to the idea of me writing and reciting something. I told them I would draft something new for the students and recite it at the event.

I don't like restrictions around my creative flow. Deadlines are helpful, but I'm more driven by the inspiration. That is the source of it all. This piece was a challenge for me because I struggled to find my creative spark to start building. I do not write with concepts in mind. I have some friends who are creatives, and I marvel at how they can have an idea of what they want to do before they put proverbial pen to paper and then set out to create what's in their minds. My creative process is more in line with old school jazz musicians because I feed off of improvisation. I improv until I find what the music is revealing to me. That's why I prefer to work with music, but poetry is always different because for me it's creating on a blank canvas. Writing music allows me to develop a relationship with the musical composition I'm listening to, and then I write as an accompanying instrument. I try to find what the music is missing and provide that vocally. Poetry is the opposite of that to me because the blank page is an empty space. There is nothing to spark the inspiration. When the inspiration strikes, it takes hold of the paper for me, and I become more like a sculptor with a slab of stone chiseling away the excess and revealing the potential underneath.

I knew I wanted this to be about my students; that was the goal that I wanted the stone slab to look like once I chiseled away everything else. I wanted them to see themselves; I wanted them to hear who they are. I wanted to inspire them and remind them of the lessons that we discussed in class about self-worth, value, and the beauty they carry. I wanted them to see that and also to know that any change in their lives will have to start with them. The system is not going to do it for you, and neither will anybody else. It didn't matter that hundreds of folks would be in attendance. Local public and political dignitaries as well as news media would be present taking in the proceedings. There could've been thousands present, but the conversation I was forming was to be said in a sacred space just for them.

The essence of the piece is the beauty we possess in the face of the ugliness that has been forced around us. It is the power that we have and how strong we can truly be when we know how to cultivate our skills and resources and use them properly. It is the unfair battle that we must wage in order to survive. We have to fight it, and our children will have to fight it. We cannot depend on them or the system; we have to find ways to bloom and blossom for our sake and the sake of our progeny. No wolf tickets ever; it is saying this is not easy; there is no shortcut way around it. We have to scrape and scrap every day to make it through. But it is possible to win some battles. It was also intended for them to see that I too am a soldier, and I fight the good fight with them. And I'm ready to support my fellow brothers and sisters in arms whenever they are ready to fight on.

For many of us this system does not teach us to dream of being free. To imagine that we can be other than what is already around us. We attend schools which are staffed with teachers that have no clue how to teach black and brown kids let alone teach black and brown kids to be free and liberated. Schools in many ways prepare young black and brown kids for lives of alienation and imprisonment. For too many of us the only way to discover our true power and a sense of freedom is through what we learn on our own.

Learning to be free is essential but equally important is learning to believe in yourself. "The Rose" speaks to this as well. The world that my students and I live in did not and will not teach us to have a sense of self that is positive. The messages we receive about who we are are constantly filled with pejoratives. If we were to believe what our society says we are, we would kill ourselves because we do not fit in and will never belong. So many illustrious minds have spoken to this very reality and a summation of their statements is the fact that we are totally dependent upon our oppressors for everything that we feel we need in our society. That includes educational institutions. We are "educated" in schools created by our former enslavers and now their offspring. What type of education do you think you'll receive at the hands of those who have been exploiting our existence since our arrival. We are not taught vital pieces of information we need for our own worth in our schools. A sense of love for self has to be cultivated somewhere else. We have to construct the institutions that do that. That's the secret of the rose. The rose is a beautiful flower because the rose knows itself. And Pac's rose grew from concrete. It grew where it wasn't supposed to grow. We have to do this every day because we've been marooned in urban America where things are not supposed to grow. We were sent here to die. This is why we are forced to develop nurseries in the most inhospitable conditions possible. Out of necessity, we become master gardeners who pioneer new techniques for sowing and growing.

In this space we can witness the fertilizer for "The Rose." Books symbolize knowledge, and knowledge symbolizes growth. Staying with the metaphor of the rose, the blooming process symbolizes the application of that knowledge for self and community betterment. There are many ways for us to learn in the modern world, which is a blessing. Information is plentiful and widely available if we know where to look and how to access it. For many of us, we are swimming in information; however there are numerous folks who are still digitally divided and unable to access much of what is out there. That's one major barrier, the simple reality that not everyone has equal access to information.

Another barrier is the fact that some of us belong to cultures that do not put much worth or value on acquiring knowledge. The devaluing of education is a response to the inadequate educational resources provided to black folks. As a result, my generation has created its own mantras to help reinforce this idea. We say things like, "Mind on my money and money on my mind." Or another popular mantra M.O.B., which means "Money over bitches." And probably one of the most iconic of all the mantras C.R.E.A.M., "Cash rules everything around me." I can go on. I'm not one for censorship; I think people need to be able to tell their stories, but the problem of an oppressed people who sing songs and create mantras to justify their self-destruction is multiplied by the force of the oppression they are constantly under. What these mantras reflect is an overvaluation of money and a devaluation of knowledge, knowledge of self, and self-development.

I am not stating money is irrelevant; money is a very important resource. Capital is an essential factor of production necessary for many things. However, if you acquire capital by preying on segments of your community, you're simply regurgitating what the masters of our system have done and are doing. Or if you have racks and racks of money with no knowledge of self and your people, then your wealth won't really profit you. The conquered began to take on the characteristics of the conqueror. What was slavery? It was M.O.B., "Money over black lives." What are mass incarceration and the exploitation of black bodies in the hood? They are C.R.E.A.M. Forget helping folks with problems they have because "Cash rules everything around me." The more locked up, the more money they make. Those in control profit off the prison industrial complex and the poverty in our communities. What is it when police terrorize black and brown communities and use lethal force to extinguish black lives? That's "mind on my money and money on my mind." Police forces are being used to protect the property and wealth of the wealthy. The wealthy got their mind on their money and use the police as a private security force to keep their property and money safe.

If it doesn't look good when the oppressor uses it, then how can it be good when we mimic the same behavior? And just like America uses cognitive dissonance to justify its treatment of blacks, we do the same thing to justify when we prey on our own to get what we need. You'll hear mantras like, "pimping and hoeing is the best thing going" to justify prostituting women and men. The business of turning a mother, sister, daughter or father, brother, and son into a commodity to be bought and sold for the sole purpose of sexual pleasure. Or "Bitches ain't shit but hoes and tricks" to justify denigrating women. Or "The hypes/knocks/fiends will get their dope from somewhere, might as well be me." To justify selling dope to your own people. Or she just a t.h.o.t., "that hoe over there," to again justify disrespecting women. He a "bitch nigga" or "fuck boy" to justify disrespecting other men. The cognitive dissonance works from the oppressor to the oppressed, but also when the oppressed who have been victimized by their oppression lash out and begin to oppress their fellow oppressed peoples;

instead of lashing out against those responsible for their oppression. This is exactly what our environment expects of us.

We know the system is not going to change, then how do we combat this? We have to learn in order to grow and create institutions that uplift and allow others to grow as well. We can't simply recycle the same pathological paradigm that has resulted in our destruction. The condensed version of that paradigm is undervaluing others for the sake of profit over everything else. That's what white supremacy, imperialism, colonialism, and the American way has been all about. We cannot take the same poison and think we'll thrive off of it.

"The Rose" attempts to capture that as well as celebrate our struggles and our uniqueness as survivors. The reality has to be firmly planted within us that we have to tend our own garden. I spend so much time writing material focused on the struggles of my people because we are the ones who this system is constantly devouring. We cannot rely on the very thing that is killing us to save us. That's asinine. There is no logic or hope in such an approach. In seeking to do something different, the first thing we must do is arm ourselves with proper information. We have a responsibility to ourselves and our progeny to stand up and fight. We have to recognize that we have power; we're still under a repressive regime but there is room for empowerment and positive self-growth. There is no fighting back without seizing control of our means of production and educating ourselves. An ignorant mind is a controllable mind. We cannot fight back being paralyzed by ignorance, so one of the first essential step is quality mass education. We have to empower ourselves through education. Once we do this, we can begin to take matters into our own hands and start to fight back and make this a beautiful struggle.

"The Dirge" (2014)

You hear the dirge of the funeral march
as the band plays on
and my heart instantly recognizes it as the same song
played since the days of slave songs
which means I'm going to stand here until the flame is gone
or the pain is gone
because I don't know how many more names like Oscar and
Trayvon
we'll have to play it for.

The populous doesn't watch out for us
nor acknowledge us
they simply dismiss our cries for help as obnoxious
until they're presented to them in a form worthy of being
nominated for an oscar
by some Academy for the best actor and score.
But sadly
the madness that maddens me
and the savagery that surrounds me
in the streets that we inhabit be
growing exponentially evermore.

Four score and some odd years ago
man, I can't even keep score
if there is a scoreboard of how many of our loved ones
became extinct and are now no more
just that simple thought makes me want to cry
until my tear ducts are sore,
or scream until my voice and vocal chords become hoarse
the only lawful alternative is to
unleash this force through verse
capable of leaving pages and earth scorched
because the truth hurts

that to them we are nothing more.

How many more Amadou Diallos and Abner Louimas
but it's been foretold
since the days of The Nina, Pinta, and Santa Maria
or 1619 when the first 19 of us got off
or should I say got lost
involuntarily drafted into this American Holocaust
you ask about the cost
it can't be computed by some consumer price index
We go from slavery to Jim Crow
to prison industrial complex
punctuated by a death sentence,
sentenced to reside in a land
where they rally behind stand your ground,
which in layman's terms we know means another nigger down.
Translated to black speak
we know it means it's open season on us now.
Can y'all feel that adrenaline rush now?
But I need y'all to hush now

Listening carefully
because the world is changing right now
while we are busy entertaining
skinny jeans sagging on corners hanging
Molly popping and boat sipping
weed smoking and banging

they have crosshairs trained
on an entire generation.

They have prisons cells and guns aimed
at an entire generation.

Deemed expendable is
an entire generation.

The government does not care about

an entire generation.

We are the only ones who care about
an entire generation.

Therefore, we are the only ones who can save
an entire generation.

Reflections of a Black Boy

There are moments when I sit and attempt to reflect on all the people I know who have been gobbled up by the streets, slaughtered by police or swallowed by jails and prisons. I honestly cannot count. If I was to limit it to one of these categories, I still wouldn't be able to count. In my brief time on this planet I've seen far too much and it's not like I was raised in the hardest of hoods. I had parents and an extended community that tried to protect me from all of that but there is no place blackness can be in America and not be touched by these morbid realities.

Everyday black babies are born. The world that they are pushed into is rigged with traps ready to snare them. As they grow, they find their spot on this capitalistic conveyor belt moving them towards the awful destinations awaiting them at the end of their black lives.

Today is Dec. 28, 2015. I'm sitting in my studio on the border of West Oakland and Emeryville, California typing away at my book, *Black Boy Poems*. West Oakland is the birthplace of the Black Panther Party for Self Defense. In 2016, we will mark the fiftieth anniversary of the party. There is a spiritual and political power pulsating beneath the surface here. If you know how to sit quiet and listen for it, you can hear it. I know I'm tapped into the frequency, and I can feel the energy of the Panthers every time I'm here, especially when I step outside my door and let my feet travel concrete and asphalt paths that those freedom fighters and revolutionaries before me trod. I think about October 1966 and what Huey Newton, Bobby Seale, and Bobby Hutton must've been looking at when they formed the Black Panthers. Whatever was in the street, in the air, or in the water, you can still catch traces of it despite COINTELPRO and other government attempts to destroy the spirit of the Panthers and Oakland.

I mentioned the date Dec. 28 because it's significant for two reasons. One, it's the birthday of one of my good friends, Ise Lyfe. Two, about an hour ago I started to receive social media notifications about a grand jury returning a decision of no indictment for officers Timothy Loehmann and Frank Garmback for the unlawful murder and execution of 12-year-old Tamir Rice.

I'll give a brief synopsis of the events surrounding the murder of Tamir for those who don't know. Tamir was playing with a toy gun at Cudell Recreation Center, a park in Cleveland, Ohio, when a call came in reporting a "guy with a gun." The caller noted that the gun was probably "a toy." The dispatcher took the call and sent the word out to police in the area. Officers Loehmann and Garmback responded and immediately proceeded to the scene. They located Tamir and drove right up to the boy, and within two seconds of Loehmann exiting his police cruiser, he began to fire the fatal shots that resulted in Tamir's death.

This led to a media firestorm. In the aftermath, reports were produced that said Loehmann had a personnel file filled with concerns about his performance on the job from his previous employer in Independence, Ohio. The deputy police chief of Independence, Jim Polak, said that, "Loehmann had resigned rather than face certain termination due to concerns that he lacked the emotional stability to be a police officer." Polak also said Loehmann was not able to follow, "basic functions as instructed" and he showed a "dangerous loss of composure" during weapons trainings. Polak said many other things about Loehmann in stating his lack of confidence in his ability as a police officer, but he summed up his vote of no confidence in Loehmann by saying, "Individually, these events would not be considered major situations, but when taken together they show a pattern of a lack of maturity, indiscretion, and not following instructions. I do not believe time, nor training, will be able to change or correct these deficiencies."

All of this was present in Loehmann's personnel file, which the Cleveland Police Department apparently felt was a plus for him as an officer in Cleveland, or they completely ignored his previous commanding officer's warnings and hired him anyway. Immediately after Tamir's murder, Loehmann was telling investigators that he and his colleague had told Tamir multiple times to drop the gun and that Tamir reached for his gun, which prompted him to fire the fatal shots. Video evidence strongly contradicted his accounting of events when footage indicated that Loehmann's weapon was fired within two seconds of him exiting the car. With all of this evidence to support Tamir's death being an unauthorized use of deadly force by a person who never should've been an officer in the first place, a grand jury in Cuyahoga County was somehow able to render a "fair" and "impartial" decision of no indictment. I'm being slightly sarcastic to make this point, but all the evidence against Loehmann was the equivalent of God on high coming down to state Loehmann was the killer and it was unjust. Still, the system found a way to exonerate a white cop killing a black child. That is the system doing what it always does.

I wrote this piece upon invitation to perform at an event honoring the lives of young men and women we've lost due to state-sponsored violence. In attendance were family members of our famous fallen; the list of attendees was as follows:

Emmett Till's Family
Oscar Grant's Family
Kerry Baxter's Family
Mario Romero's Family
James Rivera's Family
Gregory Johnson's Family
Alan Blueford's Family
Donovan Jackson's Family
Andy Lopez's Family
Jose Calderon's Family

Attending an event like this gives sobering clarity to the amount of terror and murder our communities have experienced. We gather in our spaces to grieve collectively for our fallen. The

saddest part about this list is that it's a modest list. We have so
many fallen that it becomes hard to keep track of our dead. The
invitation is what put my mind in the space to conjure up this piece.
I was reflecting on how expendable we've been deemed by our
society. Just recently, I attended another such gathering here in
Oakland at the First African Methodist Episcopal Church, and the
list of attendees read like a Hall of Fame of mourning families. I
was asked by Cephus "Uncle Bobby" Johnson, Oscar Grant's uncle,
to perform a few spoken word pieces at this event to give voice to
the experience of our people. That day I heard from the mothers
and fathers of Eric Garner, Mike Brown, Sandra Bland, Sean Bell,
Tamir Rice, Oscar Grant, Alan Blueford, and so many others. A
cousin of Emmett Till's was in attendance as well. I don't know
how you can put more heartache and pain into one room. When you
hear these parents, spouses, and family members speak, you hear
real pain. Authentic, pure, direct from the deepest regions of the
heart and soul. When you hear those words, you can't help but be
shaken to your core. I won't speak for all who attended, but hearing
those stories and knowing the system has done nothing to hold any
of the murderers accountable was enough to make any sane person
contemplate armed rebellion. These families and their beloved
fallen are the evidence of the war being waged on our people.

   We listened to the stories of these mothers and fathers. We
heard directly from their own mouths how much they've been hurt
and changed by their loss. Their words connected directly with our
hearts as they cried loudly for justice, revolution, and change.
Surprisingly, in the shadow of death, this community of bereaved
mothers and fathers had grown to provide support for one another.
The bedrock of that support was their faith. You might believe in
God; you might not, but faith in a higher power, yourself, or the
struggle is a necessary armament to carry with you as you walk
through this battlefield. The power of their faith has helped them
become soldiers in a fight for justice for their loved ones and the
survival of our people. The fight must take place because our
society has deemed us worthless. Black bodies shot down by police
and left on the street to rot for hours before any "authority" official
does anything. No attempts to revive or save the life, only
dismissive glances and disgusted faces as life bleeds out of the

body. We are worth nothing in their eyes; the black life is barcoded with the cheapest of UPC coding for human beings. As a result, we live and die so fast. A poem that has always haunted me because of it poignancy is from Gwendolyn Brooks. In her piece titled "We Real Cool," she wrote:

"We real cool
we left school
we lurk late
we strike straight
we sing sin
we thin jinn
we jazz june
we die soon"

The totality of the piece captures the grim nature of the black life. We die so soon and so often, leaving our loved ones to bury and mourn our passing. The last line of the poem always catches me because early death is the scary repeated reality for blacks in America.

In my neighborhood I often make the walk to the worker owned cooperative Arizmendi for a slice of pizza. On my way back I pass by an elementary school and kids are normally playing sports in some after school activity. The majority of those children are black. I sincerely hate the fact that some of these precious, beautiful children are destined to fill spaces in the most unwanted statistical categories that define black life. If I look closely enough I can see specters of death, cops, and prison wardens hovering in the background waiting to snatch a few of them up. What does one say to a young black innocent child filled with all the hopes, dreams, and potential of their people, but due to genetic factors beyond anyone's control, their chances at life are drastically reduced?

To put reduced life chances into context we'll examine numbers from three sources: the BJS, Violence Policy Center (VPC), and the United Nations Office on Drugs and Crime (UNODC). According to the BJS in 2008 the national "homicide victimization rate for blacks (19.6 homicides per 100,000) was 6 times higher than the rate for whites (3.3 homicides per 100,000)."

The report goes on to say the national "victimization rate for blacks peaked in the early 1990s, reaching a high of 39.4 homicides per 100,000 in 1991." In 2016 the VPC published its most recent Black Homicide Victimization in the United States report on data from 2013. The report states the national "homicide rate among black victims in the United States was 16.91 per 100,000 ... For whites, the national homicide rate was 2.54 per 100,000." Making blacks about eight times more likely to be killed than whites. In addition, the top ten states for black homicide per 100,000 are as follows: Indiana (34.15), Missouri (30.42), Michigan (30.34), Nebraska (27.65), Oklahoma (27.36), Pennsylvania (26.11), Wisconsin (24.74), Louisiana (23.33), California (21.79), and New Jersey (20.49). These numbers put black murder on par with countries that are designated so called "war zones" or "developing" which means western countries expect murder to occur more often in these places. The UNODC report Global Study on Homicide details homicides rates in all countries. Black murder rates are similar to murder rates in countries such as: Colombia (30.8), Democratic Republic of the Congo (28.3), Brazil (25.2), Dominican Republic (22.1), and Nigeria (20.0). These numbers clearly indicate that blacks live and die in a completely separate world from whites.

This might also make you think a little differently when you hear people refer to a U.S. city like Chicago as "Chi-raq," and when a rapper such as J. Cole refers to his hometown of Fayetteville as Fayettenam. There is truth in these descriptions, although some of the monikers are used to glorify the violence in the respective cities. Still, the reality is that blacks who live in America and many urban cities die like they were living in "war zones" in other countries.

I don't think you fully comprehend the pain of looking at children and knowing that a substantial percentage of them will fall in line to fill up the vacancies in all those categories. Not all black children will find their way to these miserable destinies, but the reality that a substantial percentage will should be alarming enough to this society to do something. But we are the cast-offs; we are the ones whose lives do not matter. We are the acceptable collateral damage. And this is unacceptable. I understand how America justifies it and turns blind eye and deaf ear to the suffering of blacks in America, but I will never accept it, and I won't be silent.

The piece commences by reminding my people that we are the only ones who care about our losses and our suffering; therefore, it is on our shoulders to do something about it. Relying on the authorities to make adjustments to help us is an exercise of futility. We've been facing similar issues since the colonial era in America. From 1619 to the present, the tide of terror and oppression has not ebbed. We're four centuries deep, and there has only been one brief respite. The Reconstruction era was that respite, and when I say brief, I mean brief. We're talking less than twelve years, and blacks were still being terrorized during that time.

Reconstruction is that short-lived time in America when the U.S. government actually created legislation, amended the Constitution, and used government resources to make sure rights of "freedmen" were protected. It certainly wasn't perfect, but it was a concerted effort on behalf of the American government. Reconstruction gave us the Thirteenth, Fourteenth, and Fifteenth amendments to the Constitution. The Fourteenth is arguably the most important amendment because it establishes citizenship and "equal protection" of the laws for all who are citizens. We know equal protection is more theory than reality, but the text was born out of a "sincere" attempt to grant citizenship and rights to free blacks. The window of Reconstruction lasted a little more than ten years, and then eventually the U.S. government declared that securing the rights of freedmen was no longer a priority. In 1876, President Ulysses S. Grant voiced to his cabinet his belief that the 15th Amendment to the Constitution was a mistake, saying, "it had done the Negro no good and had been a hindrance to the South and by no means a political advantage to the North." Grant's opinion was one of many that reflected the nation's lack of commitment to securing black rights even if it meant "a hindrance to the South or no real advantage to the North." As if giving somebody the rights they are entitled to should be subject to the level of comfort of others. This is how America has felt about black rights since the beginning.

In the almost 400-year history of this colony and nation, Reconstruction constitutes a shift that barely lasted longer than a decade. How do twelve years cancel out institutional hate from 1619 up until 1865? It is not possible, and that is precisely why the end of Reconstruction symbolized the return to business as usual in the white south. For the sake of argument, if we were to make the Reconstruction age a percentage of time in the black experience in America, it would equate to less than 5 percent of our time in this land. Less than 5 percent of the time blacks have been in America, the American government has actively sought to safeguard black rights to life, liberty, and pursuit of happiness. Reconstruction was far from perfect, and by no means was it the solution to black problems in America. It is a very well-known fact that Reconstruction led to the rise of white supremacist organizations like the Ku Klux Klan, which was created in 1866 in Pulaski, Tennessee. The KKK may have been the first major white supremacist organization, but others soon followed in their footsteps, terrorizing and brutalizing blacks because the government was trying to grant them societal inclusion. So while the government was trying to make things better, others were trying to make things worse. And then eventually the government lost interest in trying to guarantee equal protection to blacks and moved on to matters that were more important to the homeland. Our government has kept the same focus ever since.

This is the birthplace of the dirge. Blacks live in a society that places no value on their lives. We look for justice, but there is none to be found because the historical practice of exonerating the killers of black people is firmly established. Between the years 1882 and 1964, more than 3,445 black men, women, and children were lynched in America, and this number doesn't include the thousands of convict laborers who died by the hands of whites. In this time frame of mass lynching, only one white man was convicted of murdering black folks. Only one. The journalist Shaun King described this statistical improbability in these terms:

"What this means is that the conviction rate for illegally lynching an African-American during this time in history was 0.00058%. Fans are more likely to sink a half-court NBA shot than a jury is to convict a white man for lynching a black person."

While all this injustice was happening to blacks, the rate of conviction for murder when the victim was white had "a clearance rate of nearly 90%." We do not find justice while we are alive, and justice is seldom found when one of us dies. How do you rest in peace when your murderers walk freely, especially when those killers with badges are still employed ready to brutalize and possibly murder another black life?

They want to see us jump, rap, sing, and dance. Corporations steal from our culture for the benefit of the greater American society, while the greater American society has no concern for the general well-being of the black life. Exiled to the fringes of American life, we are left to survive the best way we can. White faces pull back black triggers, firing bullets that carry black death down the barrels of black guns, that rip through black bodies, killing black dreams and destroying black homes. The trigger pullers then go home to their families, and we are left to mourn our loss. We bury our dead in cold black holes, never fully able to heal or move on. They are remembered as hashtags, faces on T-shirts, and memes. We compose black poetry and black raps, and sing melancholy tunes backed with the slow dirge in their remembrance. The media wants to tell us that black people are mainly killed by other blacks, but the reality of so called, "black on black crime" and state-sponsored murder of black lives are two sides of the same coin. There is no difference behind who pulls the trigger and extinguishes a black life when the problems and hate are byproducts of the same racist and greedy practices grown, perfected, and applied with brutal efficiency here in America.

"Letter to Johnetta" (2015)

She's that fast talking,
lip popping,
teeth sucking,
often annoyed
quick to start something
with anybody over nothing
allowing everybody to push her imaginary button
forever beefing with her dude
and quick to cut him,
black girl.

Johnetta I see you.
I mean like for real for real I see you.
And I wish I had some magic power
or some latent mutant ability
that could allow you to see you for you.
Not what America tells you is you
not what these dudes in these raps songs say about you
or what the streets say you need to be
but who you are for you.

The story goes
Your Pops probably wasn't around
you and your moms might or might not be on good terms
probably been to jail a few times
life took a couple u-turns
that's probably how we met,
I was teaching at the county and there you were.

My job was to teach you some math,
or some new words.
Open up your mind to a new world
but in the process noticing how lost you were.

I asked you about your family
and you told me about your new girl.
What's your baby girl like?
She extra smart, she real cute
but she hates it when I'm gone.
Where her daddy at?
Oh, he locked up
he ain't gonna be coming home.

How you deal with that?
I 'on't even know.

What you gonna do when you get out?
Shoot, I ain't gonna do that much boosting anymore.

Or I ain't gonna be getting high,
I'm gonna get my babies this time.
Go back to school get me a GED
get me a cool 9 to 5.

But when they back to the streets
so often them dreams get cast off,
she go back to selling that kat off
or getting them packs off
dreams of getting them stacks and them racks tall
not understanding how we so thoroughly blackballed,

and this ain't no judgment

because it ain't our fault.
The government has historically made us into outlaws.

See, in slavery days the slave master would make us watch
as he forcefully deflowered y'all,
then crept to your quarters at night making them house calls.
And sadly, your king, meaning me
was without claws
because without cause

he could hang me by my neck
from a tree with a string
until my heart paused.

Pause!

The system made it so we failed y'all
and the strong women you are
you showed your resolve and evolved.
You had babies to raise.
Meals to cook and homes to make
to help your babies to grow in hopes that they won't break
in the face of this American hate
that attempted to emasculate your man
and put us at odds in the first place.

Since then we trying to get our rhythm back.
America hating on everything that means living black.
Then we end up hating everything inside of us
that means the same thing in fact.

See, Johnetta I know all that
but what I want now is our men and our women back.
The devil been feeding us lies
all that bitches and hoes,
bad bitch
trap queen
thug misses,
that ain't you,
that ain't us.
We are the inheritors of cultura filled with riches.
They say the greatest of tricks ever performed is by the devil
making us doubt his existence.
And what I see happening to my brothers and sisters clearly
bares the mark of his imprint.
This letter is penned with hopes that you'll remember your
beginnings
before this cloud of white hate descended

and sent us down a path or self hate and resentment.
This letter was penned in hopes that you'll remember your beginnings.
Please remember your beginnings, my beautiful sisters.
Please remember our beginnings.

Reflections of a Black Boy

Hypothetically speaking, if I were to somehow be born a fully functioning adult with a mature intellect and somebody was to attempt to explain the concept of God or higher power to me, if I then went out into the world to try to find a parallel for that idea, the closest approximation of what I'd understand in my head would be that of a woman. And sadly, just like "sacred" traditions, the truth of who she is has been coopted and mutilated by men.

We live in a patriarchal society, meaning that men, more specifically wealthy white capitalist men, have shaped the contours of American life. If you are interested in a more authoritative definition, then I suggest our dear scholar, bell hooks, and her definition of patriarchy from *The Will to Change*. For the purposes of this text we'll define patriarchy as a local and global system based upon the false assumption that men, particularly white men are superior to all living things. This assumed superiority grants them the "right" to dominate in all areas of human interaction. Their domination is reinforced in multiple ways in all institutions they create to further perpetuate male dominance and female subservience. Patriarchy is the very reason why our society exhibits a heightened focus on the male, placing greater importance on his place in the world. This is the language western society speaks. It's certainly the language that America speaks.

I can easily discuss the male experience because it is my native experience. At times, I even question if as a man I should broach the subject of the female experience. I do not like it when other groups appropriate my experience and attempt to speak on it or use it for their own personal gain. I would be hypocritical to do the same to another group, especially women. I write this conscious of that fact.

With all of that in mind and in pen, let us proceed lightly. The black woman, who suffers for the same reasons as the black man, isn't granted the same forum for analysis, discussion, and healing. Her struggle and suffering most often has to occur in silence. She has to perform the incredible feat of being the comfort for her man who is beaten down by this world while at the same time knowing full and well there is nobody responsible for providing comfort for her. Who is her shoulder to cry on when the world treats her all the harmful ways it does? She is the first to rally and fight for her man and children but often left alone when allies are needed to rally to fight for her. When it comes to the harsh realities of the struggle, the woman can be seen amongst the ranks of the politically imprisoned and fallen, giving life and limb for the survival of her family and people. She mothers the next generation while fending off the attacks of the society she has to raise her children in.

When conflict turns to fighting and blood is spilled, she is brutalized by rape and other forms of torture. When captured and in the hands of tyrants, she is bought and sold for the pleasure of her tormentors. The woman under patriarchal domination has been put through so much, but we do not respect her suffering the same way we do a man's suffering. If the black man's existence in America has been hell, then the black woman has experienced hell to an exponentially higher power. She has experienced everything the black man has plus some. We don't know the pain of having our bodies violated the way black women have been abused and raped by white America and black men as well. We don't know the pain of seeing the babies created from your body sold off into slavery, or being gunned down in the street. Or the pain of simultaneously having to nurse the physical and psychological wounds of your man and children, as well as your own. There is so much in the struggle of black women that goes unnoticed and unappreciated.

Like black men, black women live in a world that does not allow them to fully reach their potential. They are physically imprisoned in a society and then oftentimes imprisoned again by the men who make up their community who are supposed to love and support them. The black woman in America suffers from at least three major layers of oppression. First, she's black, and automatically she is undervalued because of the color of her skin. This undervaluing affects black men and women alike. Second, she's a woman, and equity between the sexes in America is still a theory. The reality of the inequity is that the gains white women have received via various iterations of women's movements have not been shared equally by all women, specifically black women. This is why there exists a sharp racial critique of "feminism." White women have benefited a great deal from their organized efforts, but the fruits of the labor have not been shared equally by all sisters in the struggle. Third, she's a black woman, which puts her in the lowest stratum of society. The oppression she faces as a black person is something all black people, regardless of gender identity, face. The oppression she faces as a woman is something heaped upon all women regardless of color, but her designation as both black and woman puts her in a category all to her own, which subjects her to the worst forms of oppression from white and black men, as well as white women. She is attacked on the three fronts that are used to define who she is.

Audre Lorde said about her role as a black feminist:

"I am a Black Feminist. I mean I recognize that my power as well as my primary oppressions come as a result of my blackness as well as my womaness, and therefore my struggles on both of these fronts are inseparable."

I will never speak on behalf of a woman because the women I know are more than capable of advocating for themselves. I am at best an ally in the black feminist movement. My mother, my sister, my partner, my aunts, cousins, nieces, friends, my colleagues, and classmates are all capable of discussing the plight of women of color in America far more eloquently than I could ever do. I have been surrounded by incredible, brilliant women all my life. I would never dare to talk at or down to, and if I did, they would put me in my place real quick.

This poem was an attempt to have a conversation with the women that I know from the neighborhood or the streets, or those that I've crossed paths with on the inside. "Letter to Johnetta" is similar to another piece in this collection, "Out." I wrote that for the men I encountered on the streets and in jails. The more time I spent teaching women, the more I began to feel guilty about not giving attention to my experience with them. Sadly, that lack of attention reflects a greater societal trend of devaluing women. Consequently, incarcerated women are the most exploited and underserved incarcerated population in America. Most programs and services in jails and prisons have been designed for men. Very few services are allocated for women, and out of those services, very few programs have been created to meet the needs of incarcerated women. I could not allow my pen to show the same type of neglect.

Johnetta became the name that I chose to represent the stories of many of the women I've met over the past few years. Black people are creative in many areas of their lives, especially when it comes to naming their children. I met a Johnetta before, and she definitely left an impression upon me. I didn't want to speak about her specifically, so I made Johnetta a symbolic figure representing the women I was holding a conversation with. The most important thing I wanted her to know was that what I was attempting to say came from a place of love. The message in the poem was crafted free of condemnation and judgment. I wanted to speak openly and honestly about what the world has done to us both, and how we need each other to survive. That last point is essential because I strongly believe you cannot confront black suffering and talk black liberation but ignore the plight of the black woman. This is one of the biggest problems I have with hip-hop culture. At times the narrative of hip-hop speaks to black suffering and empowerment while one of its consistent themes has been bashing the figure of the black woman.

I love hip-hop, but I'm critical of it because of its industry practices toward women. The world of hip-hop, like other genres of music, is a male dominated and heavily unbalanced masculine culture that often demeans and denigrates the woman. She has been commodified in many ways and is primarily exploited as a mindless, soulless physical being. She is often portrayed as a Jezebel figure, a temptress, just a body with curves and orifices for men to sexually conquer. Male dominated hip-hop has done an exemplary job of presenting women as broken one-dimensional figures. I hate that about hip-hop, but hip-hop is a reflection of the greater hyper-masculine culture of America, which has done that to women in all areas of social interaction.

The black woman inside and outside of hip-hop has been through an exhausting experience. She has been forced into a world where her very existence is an affront to her self-worth. If we want to examine some simple hard facts, black women lead all women in labor force participation rates. This means they work more than any other group of women in America. Conversely, they are the most likely to be paid minimum wage, making them prime candidates to be amongst the working poor. Black women are the most likely to die from breast cancer and not due to any biological factor, but due to the "lengthy delays in receiving follow up care and treatment." The medical industry seems to not prioritize black women's health like other groups. Black girls are six times more likely to be suspended from school than their white counterparts, and four times more likely to attend schools with inadequate resources. The most-telling reality of the devaluation of the black woman is that nobody "is more likely to be murdered in America today than a black woman. No woman is more likely to be raped than a black woman. And no woman is more likely to be beaten, either by a stranger or by someone she loves and trusts than a black woman." These stats are from the report Black Women in the United States, 2014, developed by the Black Women's Roundtable. What this states emphatically is that the black woman is under attack in every area of her life. Even in the horrific categories of death and rape, she can't find equality. While she is among the living, the discrimination is so deep that it even affects the way that she looks at herself because every standard of beauty is contrary to what she is.

Dr. Cornel West spoke of this very issue in his famous text, *Race Matters*.

"The dominant myth of Black female sexual prowess constitutes black women as desirable sexual partners—yet the central role of the ideology of white female beauty attenuates the expected conclusion. Instead of black women being the most sought after "objects of sexual pleasure," as in the case of black men, white women tend to occupy this "upgraded," that is, degraded, position primarily because white beauty plays a role in sexual desirability for women in racist patriarchal America." He goes on to say, "This means that black women are subject to more multilayered bombardments of racist assaults than black men, in addition to the sexist assaults they receive from black men."

I'll take a brief moment to discuss the issue of beauty to show one of the many categories that victimizes the black woman in American society. I want to preface this portion of the conversation with a few disclaimers. I am speaking to the stereotypes and myths that pertain to "beauty" in the Western world. I'll be speaking about different aspects of the "beauty" myth for the next few pages, but the greater conversation of this section is not just about women and "beauty." I am a man speaking about "beauty," which has been largely constructed by the privileged white racist Anglo-Saxon Protestant sexual appetite. In speaking about beauty, I am not attempting to perpetuate the myths and stereotypes of "beauty," but it is important to point out how even in the fabricated realm of "beauty," black women are demeaned for what they possess naturally.

As Dr. Cornell West mentioned, a common stereotype granted to black men and black women is that they have incredible sexual prowess. The black man is stereotyped as having the largest and most fulfilling penis of all men and being able to satisfy his partner sexually like no other man. Black women too are granted that same sexual prowess stereotype. According to the stereotype, the black woman's body has a magic that no other woman can match. These stereotypes contributed to certain cultural artifacts like the common phrase, "Once you go black you never go back." That indicates the superiority of the sexual experience with a black partner and how it will force conversion upon contact, leaving the converted to seek worship only at mahogany temples.

These sexual stereotypes are applied to black men and women, but the difference in their application is that the black man is not subjected to the same "beauty" standard/check as the black woman. The black man is granted the stereotype of having the largest and most-fulfilling sexual organ, along with being the more physically superior man. All this makes him the most desirable sexual partner. This stereotype of the black man is not counteracted by a white male standard of "beauty." Oddly, this stereotype allows for the black man to be fetishized/aesthetically appreciated for his natural gifts. However, the black woman does not share this same strange experience.

The black woman is viewed as having sexual power like no other, but Western society possesses a failsafe to strip her of that power, and that is the definition of beauty. The Western standard of female beauty is based on the archetype of the white woman. The stereotype of the black woman's sexual ability is paired with the stereotype of her being the farthest from the "norm" of beauty. Black women are deemed ugly because of the color of their skin and features that are readily associated with the black body, while white women are deemed beautiful due to the whiteness of their skin and their physical features.

We already examined dictionary "definitions" of white and black in an earlier chapter. White is defined as pure and beautiful, while black is defined as dirty, evil, and ugly. Thus, a white woman is already defined as 'beautiful," and by those very same definitions a black woman is said to be dirty and ugly. All of this creates a context where what the black woman offers in a physical sense is debased. Again, this conversation is not limiting women, specifically black women, to being solely physical creatures. However, these definitions and stereotypes are a very real part of the dominant narrative in our society, and they tell the black woman her sexual energy and body is something special, but it would be more aesthetically pleasing if her natural gifts were not on her black body.

This lends one to appropriating what makes the black woman so sexually desirable but applying those things to a white context. The white woman is the standard of beauty in Western societies and her current stereotypical phenotype is that of the Barbie doll. White, tall, slim, big chest, no butt, skinny waist, thin lips, odd geometrically shaped hips, and of course blonde hair with blue eyes. That definition is now evolving to include thick lips, round hips, booty, and tanned skin. These are traits more readily associated with black women and other women of color. Consequently, the white media loses its collective mind when a "white woman" culturally appropriates these black features and displays them for the white world to marvel at.

The problem with this is that the black woman and her features have been historically made fun of and outright attacked in western society for centuries. Sarah "Saartjie" Baartman (1789-1815) was a woman from the Khoikhoi people of South Africa. She was enslaved in Cape Town, South Africa, and eventually ended up in Britain where she was made into a zoo attraction. The reason for her being made a zoo attraction was the size of her butt. She was on display for four years in Britain and then was eventually sent to France for a few more years of circus sideshow exhibits. Baartman was eventually discarded by her handlers and died a lonely death around the age of twenty-five. Even after death, her body continued to be displayed as her dissected remains were viewable at the Musée de l'Homme (Museum of Man) in Paris for the next 150 years. Her remains were not returned to her homeland of South Africa until 2002. There are so many tragedies in her story, but what is clear is that Baartman's beautiful natural physique was completely demeaned by Western society. They looked upon her and didn't see beauty; they saw her as a freak. She was stripped of her humanity by white society and turned into something to be pointed and laughed at. A thing to be snickered at and studied to prove pseudo-scientific theories of white superiority.

The late nineteenth and twentieth centuries in the Western world saw the emergence of Black Sambo caricatures that always depicted both black males and females with exaggerated physical features. Their skin was jet black, lips were big and red, hair was nappy, and at times for women their breasts and butts were exaggerated to make them look even more foolish. This was replicated in blackface actors and actresses who appeared on stage, television, and film throughout the twentieth century. Almost every portrayal of the black woman in popular culture was unflattering and highly offensive. Her caricature was that of an ugly buffoon. She was never celebrated in her society for anything she possessed naturally.

We still see instances of this in our culture today. Our beautiful strong black champion Serena Williams is constantly insulted by the media because of how they perceive her body. She is often called manly, and some of her tennis colleagues have dressed up in an attempt to insult her by making their butts and breasts larger to make fun of Williams's physical attributes. There have been "fans" who attended her matches in blackface with exaggerated black features. In 2015, much was made of the fact that Williams is the undisputed champion of women's tennis, but Maria Sharapova, who has been defeated by Serena some eighteen times in a row with performance enhancers and all, takes home more endorsement money every year than Williams. Western society claims Sharapova is more marketable, i.e. she fits the Western standard of "beauty."

Serena just might be the greatest tennis player in women's tennis history, and a case could be made for the greatest woman athlete of all time. If you compare her with a black man dominating his sport the way she does hers, that man would not be second to anybody in endorsement dollars, white or black. Michael Jordan, LeBron James, and Tiger Woods are black men who have dominated their sports and are compensated handsomely for their dominance. I say this is due to the expectation of physical greatness from black men and no check on that stereotype. Black women can be great physically, but the check is their physical greatness doesn't make them beautiful so they are devalued. Thus, a less-talented and less-accomplished white woman can reap more economic benefit off the court because her ability doesn't really matter; her win is due to the fact that white society claims her as white and "beautiful."

White Appropriation of the Stereotypical Black Phenotype and Style

What happens when white women appropriate from black women? There are plenty of examples to choose from, but the most famous at the moment is Kim Kardashian, whose claim to fame is having a butt like a black woman and sleeping with and then marrying "famous" black men. Her fame is not based on any real tangible skill or talent, but she has capitalized on her fame and used her business acumen to generate a very successful career for herself and her family. And it all began from appropriating a phenotypical trait that many black women possess naturally and packaging it in a white body and marketing it to a white audience.

Kardashian, who ethnically is Armenian and western European, as well as many other so-called "beautiful" white/nonwhite celebrity/noncelebrity girls and women, are more and more enhancing the size of their lips, hips and butts, and bronzing their skin. Some are also found replicating black hairstyles and mannerisms all to mimic the naturally occurring phenotypic and cultural traits of black women. This is cultural appropriation at a very high level, and the inequity inherent in the appropriation is that these traits are now being celebrated on white bodies but have been historically lampooned on black bodies.

In 2014, Jennifer Lopez and Iggy Azalea made an entire song about having big butts and curves, entitled "Booty." Disclaimer: Black women do not have a monopoly on curvaceous figures, but the curves of the black woman have almost always been demeaned in Western society. I watched the video twice, once out of curiosity and a second time for research purposes. The word booty is a slang term from black culture because the curves of the black woman have been celebrated in black culture since time immemorial, while those same curves had been devalued by mainstream white society as marks of ugliness until recently when in the possession of white bodies. Like anything of importance to a people, it will be supported by multiple words for that thing. Black men in particular have had deep love for the curves of their black counterparts and have created numerous words to describe the curvaceous posterior of the black woman.

J.Lo, a very fair skinned Puerto Rican woman who first earned national attention as a dancer on the black comedy show *In Living Color*, and Iggy Azalea, a super-white skinned Australian girl whose claim to fame is doing a bad white interpretation of a stereotypical southern female black rapper, both danced around on stage in video singing about their booties. Iggy was of course using her blackface-style of performance as they twerked like black girls and mimicked other black styles for a white audience to consume.

J.Lo and Iggy were praised for being strong women who were unapologetic about their figures.

A Billboard article was published shortly after the release of the video to describe the greatness of what they captured visually. A few points from the article, Billboard claimed, J.Lo and Iggy together represent a glorious celebration of all things woman and booty. The article highlighted their confidence, power, and beauty, as well as their ability to see beauty in what another woman possesses. Then Billboard showed its evil white supremacist true colors by taking a swipe at Nicki Minaj who had nothing to do with the song or video. The article boldly proclaimed J.Lo and Iggy's booty tribute made Nicki's video Anaconda look like child's play. They actually had the audacity to take a shot at her. Apparently Billboard didn't learn the lesson of J.Lo and Azalea who could appreciate the beauty of another woman because they couldn't write the article without kicking dirt on a black woman, Nicki Minaj, essentially attempting to cancel out her presence in order to elevate the appropriation of these white women. They demonstrate the very essence of what I'm attempting to illustrate. The white woman who appropriates culture and physical traits is praised, but the black woman is belittled. The white women are extolled for exhibiting women's power; meanwhile, the beautiful black-skinned women, who J.Lo and Iggy are trying hard to be like, are told daily that their bodies and skin color do not make them beautiful and that white women make it look better.

Although I spent several sections detailing the beauty myths that affect black women, it is important to note that black women's value is not based on how men or the outside world perceive them. They are not merely physical beings. Black women are the hearts, minds, souls, and creative spirits who have driven America forward. The beauty myths are important to highlight and dispel because they are so insidious and attempt to smother the greatness of black girls and black women. All of that needed to be discussed, as well as how black men at times have served as oppressors to black women throughout their term here in America, to create the context for this piece.

The conversation of the black woman is always linked with that of the black man because of the old adage, "The enemy of my enemy is my friend." Black women and men face racism in America for the same reason, the blackness of their skin. We are bound together in our struggle for survival. In that struggle, the black man as your partner in struggle was unable to do his part in watching your back as you tried to watch his. Slavery, Jim Crow, segregation, modern day policing, and the Prison Industrial Complex have all driven a wedge between the patriarch and matriarch of the black family. The lines in the poem that carry the most visceral pain for me are:

the government has historically made us into outlaws.
See, in slavery days the slave master would make us watch
as he forcefully deflowered y'all,
then crept to your quarters at night making them house calls.
And sadly, your king, meaning me
was without claws
because without cause
he could hang me by my neck
from a tree with a string
until my heart paused.

Pause!

The foundation of the American society was established on the broken bodies, families, and homes of black people. A black man and woman who started a family during slavery times had no protections against the rape, murder, and theft of their bodies or their children's bodies. Imagine being a husband or wife, and you can't legally protect your spouse from being raped by the "slave master," and yes, black men were raped too. Imagine being a father or mother and you can't protect your children from being sold off to another plantation by the "slave master." The level of trauma in those all-too-common experiences for blacks under slavery is incalculable. As a result of that trauma, pain, and hurt, how do those partners see each other as partners? My family has lived through this traumatic experience. On my father's side, my great-great-great-grandfather Bartlett Flemister had to watch his wife, my great-great-great-grandmother Rowena Beckoms, and their first born, my great-great-grandfather Charles Flemister, be sold off from a plantation in Georgia to Alabama. My family lived through this; I carry that history in my blood.

I can't imagine what Bartlett felt watching his wife and nine-year-old son be shipped off. I can't imagine what Rowena felt knowing that her husband could not help protect her from their slave master, and she could not do anything to protect herself and son from being sold. I don't want that to come across as chauvinistic, as if a woman is dependent on a man to protect her. Also, I'm not espousing "traditional" relationship views; if you're black the system of racism doesn't care if your union is hetero or same-sex, all are subjected to the same oppression. That is precisely why, regardless of how the relationship is constructed, a couple works together to protect their union, and both partners have to do their part for the safety and security of that union.

The institution of slavery made it so a husband and wife could not legally fight for one another. Knowing this, what happens to the black family that has had all of that stolen from them multiple times? Again, I am not espousing traditional Western male-female roles. I am not saying that the man has a certain place, and the woman has her place following the man. The fact of the matter is black men and women were allies in the fight against the systemic racist abuse they faced on a daily basis. They came into it together and had to rely on each other to survive. Surviving leaves scars, and one of those scars is the realization that it is hard to have faith and confidence in your ally when he or she cannot protect you. This is a very real component at the heart of black male and female relations and the black family in America.

The challenge of loving another when you're broken daily by your surroundings is virtually insurmountable. The conversation has to be raw and open if you are addressing that historical legacy. In the piece, I wanted to bring attention to the roles that black women find themselves in just like I talked about black men and their roles in the poem "Out." Men and women both have artificially constructed roles that have been assigned to them by society. Just like the young black men smoothly fall into their roles, black women began to do the same. Many of the women I've come across are still lost somewhere in their role. Just like the roles that are scripted for black boys are filled with lies, the roles of black women are equally fabricated on foundations of falsehoods. Those roles have to be challenged and dismantled. If not, then a people who do not have our best interest in mind are bombarding us with sickened messages as to who we are to be. And their grotesque ill-informed "truth" is so very far from the truth that we know of ourselves.

As I mentioned before, black women have always been at the heart of the struggle. The story of black women is not all suffering at the hands of America and black society. Their successes are not confined only to domestic duties. We can look at slavery days and arguably the most famous and directly effective figure from that time is a woman, Harriet Tubman. Tubman perfected her usage of the network of the Underground Railroad to help blacks find their way to freedom. Everyone involved in the operation was putting something at risk, but none more than the actual conductor in the field driving the metaphoric train to freedom. Tubman risked her life more than any other conductor on the Railroad and is famously quoted as saying, "I freed a thousand slaves. I could have freed a thousand more if only they knew they were slaves." She risked life and limb hundreds of times to bring freedom by force to her people. Others in her day talked about diplomatic and political remedies to freedom; Tubman manifested it for her people by any means necessary. Her male historical counterparts are names like Benjamin Banneker, Denmark Vesey, Nat Turner, Fredrick Douglass, but arguably her example is unparalleled by all that they contributed. A woman unconquered by anyone and anything.

Post-slavery days we have more women who stand out. We have women like "Stagecoach" Mary Fields, who according to legend broke more noses than any other person in central Montana. She was a woman in a man's world but thrived in that world. And not only a woman in a man's world, she was a black woman in a white man's world. Her reputation and character was so respected that she openly defied segregation policies in the city where she lived, and nobody did anything about it. She became the first female U.S. mail carrier in her region and never missed a single package. Stagecoach was bad.

These are not isolated instances. We can go through the history and continue to highlight examples of black women overcoming the strictures of two societies to become successful in their own right. Mary McLeod Bethune and the Bethune-Cookman schools, Madam C.J. Walker and her industrial success, and Ida B. Wells and her fight for black rights and women's rights. The NAACP had women in positions of leadership and as the legal minds behind various initiatives waged by the organization. We know the example of Rosa Parks and her role in what eventually became known as the Montgomery bus boycott. And some historians mention how Dr. King was pushed to become involved in the civil rights movement by Coretta, and without Coretta, King's role in the movement would not have been possible. Women have been at the forefront of the vanguard all along.

In historical reflection and retelling, the black liberation movements become very patriarchal, but none of it was at all possible without the strength and support of black women. We remember our Dr. Kings and Malcolms and organizations like SCLC and SNCC, the Nation of Islam, as well as other groups that contributed to the struggle, but at the backbone of all those groups and movements you found women to be the primary supporters and many times part of the leadership. Immediately following the civil rights movement, you find women in leadership positions all throughout the black power movement. A woman I am blessed to know and consider a mentor, Elaine Brown, became the Chairperson of the Black Panther Party in 1974, instantly making her the leader of the most revolutionary organization in American history. Under her leadership the party flourished and in that position she was arguably the baddest and most powerful black person in America. And as she's told me on several occasions, she's still bad. At one point in time, a significant portion of the leadership of the Black Panther Party were women. Other important figures from that era were Assata Shakur, Angela Davis, Kathleen Cleaver, Fannie Lou Hamer, Erika Huggins, Dr. Betty Shabazz, Sis, Clara Muhammad, and Shirley Chisholm. Since day one, women have always been involved in, and at the forefront of every aspect of black resistance.

The power exemplified by the previous examples is an essential aspect of the narrative of the black woman in America. We hold to that example and honor it. That awesome power is born out of the fact that they have been given the shortest end of the stick and are still able to create miracles everyday with what they have been given. This is no easy task, and the pain and trauma from finding ways to survive this hellish reality are real. This fight waged by the black woman has led to another stereotype of the "strong black woman." It is used in a way to ignore her pain and suffering because she can handle it. In other words, no need to support or comfort her because she can deal with it on her own. No one is an island; we all need love and support.

If society was different, if it gave black women equal access to the spoils of America, we would be able to celebrate the minds, accomplishments, inventions, and innovations birthed by black women much more than we are able to do now. But the multiple layers of oppression are thick and weighted heavily across the backs of black women. Society fails to see and respect the intellectual gifts of black women and instead shuns the majority of their creative ability, unless it is tied to a man's sperm. But the resounding truth is women are powerful and valuable with or without men. They do not need a man to validate their greatness. Women have been doing great things throughout their existence, and they will continue to do so. It's an insult to try to confine their greatness to their "beauty" or their reproductive ability.

"Letter to Johnetta" attempts to bring light to the realities of the women I've met in jails, prisons, and on the streets of the Bay Area. It is so easy to only highlight beauty because from a patriarchal lens that is what men want to see women as. My teaching has afforded me the opportunity to learn from the lives of the women I meet. I wanted this poem to reflect the very real connections I've established with my students. I wanted them to see that I see them and convey to them the reality of our shared struggles. Like the poems "Out" and "The Rose," there's a similar formula to the way the poem is written. First, it's written to grab the attention of its intended audience. I try to create a context that is familiar to draw the listener in. Then I begin to introduce problems that the character in the poem is facing and try to show love and support for the intended audience. Finally, I try to show that the only way to solve our problems is together, and that I'm here to do my part to help us win.

I feel "Letter to Johnetta" is an important poem because there are a number of songs and poems about the black "queens," Nubian sisters, and well-to-do more "socially adjusted" women, praising them for who they are. On the contrary, there are very few songs and poems about women who are not classified as such, done in a manner that isn't about calling them out by their name. It's a horrendous dichotomy of "you're either a queen or a bitch." You're the mother of civilization or ratchet. That's what happens when men are allowed to dictate the story; women become reduced to a false binary of what men like and don't like.

"Letter to Johnetta" is written outside of that dichotomy. It is my attempt, firstly, at an honest message filled with love and concern for the plight of black women, and secondly, the connection between black men and women. Black women have been discarded by society. This poem was to say that black women matter, as well as to address the poisoned messages that are fed to us on a daily basis to distract us from who we truly are. The poem also includes a subject that I feel isn't really discussed openly enough, and that is the often turbulent relationship between black woman and black man. I address the deliberate steps taken by this society to drive wedges between black men and women. Again, not saying that a woman has value only in relation to a man. Yet and still, we both face similar institutional discriminatory treatment by this society, and we will have to work together as partners to save ourselves. Although women shine independently, we are inextricably connected because we are the only ones left who are concerned about our survival, and together we are stronger in fighting for our livelihood.

The piece finishes with appeals to understand the mind-control programming directed at women and the historical traumas that have prevented black women from being their authentic selves. Both black women and men have to shed the roles imposed upon us by a society that does not care for our health and well-being. It is up to us to rectify our condition in this society. Black women are extremely important because they have been the lifeblood of every major movement toward black liberation in America. There is no black liberation without the liberation of black women. We need all black women and men to work together with equality and justice if we are serious about revolutionary change in our world. This is the heart of "Letter to Johnetta." May the words serve as inspiration and a benefit to our sisters and brothers. May we both find our way together to our true selves and may we struggle proudly until we make our way OUT.

Material of Martyrs (2015)

I am made from the material of martyrs
hewn in the hollows of vessels whose hulls housed
the most horrific horrors history has known.

Fashioned in a furnace
fueled by the fires of hatred and fear

I emerge mangled and misshapen
the merciless hands of manufacturers
attempt to molest my essence
maneuvering my body in multiple directions

Am I not man and brother
Am I not flesh and bone

Their eye is incapable of envisioning that reality
my truth is engulfed,
superimposed are their mental projections
by-products of their fantasy and fancy

They cannot see
that I too
am blessed By the One,
adorned in a bold, brilliant
and beautiful brocaded dark cloth,
eerily iridescent
incandescent and majestic

Their eyes marvel
then their envy intervenes
their hearts conspire jealousy,
their souls grow deficient and desperate

Their desire is to own the economy of me
incarcerate those of this ilk.
Appropriate our creations
for the expressed purposes
of commodity and control

And they believe their victory is nigh

What they don't know is
intricately woven into the fabrics of my robes
are rebellion and resistance.

Yeah, these wears are wrought with revolution

Regalia is ripe with the royal hues of our royal ancestors

My garments are replete with struggle and survival
Bespoke apparel
customized by the knowledge and wisdom
amplified by
shotgun shells flying from barrels in the Audubon.
No brand names
Just black names
etched in each strand of cotton,
linen,
silk,
polyester,
and rayon
I have on.

I wear Addie Mae Collins,
Denise McNair,
Carole Robertson,
Cynthia Wesley,
Medgar Evers
and Trayvon

I'm covered in some Martin King,

Fred Hampton,
Fred Gray
Emmett Till,
Sandra Bland

I'm clad in that plaid pattern
ropes make on flesh
when tied around necks
as nooses

This is not some fashion week exclusive

This is bruises and blood,
bullets and billy clubs,
burning crosses,
ballot boxes,
brutality making us into
burnt offerings at the altar.

If you look here, my man, you'll see
This ain't swag
This is sophistication
stitched through generations
it's deep in the lines and seams
and my kind knows the reality
of what every thread means.

You can't buy that
you can't try that
it's not off the rack
or couture
this is that authentic black culture

And I've found this cut and fit
is tailored to my size
ain't no other suit for me to try
nor would I want to try
and this is why I make this look so good

because I wear this with pride.

Reflections of a Black Boy

What does it mean to be black in America?

"Representatives and direct Taxes shall be apportioned among the several States which may be included within this Union, according to their respective Numbers, **which shall be determined by adding to the whole Number of free Persons, including those bound to Service for a Term of Years, and excluding Indians not taxed, three fifths of all other Persons.**" - Article I Section II US Constitution

This is the first official answer to the question of what it means to be black in constitutional America. Three-fifths of all other persons. Not to be counted or considered a full human being, to be considered by law 3/5ths or 60% of a human being.

The catastrophe in our existence is that the exploitation and extermination of life has been for one main reason, capitalistic greed. It's a greed for power, money, property, and other forms of wealth for the benefit of a select few and the slight but significant elevated status of middle- and lower-class whites. That greed has manifested itself in many ways and spawned numerous justifications, theories, and philosophies to support it, but the genetic essence to the social underpinning of our plight is capitalistic greed.

We know the motto of the Spanish conquistadors was for "Gold, God, and Glory." Once they laid their false claims to lands, they worked hard to establish colonies to extract wealth from the land by any means necessary. In the process, they almost completely obliterated all indigenous populations they encountered. Other European countries soon followed and began to emulate their example. It didn't matter whether the labor came from indigenous natives, other poor Europeans, or Africans. Eventually, for the sake of efficiency, shrewd business minds concluded it would be more advantageous if the labor was to be provided on plantations in South America, the Caribbean, and North America by Africans.

Free labor is great for greedy countries, economies, and corporations. The first major undertaking in the operation of colonial empire building was acquiring large swaths of land that could be utilized for resource purposes. To accomplish this, the indigenous people all throughout the Americas were systematically killed off and displaced from their lands in the pursuit of wealth and expansion of empire. In the example of the United States, we broke every treaty ever made with the indigenous nations because the lust for wealth was greater than honoring agreements made with innocent people. The American machine was inventive in all the ways it justified the theft and slaughter necessary to acquire indigenous lands. The justifications were necessary to salve the conscience and quiet the guilt rising in the soul over the barbarism and greed.

The indigenous peoples were not the only ones victimized by the rise of America and weren't the only ones who received the justification treatment to excuse their systematic exploitation and extermination. Many white Americans during the time of legalized chattel slavery felt slavery was immoral, but because it was so lucrative people found it hard to take a moral stance on the issue. This is somewhat understandable but not excusable. If your entire livelihood is based on the exploitation of another group, the fact that you earn a living from that exploitation makes it difficult for some to say, this is wrong, and then act upon that feeling, and stop doing it. This is what America faced and America failed. Sadly, America still fails in this present day when confronted with numerous moral/ethical issues in the face of potential profits. Both the South and North profited greatly off of slave labor. Textile mills and other industrial apparatuses in the North received cotton, cash crops, fossil fuels, and other resources for cheap from the South because the labor was provided by captive beings. The mighty American empire was firmly established upon blood money from slavery and indigenous forced removal.

Millions of lives were lost to make this union what it is today. This is why in the piece I say, "I am made from the materials of martyrs." We were, and still are the collateral damage of this industrial empire. Treated like surplus resources to be disposed of however they saw fit. Blacks in America and the Indigenous people of these lands share a common and, at times, a divergent experience but the cause of our suffering emanates from the same place. Our oppressors who are fueled by their greed operate with the basest goals of all time, so much so that they are willing to enslave generations of people or wage wars which kill off millions of innocents to secure resources and markets.

All people, regardless of time and place, are capable of greed. Western society, and white civilization isn't the first and won't be the last group of people in power to succumb to greed. They definitely have done it with a unique flair that has left an indelible mark on the world. Our planet will never be the same as a result of what Western civilization has brought to us. The year 1492 was the beginning of a new world order that has resulted in irrevocable social, political, and planetary shifts. Greed and the pursuit of base desires are not a monopoly that Western civilization owns the deeds to. My ancestors were sold into slavery by other "Africans." Currency was exchanged between the African slave catchers and their European business partners, who were interested in cheap labor. The catching and selling of slaves eventually became an industry over the centuries of the trans-Atlantic and Arab slave trades, which mainly affected African populations. Greed played a role in the perpetuation of these heinous acts. It is true that many African cultures had a different experience with slavery. It wasn't the same type of barbaric chattel slavery pioneered by Europeans in the Americas. Still, the pursuit of money led many to capture men, women, and children and put them up for sale for Europeans and Arabs to purchase. With an unapologetic acknowledgement of that historical fact, the pursuit of profit motivated by greed was elevated to an entirely new level by Europeans in America.

I use the term material because black bodies became commodities to be bought and sold. The only legal definition for blacks in early constitutional America was that of property. The constitution legalized this property status in Article I Section II with the 3/5ths compromise and in Article IV Section II via the fugitive slave clause. Both articles were definitive statements making black people held in bondage property of such and such state and by extension the United States. Black people were a tool of the agricultural apparatus that was providing major money for the American economy. Black bodies were simply a cog in a wheel turning the motors of a much larger machine that was the basis of the burgeoning economy of a new nation. We were beast of burden. Raw material. And like all resources used in the agricultural and industrial process, we were used up until we were no longer useful, and when that occurred we were discarded. Like a molting mantis casts off his old skin, his husk is sent to the floor and replaced by something new. Black husk-like bodies began to cover the floors of America once the last bit of life was wrung from their muscle and bones.

This greed bred two distinct philosophical cousins to justify its existence as a means for building America. Those cousins are racism and white supremacy. The philosophy took years to be birthed and developed, but racism and white supremacy thrust themselves onto the world's stage and made bold claims that white people were the best people on the Earth, and it was because of this self-proclaimed fact that they had the right to use all resources on the planet, including people, the way they saw fit. They were the caretakers of the planet and could exhaust resources to their liking.

This is the background to "Material of Martyrs." The systems of white supremacy, racism, and the beast-like greed displayed by this society are horrendous, callous, and cold. Thus, the language chosen for this piece is very mercantile. I selected language that paralleled the brutal mechanizations of the machines at work. I wanted to emphasize the cognitive dissonance of turning a human being into a tool of production. That was their intention when they had control of black bodies. This dehumanizing view of man as beast of burden became the backbone of the system of American and Western civilization.

However, as the piece shows, contrary to what some may have thought would eventually happen to blacks when they were no longer of use, we survived. We escaped it by some miraculous sequence of events and have risen to create something new despite all that had been done to limit us. We wear the marks of this inhumane experience. It is constantly present around us and in us. It covers us up completely, yet we still have the audacity and the ability to look beautiful and create beauty in this world for ourselves and others. I am made from the material of martyrs. I am the son of those who were brought here to toil for the pleasure and profit of others. I am the son of those who survived that and are attempting to thrive in the present. I wear their struggle on my chest every day of my life. So much so, that I now shine brightly because of those who sacrificed to give me this clothing. We are the material of martyrs and those before us have woven a beautiful fabric that has been passed down to us so that we may warm ourselves with their sacrifices and struggles, to carry on their tradition of fighting for freedom, and to live with dignity and pride.

Black Child (2015)

Black child, my child,
with all the sincerity I can muster
forming the most unbiased and humble opinion,
I say to you
that you are the envy of all of creation.

It is a universal fact that your genetic inheritance
is straight from the material that spawned civilization.

It was men and women in your blessed hue
who walked this planet first.

They pondered the realities of life on earth
and passed on their precious gifts to you.

When you stand in the power that you posses
The sun, the moon, the stars, and everything upon the earth
and in the heavens
feel that slight twinge of their heart strings
as your elegance and grace is laid bare before them.

You are the personification of the highest definition of beauty
which is so sacred it is incapable of being spoken by a human
tongue,
an anthropomorphic presentation of all that can be right in the
world,
A noble embodiment of freedom and struggle.

You are love and you are loved.

And I must apologize for the world that I have to bring you into.
Black child, my child
know that I have tried,

and others who are more worthy than me have tried with life and
limb
to create a world that would not offend you.
It is a fact of this life that I must prepare you
for the evil that men do.

Black Child, my child
know that I have endeavored with every effort
to carve out a sliver of this world to place you in
where you will not be blemished or tarnished
by the venom and garbage
of heartless hardened men
who have yet to hearken
to the sweetness of your song.

They say ignorance is a state
which equates lack of knowledge or information
Modern man is a woefully ignorant,
a penniless
indigent pauper
whose transactions are bankrupt

for, if they listened, then they would know.
They would know the beauty that produced you
and is produced by you.
They would recognize the seed of the tree of knowledge
by its roots and its fruit
they would be transformed by the lessons you have buried in
your flesh.

Through knowing you they would know themselves.

But they reject,

they cover up,
wipe away,
smudge out
like a tantrum touting toddler claiming everything is "mine"

Their hearts and souls become decrepit
blind and illiterate,
deaf by choice and
dumb with distinction

all to protect the trivial trinkets of western adornment
they believe belong to them.
They believe these things make them more beautiful than you
Spiritually and morally destitute and inept
They are unable to feel the braille that is written in your soul

This is how jealousy,
envy,
hubris, and arrogance
have manifested in what could've been a great people.

May their example be a cautionary tale to you, Black Child.
Do not accept their ways as your own.
You were made to sing and dance in the sun.
The moon bore witness to your song.
The stars shine bright in tribute to your smile.
Black child, my child
never forget who and what you are.
This wisdom of the elders has been passed on for generations
since time immemorial and now I present it to you.

Many will attempt to change,
corrupt,
influence,
steal,
appropriate,
confuse,
challenge,
humiliate,
denigrate,
judge,
and hate you for being you.

This is part of your sentence as a Black Child,
but you must always know that you are greater than.
You are the first.
You are the fulcrum providing the balance
the universe rests upon.
The world is again waiting for you to assume your rightful position
of leader in the cosmos.
May we all live to see that day where you, black child
again lead us safely home.

Reflections of a Black Boy

Being a black child in America is my Great-Great-Grandfather Charles Flemister who was born a slave and was eventually sold with his mother from a plantation in Georgia to a plantation in Alabama for $1,500.

Being a black child in America is being a 14 year old innocent black boy who is tried and convicted of murder in one day, sentenced to death, and then executed by electric chair. George Junius Stinney Jr.

Being a black child in America is going to church on a beautiful Sunday morning in Birmingham, Alabama. Instead of laughing and joking with your friends all of you become victims of a white supremacist terror plot when a bomb goes off killing you all instantly because you're black.

Being a black child in America is playing with four of your young siblings at 6221 Osage Avenue in West Philadelphia, PA on the morning of May 13th 1985. The day that Philadelphia police decided to drop two bombs on your home knowing in advance that women and children were in the residence, killing all five of you and six others.

Being a black child in America means you have no childhood because law enforcement personnel and the larger white world always see you as older and bigger than you are. The added age and size create fear in the body and mind of the onlookers. They don't see a black child playing with a toy, they see a potentially armed criminal ready to commit a crime. In response, police pull triggers on you because the moment they see you, they're already in fear of their lives.

I have yet to become a parent. Becoming a father is a future blessing I hope will be mine someday soon in my life. I have many near and dear friends who have moved into that phase of life and are faced with the reality of trying to raise a black child in a world that has little to no love for their existence. It makes me think of what my parents must've dealt with while raising my older sister, Kira, and me. I recall conversations with both of my parents about how I needed to be "careful" and "aware" when I was in public or when I was in white areas because my lack of awareness could result in problems. When you are black, those problems can mean death, incarceration, or serious physical injury. We had those conversations often. I do not know what guidebook my parents used to raise their two kids, but they made a lot of right calls.

One bit of wisdom they had that I didn't fully understand at my young age involved toy guns. I'm a child of the '80s; I remember one Christmas before we stopped celebrating Christmas, my parents spent their hard earned money on a new video game system for me. I was now the proud owner of a Nintendo Entertainment System. That mug was fresh. I had the standard games that came with it, "Mario Bros.," "Gyromite," and "Duck Hunt." In order to play "Duck Hunt," you had to use the gun controller that came along with the system. My parents weren't having that at all. It was a rule in the house that I was to never have toy guns. I didn't understand why, but as I got older their logic became painfully clear. The years passed, and I witnessed countless black bodies having their lives extinguished by law enforcement agents for holding toy guns or having anything in their hands that could be interpreted as a threat.

This is what it means to be the parent of a black child. You have to prepare your child for a world that is filled with constant harm because of their skin color. White kids get to have a childhood where they can play with toy guns, and their "unruly" behavior is dismissed as it's just kids being kids. Black kids and their "unruly" behavior can result in far more severe and permanent consequences.

It is a point of fact that black kids cannot do the same things that white kids can do in America. That's not a question of ability; it's the reality of race in America. The stakes are much higher when you are black. My parents wanted me to be free and have a childhood, but they also made it clear that they wanted me to know I was black and had to be more careful than other kids around me. I wasn't traumatized by that lesson. I didn't fully understand it, but the seriousness with which my parents taught it to me made me pay attention.

Early on I became aware of the color boundaries of my hometown. I was from the East Side, where the majority of people of color lived in San Jose. The West and North sides were where most of the white folks lived. We seldom traveled to those parts of the city. My neighborhood was made up of mostly Mexican families. Sprinkled in-between were other immigrant families, mainly folks from Central America. In the middle of all of that was our black family. The police were often in our neighborhood because of America's institutional selective policing of areas with "poor" people of color.

The lessons my parents taught me became a piece of equipment that I added to my armor as a black man in America. I recall when my father sat me down to have "the talk." Depending on what type of home you were raised in, you might think "the talk" refers to sex. If you're from a black home, you know there are two talks, the first being "you're a black child in America" and how you need to deal with police, and the second one was "you better not get no girl pregnant" or if you're a girl "you better not be coming home pregnant." My father gave me the advice you have to give to a child whom you know might be confronted with officers who could possibly take your child's life. He told me to be respectful and listen to what cops are saying to end the encounter as quickly as possible, but he also told me if I felt threatened and there was a chance for me to get away, then I needed to run. Some people may disagree with that advice, but according to the Department of Justice, blacks are two times more likely than whites to be confronted with force when dealing with police.

In my hometown of San Jose, blacks are virtually nonexistent. I laid out some statistics about blacks in the city of San Jose in an earlier chapter. Currently blacks constitute 2 percent to 3 percent of the San Jose population. This almost imperceptible group of people is somehow 10 percent of all SJPD arrests and statistically the highest percentage of people force is used against upon arrest.

In back-to-back years of 2006 and 2007, blacks were 17 percent and 15 percent of all arrests where force was used. I had to use stats that old because police departments have the odd habit of being reluctant to investigate themselves for potential wrongdoing or bias. So if you're a parent of a black child and you know the dangers that exist in the society that can befall your child, you must give your child advice that might seem contrary to "normal" logic because that "normal" is not based on a paradigm that considers your skin color. Normal in America is being white and what the "white" response to a situation with police would be. Normal is the white boy and known white supremacist terrorist Dylann Rouf shooting up innocent black churchgoers being apprehended gently by police and then taken for a meal at Burger King before being admitted to jail. Be you a criminal worthy of death or innocent, white folks have a completely different understanding of "normal" when it comes to interactions with police officers. Normal for blacks is our young boy Tamir Rice shot and killed by Cleveland police for being black and playing with a toy gun in a park. That scene has played out multiple times in Black America, and this is why black parents have taught their children a different set of rules for attempting to survive racist America.

My father and mother knew this. This is the reason why my father sat me down numerous times to tell me how to survive in the streets of America as a black boy who hoped to one day become a black man. Those lessons included how to survive in Black America as well as White America. I had to learn the traps of the streets we lived on, and the bias of those who placed us on those streets. Pops told me, "If you see folks fighting you go the other direction. Don't stand around and watch." This is how innocent bystanders can get caught up in conflicts on the street, and if the cops come, one nigger is as good as any. You might've had nothing to do with the incident, but being in close proximity is all they need to grab you. He knew that one interaction with police could result in my body being beaten or exterminated. If not, then there was a possibility that I could be violated by law enforcement upon arrest, while being transported to the police station, or once in police custody.

Just recently all officers who were involved in the arrest and transportation of Baltimore's Freddie Gray had all charges dropped against them. The medical examiner ruled Freddie Gray's death was the result of a homicide. Somebody was responsible for killing the boy. He was arrested for committing no crime and somehow between arrest and arrival at the station his spine was severed to the point that he would later die from those injuries. Three of the six officers involved actually had days in court and of course the "judicial system" was able to somehow prove these officers weren't involved in the homicide. The logic the system is telling us is this: the medical examiner rules it was murder, there were only six people who could've been responsible for the murder, and they were all cops. A court of law in 2016 has created a new legal precedent because we have just witnessed legal murder without a murderer.

It is simply insane but many of us still want to put our faith in this system. America is a land where a black person can be completely innocent, unarmed, or a child and still be met with the full force of the law. It gets so ridiculous at times that even the true experiences of black folks seem impossible. Black people have been sent to prison, and the main piece of convicting evidence has been a person's dream. That's not a typo, a dream, as in a person was sleeping, and in their REM state they experienced a vision in their mind where the black man was the perpetrator. This "dream" was used as evidence in a "court of law" and a "jury" of sentient "educated" human beings convicted and sentenced a black man, Clarence Moses-EL, to forty-eight years in prison.

A dream is enough evidence to convict a black man in America, but a video that clearly shows a white officer shooting down a black boy within seconds of him exiting a car, coupled with volumes of evidence stating this officer should never have worn a badge, isn't enough evidence to even bring charges against a white man in America. You have to understand this to be able to see why a black parent would tell their precious child to be very aware when police are around and run if you feel your life is in danger.

I learned these lessons very early on and applied that understanding as best I could. You can have a master's or a doctorate level understanding of surviving America as a black person, and it is still not a guarantee that you'll survive. It's not like there comes a time when the lessons are no longer applicable. It's a lifelong practice in this society. Knowing that and reflecting on this poem really makes me think of the mind state of a parent who is responsible for protecting the life of a young black child. What do you do? How do you feel? What are the thoughts that run through your mind when you let you child walk outside your door? Especially in today's world of #BlackLivesMatter, which is a response to the intentional and institutional devaluing of black lives. Or when every few days we witness through social media another black life being abused or taken by some authority figure. It doesn't matter the age of the child. Their skin color marks them as carriers of all the stereotypes attached to black skin. They will not be judged for the content of their character, they will be judged and presumed guilty because of the color of their skin. How do parents deal with that reality? How do parents of black children feel when they see another black child abused or killed by law enforcement agents, and they know deep down in their hearts that the child could be their son or daughter? The knowledge that you are placing your child in a world that at any moment can swallow up your precious flesh and blood, all because he or she is the wrong color all the time, is scary.

Ta-Nehisi Coates refers to the taking of black bodies as "plunder." This word connotes a theft of multiple levels. For the parent, the plunder of their flesh and blood represents the theft of everything they had ever put into that child. Coates describes in candid terms the visceral pain resulting from that plunder:

"all the shared knowledge and capacity of a black family injected into that vessel of flesh and bone. And think of how that vessel was taken, shattered on the concrete, and all its holy contents, all that had gone into him, sent flowing back to earth"

This is what is at stake. The loss of the most precious thing a human being has ever held. A parent raises their child with all the love, hopes, and dreams of a brighter tomorrow. All of which was passed on to them when they were born. Their birthright is the legacy of their people. There is nothing more valuable on the face of the Earth than that. The thought of this vessel that is the most beautiful piece of you being desecrated by infidels who show no respect for the sacredness of the temple erected literally out of your flesh and blood is enough to drive a person to war with the killers.

As I sat at the wake for my former student Mario Woods, I kept my eyes on his mother Gwen. I watched her sway from the pain she felt from the loss of her son. I watched her as she looked down upon the casket filled with the body she use to hold as a baby, or console when he was injured, and tears streamed down her face. I heard her cry out loud with the most gut-wrenching soul-stealing cries that can come from a human being. She is not alone; there are far too many black parents of black children who have been in that same place here in America. Crying, shrieking their souls out over their lost sons and daughters. America does not love us, does not greet us with open arms; we are not sheltered by the warmth of her bosom. We are pointed at with a finger that caries suspicion and fear. The fear is irrational but the outcomes are very real. Death and destruction, the plunder of black bodies.

The root cause of all of this is racism, white supremacy, white ignorance, and the pursuit of wealth to fuel the continued domination of Western civilization. When you step outside the false lenses of all the above, you are left with the reality that all people are the same. All children should have the right to grow up safely and live peacefully in their world. The lenses block these biological realities and make one think like the highly honored and esteemed President Abraham Lincoln, who once said, "There is a physical difference between the two, which, in my judgment, will probably forever forbid their living together on the footing of perfect equality, and inasmuch as it becomes a necessity that there must be a difference, I, as well as Judge Douglas, am in favor of the race to which I belong having the superior position ..." This type of speech and thought is what has allowed America to continuously disregard the value of the black child. This is how the poem "Black Child" came to be. If I become a father, my wife and I will have the privilege of raising a beautiful black child in a world that bares its teeth at our child from the womb. It will be our job to raise, safeguard, teach, and love that black child despite the dangers, lies, and hatred that exist in the world for our child. It is not an easy task, but it is the responsibility of any parent who has the blessing of becoming the mother or father of a black child. We must do our part to ensure the safety of our black children.

Death Toll (2015)

I once said before, We hold each breath close
like Uncle Sam holds
political prisoners on death row
he scared to let go
he fears the power
of the child of the ghetto

but this death toll
is at my threshold

and if you didn't know
this being black in America ish is stressful.

Never knowing what's gonna happen when you set forth
and step forth from your front porch
maybe that's the reason
why I'm contemplating death more

Like

what's it gonna feel like when my flesh cold
they place my body in that fresh hole
and I hate being so necro
but negroes and death go
hand in hand
like kids back in the day who used to thumb wrestle,

that grim reaper be on our back like an echo
echo
echo
echo

I've seen police choke a nigga until his breath go

I seen them point that glock at his top
cock back that shot
and then let go

Cop must've thought he had a bulletproof dome like Destro
The boy had locks with a front license plate in the glove box
so tell me what he dead for.

I seen them arrest a sister for failing to signal
while driving through a pedzone
should've been a citation
still they took her to jail
and 3 days later she dead though
and they think we stupid enough to believe
that suicide is the reason why we laying flowers at her headstone.

I seen them shoot a man shopping at Walmart
for an air rifle outside of Dayton metro.
Cops magically appear on the scene
with guns out like presto.
Shots get fired while he looking at them falling price specials
now he under at the morgue under a white sheet
with a tag on his left toe.

That's death toll

These American streets are a morbid expo
of lifeless black bodies lying exposed
they try to assure us that this ain't no retro Jim Crow
but we know this that new version 2.0
Michelle Alexander said so

This here is my manifesto

We sick and tired of dying
we putting an end to dying
by our hands

or the hands of white violence
I know I have agency
over this hate in me
but I experience some latency
when I think about those 9 killed
by that white boy at the AME
you can look at my face and see
black rage in the place to be
what you expect
when y'all doing this so blatantly

my country, tis of thee

you have made me a strange and bitter fruit
which you harvest from your tree of liberty.

Roots are buried deep beneath the soil,
four hundred years of racial terrorism and turmoil
better beware before this melting pot start to boil.

You are not equipped with empathy,
you do not have the capacity to change.
You are so thoroughly programmed
that you cannot see the error of your ways.
And my people have changed.
This ain't that docile hat in hand
Stepin Fetchit step to the side,
We that wretched of the earth,
with a ratchet tucked
west side til I die.
We already accustomed to dying for no reason.
And once these lines remove the poison
and blindfolds from my people's minds
whose favorite past time is killing they own kind
they gonna want to get even.

So what does this mean for America as a whole?
keep killing my people stealing those we love from our homes,

And you'll leave us with no other choice
but to show America the true definition of a death toll.

Reflections of a Black Boy

Since 1980 close to 300,000 black men have been killed in the
United States of America. Wyoming is the lowest populated state in
the union. According to census numbers from 2013 there are
582,658 people in that state. In almost 35 years enough black men
have been killed to approach the population of a state.

No matter how descriptive an artist can be in detailing the
experience one may have in America as a result of being clothed in
black skin, you'll never be able to understand it without living it.
The poet laureate of my family, Prentice Powell, said this, "Being a
black man in America is a full time job ... being a black man in
America is to be a black man in America and unless you are a black
man in America, you will never understand what it's like to be a
black man in America." The institutional hatred for black life is
embedded so deep in the soul of the society that without its
presence, the society might not know who it is anymore. There are
many faces at the bottom of the well; the faces change depending
on the time and place in America. The two permanent roles at the
bottom have been faithfully played by the indigenous natives and
Black Americans. Indigenous people were so thoroughly hit by the
rise of America that many nations and tribes have become virtually
extinct. Entire peoples and histories wiped off the face of the Earth,
completely removed from this plane of existence.

Black people were forcefully brought here to the Americas
solely for the purpose of exploitation, specifically for their labor in
building up the new colonial economies. Over time, the thirteen
British colonies and then eventually the United States thoroughly
legislated the subservient/less-than-human position of blacks in
America. In the Declaration of Independence, Jefferson eloquently
opines that, "all men are created equal, endowed by their creator
with certain unalienable rights." Although, the DOI is not a legally

binding document of American jurisprudence, it's still essential to the creed and culture of America, inaugurating the rich hypocritical history of America and its treatment of blacks and Native Americans. Jefferson spoke so boldly of universal equality in his declaration, but it seems he was only referring to equality and independence for wealthy white men, for he would later go on to write extensively about the inferiority of blacks and his belief that whites were superior to them in every regard. Imagine Jefferson dipping his quill pen in an ink reservoir scribing those great words of equality and freedom while owning slaves and carrying on a "relationship" that should be better termed as raping a woman he held as a slave, Sally Hemings. I don't know if it's possible to have a relationship with someone you own as a slave. This "relationship" eventually produced multiple offspring, which according to Jefferson's opinions of blacks meant they were of "inferior stock."

The Constitution was the next to make a bold claim and legislate an oppressed status for blacks. In Article I Section II we read the text for the 3/5th compromise that states how 3 out of 5 slaves can be counted for tax purposes and for determining population for representation in the House of Representatives. The application of the 3/5ths compromise was specific, for tax purposes and determining population, but the reality legalized a de facto understanding of the position of black life in America. We were arbitrarily deemed 3/5ths of a human being; the social reality of this was the legalized subhuman status of blacks in America.

Dred Scott further added to the American lineage of government oppression of black life. In the now infamous Dred Scott decision, the Supreme Court ruled that Dred Scott and his wife had no claim to file suit for their freedom against their slave master on account of him moving to a free territory. Chief Justice Roger B. Taney further attempted to clarify the issue by stating in no uncertain terms that the founders of the country never intended to give rights and freedom to blacks, and that slaves, as well as free blacks, "had no rights that the white man was bound to respect." This is 1619 to 1857, 238 years of colonial and constitutional oppression and degradation. For all intents and purposes, Taney was stating that blacks have no claim to a free life in America. Their sole purpose is to be beasts of burden for the benefit of White

America. His opinion was not a minority opinion then or now in America.

Welcome to the deep dark birthing place of "Death Toll." Our entire existence, is one of total exploitation. We're used for pleasure, labor, entertainment, sport, and when the need arises our bodies can be exterminated with the explicit consent of the state or complicit consent of American society. White people can't and never will understand this plight. This is the privilege that they have guaranteed themselves. They've shielded themselves from ever having to look at any of the atrocities they've heaped upon black life. Their society will never convict themselves of their crimes—past, present, and future—against us.

I often wonder if there is a way to quantify the number of black lives America has taken. That would force us to tally the numbers of slaves violated through the slave trade in Africa, middle passage, and here in America. Add that to the numbers of those who languished on plantations and those brutally beaten and killed while enslaved for American economic progress. Post-slavery, we'd have to count the numbers of free blacks tortured and brutalized for the preservation of the white social order. Those lynched. Those killed in white riots against black citizens in black towns/cities. Those arrested on frivolous charges to be sent back to slavery via convict leasing or forced back to slavery via debt peonage or sharecropping and tenant farming. You can't; it's impossible to calculate the loss.

There are moments in American history where white folks out of fear, rage, anger, or some other arbitrary reason simply raided and razed entire black communities to the ground. The American narrative has memorialized certain moments of American suffering. Pearl Harbor is a red-letter date, and we are always told to remember 9/11. I am not making light of the loss of life at any time. Death perpetrated by heinous acts is always tragic. What's even more tragic is when your own country is the perpetrator and completely ignores the suffering and trauma it has inflicted upon your people. In 1921 in Tulsa, Oklahoma, the U.S. government firebombed a lawful black community to reiterate the narrative of white supremacy again. Men, women, and children all died in the bombing, riot, and subsequent fires. They were killed with American planes and bombs. They were not insurgents or enemy combatants, as if those terms justify America killing people. There is no justification for what happened to the people of Tulsa, but America is so bold when it comes to its treatment of blacks that it doesn't even search for justification, America simply ignores it as if it didn't happen.

In the modern day, black life is so cheap that this society does not even pause for reflection and consider possible ways to change when black bodies die. Blacks are overrepresented in pretty much every category of death possible. That includes death by the state, capital punishment, officers extinguishing black lives, health-related deaths, death of our babies, and of course death in the streets. Black life is cheap in America. White supremacists still enjoy their pastime of killing black people, and America doesn't really even bat an eye at it when it happens. Use Islam in any way to kill Americans, mainly white Americans, and our government will move heaven and Earth to try to find the next possible terrorist. We'll pass new legislation like the Patriot Act and create new divisions of government, like the Department of Homeland Security, and use every piece of technology we have to root out through digital spy networks the next possible terrorist.

Be a member of the KKK, the oldest terrorist group in the United States, and America will claim you're protected under the First Amendment. Be a white supremacist who talks about openly committing terrorist acts and killing black folks online, and the government and other law enforcement agents will act as if they can't see anything. You can be on Facebook and Twitter or other social media forums posting all day about your hatred for blacks and desire to kill them all, and our society will act as if they never saw it coming, or treat it as if it's not really a big problem. America doesn't care about black people to the point that we still allow the Confederate battle flag to be flown, which is a symbol of slavery, insurrection against the U.S. government and white supremacy. I can go on. A young and relatively sane Kanye West in the aftermath of Hurricane Katrina spoke about President George W. Bush and his lack of care for black people. It doesn't matter who is president of the United States, white, black, male, or female, this country and society does not care about black people. And this is exactly why we are allowed to die so often.

The expectation of our society is that we are to die. We are the ones to be jailed; we are the first ones to be thought of as criminals and imprisoned as criminals. The American landscape is so rigged that we're simply fulfilling the prophecy they've shaped for us. America is not interested in changing the landscape or our roles. "The black man has no rights that the white man is bound to respect." The first definition for us in this society was chattel, property, similar to owning an animal or livestock. When a society expects you to die more and be imprisoned or impoverished more, you are treated as less. That is our historical reality which shapes our place in contemporary society.

The mental, physical, and emotional response to that reality is what inspired my pen to write "Death Toll." If you examine the words in the poem deep enough you'll feel my pain, my anger, and frustration for how my people are treated and discarded so easily. "These American streets are a morbid expo of lifeless black bodies lying exposed." Many of us have seen footage of Mike Brown's body bleeding out on a street in Ferguson for hours. This is a scene we've witnessed far too many times. Closer to home Kenneth Harding Jr. and Derrick Gains received similar disdain in San Francisco as their lives bled out their bodies while first responders were unwilling or prevented from providing medical assistance.

I am not a gambling man but at all times in America I know I'm gambling with my life. "Never knowing what's gonna happen when you set forth or you step forth from your front porch, maybe that's the reason why I'm contemplating death more." There is so much at stake everyday being black in America. And as the poem says, "I hate being so necro but negroes and death go hand in hand like young kids back in the day used to thumb wrestle ..."

As a result of the death and the brutality that often goes unpunished by the system, there are those that talk of revolution and using violence to overthrow the system. I am not saying that this cannot happen. This country was born out of a violent rebellion against the British. The continental forces were able to be successful enough to cause the British to make a decision about whether or not they wanted to keep fighting. The British chose to give up the fight and focus on building up their global empire. I don't know what a violent rebellion would look like in America today if one were to take place, but what we do know is that the American government has a military industrial complex that is unmatched by any man made force on this planet. If a fight were to take place the fighters would be waging war against the people with the biggest and greatest amount of guns on earth. If people were to take up arms and fight, they would most assuredly be killed. That doesn't mean they couldn't be successful but death would be high. This is beyond the Jewish story of David and Goliath. There are around 40 million black people in a country whose population is close to 320 million. If we compare the population numbers of whites to blacks, then we'll see blacks are almost outnumbered by 210 million people. The talk of violent revolution is moving, it's stirring, but how tangible is it? We are constantly inundated by news of abuses, murders, and police executions, this raises the flames of armed rebellion in the hearts of men and women. Assessing the potential battlefield before us we have to admit they are united and strong, while we are unorganized, and in our disorganized state, we are weak.

There is no full scale military effort for the freedom and liberation of black people, yet, and still, fighting but not with arms and munitions for our survival in this society occurs on a daily basis. This fight in and of itself is revolutionary in nature, and it is that fight that makes us insurgents in our own land. This is what makes me a solider that knows that any day in America could be my last. I walk outside knowing that death is waiting for me somewhere. Mainstream America has provided us with no shelter, so we exist physically and emotionally on the margins of society. And we know all too well that our lives perpetually hang in the balance. Every decision or non-decision can be read as necessitating lethal force. A police officer saying, "show me your ID," and you began to reach for your wallet in your pocket can merit forty-one shots. Or simply walking in your father's neighborhood and an overzealous/racist neighborhood watch civilian wannabe officer can chase you down, pick a fight, and kill you. And then eventually be found not guilty after being told numerous times by law enforcement not to engage. You can be sleeping in your car and pose no threat in your unconscious state and still be perceived as a threat and have your life taken.

The slight increase in your heart rate when an officer pulls behind you while you're on the road is one of the many signs of this occupation and war. Black people have been killed for centuries in America for no reason at all. We all carry the trauma of senseless death in us. We know that each day could be our last if the right or wrong circumstances arise. Complying does not guarantee survival. It's a crapshoot every time. And we've died enough. There is no tried and true formula for survival. America hates us all in all our glorious diversity. You can be in the finest business suit and hold degrees from the most prestigious American institutions, and they will hate you. The years of 2008-2016 have clearly demonstrated this lesson with President Obama. You can be from the worst hoods in America and sag your pants all day long with all other forms of stereotypical black deviance present, and they will hate you. It makes no difference. We can talk like corporate America or in street vernacular; we are all still potential victims of white American hate. They kill us in churches, schools, cars, homes, stores, and on corners. They kill us if we're babies, kids, teens or adults, awake or sleep. For blacks, death is everywhere.

I hate to see how some of my people get caught up in trying to demonize those who dress, act, or talk outside of the "white norm." America won't respect us more if we "pull up our pants" or do what Bill Cosby was trying to advocate for and stop acting street. It's semantics. The reality is you are hated simply for being black; Obama is insulted and ridiculed and possibly had attempts made on his life, just like Oscar Grant, Trayvon Martin, Laquan McDonald, Sandra Bland, Rekia Boyd, Mike Brown, and so many other names. The outcome is the same. Change clothes, change your diction, change whatever, you cannot change your color, and that is primarily what America hates us for the most. Being black in America regardless of how you dress or sound comes with these oppressive suffocating stereotypes that boil down to fear of black bodies, which makes it easier to kill black bodies. Black means death in America, and this is why we die so much so often.

The poem ends with a warning for America; you can only push a people so far before they begin to fight back. It is foolish of America to think that a response from the people they are brutalizing will not manifest in some form. If and when black people begin to fight back, they will die too. It is sad that this even has to be considered but you cannot keep abusing and killing a group of people and expect them to not respond. In the present and near future there will be more what the white media terms, "riots," rebellions, or uprisings. People have had enough of unjust killings and injustice in the form of cops, lawyers, grand juries, and judges. The writing is on the wall, black people in America are being pushed to their limit, and when they do respond there will be more death. What the death will lead to, I don't know, but what it will cause in the immediate is an increased death toll. What will those bodies die for? Only the victor will have the right to define that.

You (2009)

Where swamp waters flow
Where fat Mosquitos fly
A young daughter grows
Around where gators lay.
It's black magic, mathematics, lots casted
Cowry shells, chicken blood, putting roots on the slave master.
Where you might see a black man hung up in them branches,
Where we close to, homie? Man, I think we close to Natchez.
It's that dirty dirty
Share cropping, cotton picking, bright and early
lashes on our back and our flesh is burning.

I see her in an old faded picture
her soul plated with scripture
skin light and face tight
because of the mixture
of the slave master who made em suffer
and her Native brother
and the blood that come from the land of her mother
It all runs through her vein.
No more shackles cause freedom came
Grandma Dolly was her name.
The next generation came when the century changed over
my great gram saw the world go to war over Franz Ferdinand.
Color like a rubber band holding us back
that's something my folks in the south understand.
If you black you wasn't viewed as a man.
My great gram was light, couldn't pass
still viewed as second class citizen
passed down through the lineage.
Essie May my Grandma born in Meridian
around the great depression
Jim Crow stole our innocence

left us with bitterness.
Moms keep them sons at home
because out there they're lynching men.
Grandma was witness to it
because she was living through it
separate but equal schooling
strange fruit
seeing her classmates strung up in them nooses.
It's a nightmare but it's real life
she met up with a man who made her feel like
the sky the limit
but he playing both sides of the fences.
My Grandma pregnant with my mom he ain't trying to listen.
So she started living
for her daughter
tried to make sure that she got
more than everything she was given
in that delta of Mississippi,
my mom was young and pretty,
her pops was never there
he everywhere with other women in the city.
Left her for her moms to raise
she a single black mom now
looking at harder days.
She worked odd jobs trying to put food on my momma's plate.
But it ain't easy for her many times she thought she'd break.
She meet another young man now so she thinking she's safe,
she didn't know he type to flip out once he get a taste
and that liquor get in his system.
My moms she paid attention
she dreamed of one day raising a young man who would be
different.
So everyday in her womb I would sit and listen
to her tell me about my mission, she said, "you!"

It was a cold night in November
the sign of a Scorpio
her younger brother died just a year before from overdose.

My birth brought life back to a family that's trying to cope
she held me close and filled my ears with hope.
Then she named her boy Tyson,
after the actress Cicely
before I spoke in poetry
my momma already envisioned great things in store for me,
now I'm living out my destiny
doing my best to be
everything that she wanted for me.
She told me to stand strong,
she told me to shine,
she told me to respect women at each and all times,
she told me God buried something great in me deep inside,
and that the world gets to hear it every time I speak a rhyme
she said, "you!"

Reflections of a Black Boy

"Mississippi Goddam!" - Nina Simone

According to the Equal Justice Initiative's 2015 report Lynching in America "Georgia and Mississippi had the highest number of lynchings between the years 1877-1950."
In Mississippi the largest numbers of lynchings were found in Hinds and Lowndes counties. Most of my Mississippi relatives have lived in and still live in Hinds County today.

As I stated in the intro to this book a portion of the title is an homage to Richard Wright who is one of my greatest literary influences. I haven't discussed Wright much in this text but I put this poem in the book because it allowed me to explore another connection I feel I share with Richard Wright and many other black folks in America, and that is the Magnolia State. Mississippi has produced some of the most incredible black folks the world has ever seen. Mississippi is also the only state that has the confederate battle flag in its state flag. As our sister Nina Simone wrote,

"Alabama's gotten me so upset
Tennessee made me lose my rest
And everybody knows about Mississippi Goddam"

    Mississippi is arguably the worst state for blacks historically and possibly in the present day as well. Currently Mississippi, is the poorest state, has the highest unemployment, and worst public school system. Mississippi also has the unwanted honor of being the most obese state in the country. Blacks are the ones most impacted by the poverty, unemployment, schools, and food-related health issues.

    Mississippi was admitted to the union in 1817 as the twentieth state; by the start of the Civil War, Mississippi was the largest cotton-producing state in America. The United States was the world's largest producer of cotton, thus making Mississippi one of the most important cotton-producing regions in the world. The growth of Mississippi as a state is directly correlated with its dependence on the slavery apparatus. The population and economy of Mississippi developed as it increased its dependency on slavery. Cotton became the primary focus of the plantation economy. To become the champion state in terms of cotton production, Mississippi had to import more and more slaves. By the start of the Civil War, Mississippi had more than half a million slaves within its borders. That was more than half the total population of the state, and one-eighth of the total slave population in the United States. The entire economy of Mississippi was geared towards slavery. It was a system in which very few plantation owners made incredibly large sums of money by brutally exploiting enslaved blacks. Poor whites didn't fair too well in the slave economy either, but their status at least on the outside appeared to be better than that of slaves. Mississippi proudly had the greatest concentration of wealthy people in America prior to the Civil War. The biggest money in America was to be found around the Mississippi Delta. With their power through wealth and property, the rich planter elite held the state hostage and created policies and social/cultural mores that allowed them to maintain power and control, while at the same time maintain an oppressive system of institutional degradation of black lives.

This is the skeletal structure of Mississippi. This is the DNA of its society built on the oppression and exploitation of black bodies for monetary gain. Blacks were a majority in population in Mississippi for decades before and after the Civil War. Whites represented a minority population in the state. If they were to maintain control of a majority population that had every right to overthrow their authority, then they would have to maintain that control through force, violence, and terror. Mississippi was not afraid of using violence and terror as a means to institute white dominance in society. This is why Simone sings, "Mississippi Goddam." If we were to create a list of the worst states to be black in, Mississippi would most likely come out as the worst of the worst the majority of the time that list was compiled. Blacks in Mississippi experienced the most brutal treatment during and after slavery. Mississippi has the historic distinction of being the place where Medgar Evers was murdered before his family in his driveway. It gave birth to some of the worst slave codes and black codes ever seen. Mississippi is legendary in its terror, brutality, violence, resistance to integration, and exploitation of blacks. The fact that so many blacks have roots in Mississippi means that the legacy of that trauma, abuse, torture, and oppression lives on in us wherever we may call home.

Wright was born and raised in Mississippi. He eventually migrated to Tennessee before leaving the South completely, but his foundation is Mississippi. I'm from at least four generations of Mississippi on my mother's side. Sadly, I don't know my mother's father's lineage because she didn't even know who her biological father was until she was in her forties. We know who the family is now but are not connected with them and are not familiar with that side's family history. They were from Mississippi though. What I know for a fact is my mother's side and that makes me the byproduct of four generations of women who survived Mississippi. Grandma Dolly, who they say was mixed with native blood, my Great Grandma (Big Momma), my Grandma (Grandma Essie), and my momma. Kira and I were the first in four generations to be born outside of Mississippi.

Richard Wright would eventually leave the state of Mississippi for Tennessee, Illinois, and then the United States for France. In all the places he was to see and experience his Mississippi upbringing was still a major part of him. I am California born and raised, I'm a Cali boy down to my socks. I love the opportunities and experiences that my home state has afforded me. I'm thankful for what I have been exposed to here in California, but as much as I am California, there is no denying that I am also Mississippi.

That land and the struggles of the peoples in that land have carried the blood of my family for generations. I'm a transplant. I am the seed of Mississippi planted in a fertile alien soil. My family had to leave like Richard Wright in order to fully realize potential of who they could be. Mississippi had been the beginning and ending of so many black lives and families. It had served as a cotton-tinted glass ceiling preventing any inkling of success. Every era of black life in Mississippi was hard. Slavery, to Jim Crow, to civil rights to the new Jim Crow. If you're black and you want a chance at a good life, then Mississippi was not the place for you to be. This is why there were numerous migrations out of the state of Mississippi over time. So many blacks made the decision to leave Mississippi that their departure changed the population demographics and made whites the majority. Whites would never have become the majority in Mississippi if it were solely based on birth rates. The horrendous life that blacks experienced was the catalyst for blacks to move which eventually gave whites a majority in the population.

Thousands of blacks attempted to leave Mississippi immediately after the abolition of slavery in 1865. Over the course of the next few decades, blacks continued to leave Mississippi in droves. Wright was born in 1908, forty-three years after the abolition of slavery. My family, like Wright, became part of those mass migrations from Mississippi. Wright ended up in the Midwest while we ended up on the West Coast. The route my family took went from Mississippi to Germany and then to North Highlands, California, right outside of the state capitol, Sacramento.

California, contrary to what some might believe, is not some paragon of equality and fairness for blacks. Black people have suffered from racism and oppression in California as well. You don't get groups like the Black Panther Party for Self Defense or the Brown Berets or Cesar Chavez UFW (United Farm Workers) without having a context that is rife with racism and discrimination. Those movements are byproducts of years of discontent and systemic abuse. My mother and grandmother eventually found themselves attempting to survive in this context. California afforded my family more opportunities than Mississippi, but it came with costs, just like the experience of Wright in Chicago. He was better off and had more access to things he desperately wanted but American racism is alive and well in all parts of this land. Racism is diverse but equally diabolical anywhere it appears on the horizon. It serves as a crippling force in all of its forms, and each is harmful to black lives.

Although my family relocated to California, Mississippi is still our home. There is no way to relocate all of my family blood that is buried in that red soil. More of my family still lives in Mississippi than any other part of the United States. I have cousins, great aunts, and uncles who still call Mississippi home. My sister decided to move back to Mississippi and has built her family and practice there. I have two beautiful nieces in Mississippi right now. I am not ashamed to say that I am equal parts California and Mississippi.

The decision to leave Mississippi was not an easy one but it was necessary for a chance at a different life. In an attempt to find better, and to make better for themselves and the ones to come, my family moved west. We sought a more fertile soil for the seeds of our family to grow in. It has not been easy, but we've experienced some success. And every day we continue to strive on with Mississippi and all the lessons she taught us, be they good or bad in our hearts.

The content of the piece is very special to me because it tells the story of the matriarchs of my mother's family. It's a story of four generations of women and some of what they had to deal with in surviving being a black woman in the American South. The piece ends with my mother hoping and praying the best for her son, but it's a story of the power of women. I know that I come from strong women who sacrificed a great deal so that theirs could live. Maze featuring Frankie Beverly told the world about the gifts and the beauty of the southern woman in their song "Southern Girl." Mr.

Beverly put that velvet like vocal through the mic and sang a praise for our sisters south of the Mason Dixon line. Maze's song pays homage to the glory of all the women of the south but the truth is ain't no southern girl like a woman from Mississippi. She has survived the worst, and she's still here.

I'm indebted to the women of my family, and I'm thankful to be one of their progeny. I hope that I carry some of what made them excellent. I pray that my efforts as a man and a human being make them proud and make their struggles and sacrifices worth it in their eyes. Mississippi and my family have an old love/hate relationship. It has birthed us and put us in the dirt far too early. It has forced us to toil its rich soil and allowed us to plant and reap some of what we've sown for ourselves. It hasn't given us any quarter at any time. We would never call it a friend, but it's home. It's hard to have love for a home that has had no love for you, but Mississippi is home and for better or for worse is in the heart.

A Word on Mario Woods

After the completion of this text I was asked by my school to help facilitate the graduation ceremony where Mario Woods was supposed to walk the stage. I was approached by my supervisor to see if I would be interested in leading the portion of the program that would be dedicated to recognizing Mario and presenting his diploma to his mother. I humbly accepted that responsibility. I felt honored to be charged with that duty, and after leaving school that day I was inspired to write a few words to speak to my experience with Mario. What follows is the poem that I wrote, but I wasn't able to recite the version that appears here; I was requested to recite an edited version of the poem at the ceremony. After the event I was contacted by the communications director of the United Educators of San Francisco. He asked me if I would be interested in writing an article about Mario for publication in the UESF newsletter and possible publication in a major national periodical. What follows after the poem is the draft version of the article I wrote about Mario entitled "A Word on Mario."

A Poem for Mario (2016)

I see him
In my mind he still sits
in that same place.
Young black face
tucked in the back of the class.
He's quiet, not quick to cat off
or laugh as time pass
because he's busy trying to master his own path.
I see the pain inside.
I see he don't want to remain inside.
I see the brain inside.
At times he'd raise his hand high to share some of his insight.
I see he gets it.
I see the boy, he's young, black and gifted.
We both see that our blackness leaves us trapped in the system.
He's gotta date, he's gonna hit those gates soon.
A new start,
motivated by the promises he made to his mother that he carries
in his heart.
He's a good dude, but he ain't perfect.
Truthfully, none of us are,
and as far as the word go,
may he who is without sin cast the first stone.
There won't be any rocks flying,
but on that day them shots were flying,
like a firing squad who wouldn't stop
until he dropped and was dying.
Hearts dropped and broke and couldn't stop crying.
Now his folks shocked as I am
trying to calm the violence rising inside them.
And I know this shouldn't be a eulogy keynote.
I should be standing, smiling right beside him,
watching him walk off with his diploma a brighter future on the
horizon.

But you and I are left to think of what might have been.

Mother Gwen lost a son,
Others lost a family member or a friend,
Me, I lost a student.
May we never lose our love for him.
May we never lose our hope that we will win.
And his leaving us will not be in vain,
for we will make sure this never happens again.

Rest in Power and Peace, Mario.
Justice for Mario Woods

Reflections of a Black Boy

Miracle of life
Mother gives birth to child
Mother holds child for the first of many times
180 seconds
Child is taken away by doctors
Mother loves child every second of his life
831,945,600 seconds.
Swine genetically modified
stampede sacred ground with weapons of mass destruction
leaving nothing behind.
9 hooves on triggers
40 plus shots
21 direct hits
5 second barrage

the final grains of sand succumb to the pull of gravity

831,945,595
831,945,596
831,945,597

831,945,598
831,945,599
831,945,600

sands spills all over the floor
death spills out onto the floor
ashes to ashes
dust to dust

UESF Article

I have taught high school courses in the San Francisco jail system for more than a decade. The San Francisco Sheriff's Department decided to establish a school within its incarcerated facilities in 2003 to try to reduce recidivism and ameliorate the effects of the school to prison pipeline. Despite the challenges of providing education in an incarcerated environment, the school has been a major success. In 2014 we were awarded the Hart Vision Charter School of the Year Award and just last year we won the prestigious Harvard Innovations in American Government award. In my time with the school, I've witnessed tremendous life-changing successes in the lives of some of my students. Conversely, I've witnessed painful tragedies which have resulted in too many untimely deaths of those who once sat in my classroom. Recently, one of my former students had been christened the latest black face gunned down by law enforcement. On a cold day in December in San Francisco, powerful forces conspired to involuntarily draft him into the world of hashtags and memorial t-shirts and posters. My student had become the latest black faced burnt offering on the altar of America.

His name was Mario Woods; you may have heard of him by now. His death was witnessed by millions of people due to cell phone cameras and social media. The problem with only seeing the last minute of someone's life is it can in no way inform you as to how they lived. The mainstream media did what it often does when badge kills black body. It moved heaven and earth to find numerous ways to demonize the person of Mario. Television, print and web-based news highlighted his "checkered" past and his "record" with law enforcement, as if prior history is a lethal offense and said individual with history is to be executed on sight with impunity and lacking due process. Headlines branded him a drug addict, gang member, and other socially invective epithets that like those twenty police bullets assassinated his character. Mario was found guilty by the media of being poor and black and sentenced to death by social denigration. Those that did not know Mario and didn't attempt to question the fabricated narrative of the press were more likely to believe what was being "reported" about him and feel his execution was justified.

I knew a different Mario. I too, was one of the millions who witnessed his horrific murder online. But the difference between me and most of the world is I knew the one who was on the other side of those police revolvers. On December 2, I was scrolling a social media timeline and a hashtag followed by ten letters that I had seen multiple times on one of my school rosters kept appearing.

San Francisco is celebrated as one of the world's greatest cities but its popularity far outweighs its actual physical size. It is a 7 x 7 square mile city in which the gentrification effort led by the tech community is well underway. The historical black and brown populations are being forced out at what seems like close to light speed. There are still a few black and brown enclaves in the city, but at the current rate it's just a matter of time before they are whitewashed completely. The schools in the Fillmore or Bayview Hunters Point or the Mission are usually the worst in terms of academic performance. Social services are nearly invisible in these neighborhoods. The poverty and the depression are heavy and very real. The people, their spirits, and the cultures they have created are beautiful but a community cannot thrive on prayer alone. Poverty and systemic discrimination are powerful corrosive forces that can strangle the life out of a community. People eventually begin to succumb to the pressures of their surrounding environs and act out in a manner that they wouldn't if quality education, services, and access to good housing and employment were present.

This is the world that Mario was formed in. He was raised on the oft-unforgiving blocks of Bayview Hunters Point. He was a smart kid who really loved and supported his mother. You didn't have to look too hard to see his talents and intelligence. Still, he lived in a place where very few young people his age saw a way out that didn't involve surviving the traps of the street. He wasn't a tall man. He didn't have a physically dominant presence, but he had a presence. I was always able to tell when he was in the room even though he was fairly quiet. There was a silent confidence to him like he knew a secret about himself that nobody else really understood. He had his struggles with the world around him but he had confidence in himself that he would find his way through. I noticed this about him fairly early on while he was a student in my classroom. I taught Mario math on two separate occasions in 2009-2010. His first trip to my class didn't go too well. This could've been the result of multiple factors. Jail is not the easiest place to learn anything. One of the most celebrated young minds of the twentieth century Tupac Shakur said, "Prison kills your spirit, straight up. It kills your spirit. There is no creativity, there's none of that." There are many stressors one faces while incarcerated. I do not know what Mario was dealing with at the time, but he did not fully apply himself to the curriculum for some reason. I also realized it wasn't because he was unable to understand the work, there was something that was holding him back, and as a result he did just enough to pass.

The second time he walked through my doors and took my class he had a different level of focus. Whatever was holding him back was no longer there, and he earned one of the highest grades in my class during that semester. He passed my algebra class with a B+. The silent confidence was radiating from him. We were both able to see that secret that he had hidden. He and I both knew that he was intellectually capable and could focus enough to figure his way through whatever he would face in life. This was the Mario that I knew and grew to respect. He left my class feeling accomplished and even more confident that he could change his life for the better.

He had to serve time in prison, but upon release he found his way to a residential program and into one of the community arms of our school. Mario had already completed his GED but under our charter a student could convert their GED into a full high school diploma by completing additional course work for credits. Mario made the decision to do this because he knew it was something his mother always wanted for him. Mario applied himself with the focus that I witnessed while he was in my class for the second time. He was known as a positive influence in his class, often motivating and helping other students accomplish their academic tasks. And in July of 2015, he completed all of his requirements to earn his high school diploma. He had also recently found work and acquired a new driver's license. He was on his way to the life that he and his mother wanted for him.

Fast forward to Dec. 2, 2015. A complaint comes in via a man who was stabbed in the Bayview area. A general description is given of a black male of a certain height and complexion. Officers begin to make their way to the area and search for a suspect. Eventually Mario and a few officers cross paths. As of now we do not know if Mario was the person who stabbed the victim. We are told in police accounts that Mario was holding a knife, and it can be heard on video that voices in the crowd were urging Mario to drop something. The California penal code does not state that stabbing a person or being suspected of stabbing a person are lethal offenses. I am not attempting to be dismissive of the victim or the victim's family either. If a wrong was committed, then that wrong needs to be addressed and dealt with appropriately. The metaphor of justice is a scale connoting balance. The wrong committed throws off the balance of that scale. The idea of justice served is when all parties affected by the "wrong" are restored to a state of balance. The victim, offender, and community are all parties to the wrong, and all deserve justice. I'm quite sure the victim and their family wanted justice regarding the stabbing, but I don't think it looked in their minds like it did to us online. Mario was surrounded by ten officers who all had their weapons drawn on him. The official report states the officers tried to de-escalate the situation with non-lethal rounds by using beanbags. This did not give them the result that they were looking for so their circle began to close in on Mario as more directives were being yelled at him. Mario begins to stagger and walk off with his right shoulder against the wall away from the majority of the police officers. The report states that officers began to shoot when Mario made a threatening gesture with his knife-wielding hand at one of the officers. Their account is contradicted by the video footage that shows he made no such "threatening" gesture, but police still fired. The timing of Mario's murder is important because this all took place five days after a white man, Robert Lewis Dear Jr. shot up a Planned Parenthood in Colorado Springs, Colorado, killing two civilians and a police officer but somehow was arrested non-violently. Meanwhile, in San Francisco, California, a young black man who was suspected of stabbing a person, who when confronted by police attempted to walk away and made no threatening gesture, was shot twenty times. Seventeen of the shots were through his back, according to the autopsy report.

Yesterday was Jan. 20, the date that Mario and his mother Gwendolyn Woods were both looking forward to. This was the day he was to walk across the stage, maybe even say a speech, and look out into the crowd and see his mother's proud smile upon him as the state of California placed a high school diploma in his hand. This was to be the first of many more major accomplishments but instead of Mario, it was his mother who was to walk across the stage with a bouquet of colorful sad flowers and tears streaming down her face. I was to play the role of the teacher who had only a few weeks ago attended Mario's wake with some of my colleagues and was now at the podium reading off his name knowing full well that he would not be bounding up those steps in cap and gown with a smile on his face, hand extended for a firm handshake and hug.

As teachers, we are not parents, but through education we give life and energy to our students. We spend time and develop deep relationships with our populations. We hope that they will be able to go into the world and find their path to a long and fulfilling life. We pray that we will send them into a world that will not shoot them down or allow them to be consumed by the prison industrial complex. This was my hope and prayer for Mario when he walked out my class after earning a B+. I knew it would not be an easy path, but I sent that positive energy into the universe for him, like I do for all of my students, that he would find his way. One of the saddest parts of this story is that Mario was actually on his way. He may have made a few missteps but he was much closer to his path than ever before, until that afternoon on Dec. 2 when SFPD officers determined a short black man who may have been holding a knife was a mortal threat. They pulled triggers and extinguished more than a life, it was a dream shared by Mario and his mother. It was a hope and a prayer of many teachers who had helped Mario achieve his goal of a high school diploma. It was the love of family members and friends that was snuffed out all because ten officers could not find a way to arrest a man who was walking away without using lethal force. If officers in Colorado Springs, Colorado, can figure out a non-violent arrest technique after two civilians and one of their own have been shot and killed by a suspect armed with an assault rifle, then SFPD, which supposedly resides in one of the most "progressive" and "diverse" cities in the nation, should be able to figure a way to do that as well. As I said in the poem titled "A Poem for Mario"

"this shouldn't be a eulogy keynote.
I should be standing, smiling right beside him,
watching him walk off with his diploma a brighter future on the horizon.

But you and I are left to think of what might have been."

Mario should not be dead. He should not be another name added to the long list of hashtags that serve as indictments of America for devaluing the black life. This is precisely why so many yell out #BlackLivesMatter. We yell but America turns a deaf ear to our protest and slaughter. We will keep yelling, and we will honor those we've lost. Like Mario, I too am a black man, and what many of us know too well, the brother Karega Bailey said, "Truth is, we're all just one bullet away from being a hashtag." This is because the Mayor Ed Lee, Chief of Police Greg Suhr, and other higher-ups will parry and deflect using language like procedure and better training. They talk of arming SFPD with tasers and possibly more de-escalation techniques. These "changes" may or may not occur, and in the interim officers and civilians are still on the street.

What we have to confront is the fact that we do ourselves a serious disservice when we believe a person is infallible due to their profession. The commonality between police, teachers, and doctors is that they are all human, and it is because of this fact that they are fallible. Humans are an incredible species. We are capable of tremendous greatness while at the same time equally capable of mass destruction. Humans are also affected by their environment; we inherit and learn the prejudices, biases, fears, and stereotypes of our culture. We don't shed these by putting on a suit and tie, lab coat, or a uniform and badge. We have to acknowledge that there are good, mediocre, and bad cops, just like there are good, mediocre, and bad teachers and doctors or any other profession. If a teacher is not performing their job according to standards and state law, they can be stripped of their license to teach. If a doctor violates their Hippocratic Oath and harms patients, there is a mechanism to deal with such violations. Hence, the concept of malpractice. Doctors can be stripped of their ability to practice, as well as other forms of punishment. Why is that important? Because doctors carry a patient's health, and oftentimes life, in their hands. Their mistakes can literally mean life or death for a patient. Mistakes of police officers can be just as fatal, but law enforcement is cloaked in a shroud of invincibility and instead of blame being placed on the person(s) who violated, blame is often shifted to the victim, especially if they are black. This prevents the system from ever having to hold itself accountable for wrongdoings because the system finds ways to excuse the behavior.

Mario and I both belong to the most stereotyped and feared group of people in American society. We are adorned in that black hue that causes some to cross the street when they see one of us approaching. We are decorated in the color that makes one who sees me dressed in jeans, a Black Panther Party hoodie and a red, black and green snapback hat assume I'm a thug or gang affiliated instead of a celebrated educator, artist, author with multiple degrees, and a master's in education. We are presumed guilty and viewed as violent threats because our humanity is not the first thing seen, the stereotypes of the black life hijack first encounters and impressions. This is partly why black people are the most likely to be arrested with force or found on the other end of a police bullet. I am a man. I am a human being. Mario was a man and a human being. All humans regardless of color, creed, language, religion, age, sex, political affiliation, or sexual orientation deserve justice.

Black Lives Matter, justice for Mario Woods, end police brutality, and criminalize the actions of those who violate their sworn oath to protect and serve and instead terrorize, maim, and kill because all deserve justice.

Aftermath, Thoughts, and Reflections

This work has been a cathartic exercise for me. I know some people will read this collection and they will label me a hate monger, a racist, and maybe some other stuff I'm not even familiar with. They are free to do that, and I'm free to own my response, which is no concern at all. My reality has shown me very clear lessons about the black experience in America and I do everything in my power to take heed to those lessons. It does not matter what America chooses to label you, the genetic marker of black skin in America is damning enough. I can be the most nonviolent church going black Republican pacifist or the most revolutionary pro-black big Afro-wearing, fist in the air waving, gun-toting Black Panther reincarnate; in the mind and eye of America we are all the same. This country refuses to see us as anything other than a nigger. I can be in a suit in the Oval Office or sagging my pants in West Oakland; I can be a medical doctor or an academic with multiple degrees and distinctions, but to the America power structure I am still a nigger. The perceived threat of the nigger is real to the American psyche, regardless of how it is dressed up or down. Label me what you will, I know who I am, and your attempt at falsely labeling me will not change who I know myself to be and what I feel I must do as Tyson Amir, a black boy in America.

America has a blueprint for me and refuses to see me outside of that schematic. The labels come with the territory. In fact, the labels are already there regardless of whether I stand up and fight back. I don't fight for the people who choose to label me out of fear and ignorance, and therefore I don't care about their opinions. I know who I am, and I refuse to submit to the ill-conceived labels they attempt to superimpose on me. My parents and my community took great care in making sure that I would know who I am, and it does not matter what they do; I'll never lose that understanding. Their ignorance and fear might result in my untimely demise but we know that's a risk every black person faces stepping outside their door any day of their life.

These words and this critique of America is not about hating white people. I know I don't hate human beings. I hate the actions of certain human beings. I hate systems of inequity that are predicated on false pretenses of color bias. I hate what America has done and continues to do to black people. As well its treatment of the indigenous natives here in the Americas. I hate it all. And I have every right to hate those things. I do not buy into the fallacy of the American dream; it's a false reality that is only possible because of the tremendous amount of death, destruction, barbarism, and unspeakable crimes against humanity America has perpetrated to create it. My ancestors are part of those bodies stolen and exploited to build America. My bloodline has served as witness to the making of this "dream." For them and for my sanity I cannot accept America as it is and for what it has done. My family has witnessed generations of exploitation and oppression here in America. This work is for them and for those who are living right now who do not accept America as is. This is for those who will not settle for anything less than freedom and equality for all.

Struggle is essential for survival in America if you are a person of color, especially if you are black. This society takes aim at all aspects of black life. We are under attack mentally, physically, spiritually, legally, culturally, and socially. Fighting back against this system is the only way for us to preserve our dignity and sanity. If you do not challenge the system, you will succumb to its dictates. It will engulf all aspects of who you are. We cannot accept that as our fate. This country has already taken so much from us; we will not allow it to take our hearts, minds, and souls. This is why I say this work is cathartic because it has allowed me to use a new medium to give voice to long-held thoughts and feelings. I use my music and poetry as vehicles to express various viewpoints but developing a compendium such as this has been a different labor. This body of work is an entirely new approach that has allowed me to present these ideas in what I hope is a more cohesive but potent fashion.

The idea came to me to collect my writings, which I view as commentaries on the black experience, while I was abroad. I have very close friends who have published bodies of work: Ise Lyfe's *Pistols & Prayers*, my brother Amir Sulaiman's, *Love, Gnosis &*

other Suicide Attempts, Adisa Banjoko's *Lyrical Swords* and *Bobby, Bruce & The Bronx*. I too wanted to enter the realm of poetic author but I wanted to do something more. Ever since I found my voice as an artist, I've been writing the black experience. It's the experience that I know best, and my pen writes most effectively when it knows the subject matter well. My entire catalog is filled with various episodes of black life. I'm thankful that I have been blessed with a pen that knows how to speak to my people; it's one of the things I feel I do best as a writer.

I wanted this compilation to be something different; I wanted it to be more than just poems and verses. I wanted people to be able to really feel the visceral emotions behind each word in the pieces. I do not know how it happened but I realized fairly early on that I have been selected by the Higher Power, my people, or a combination of both to carry the stories of those before me and with me. The pain, trauma, hurt, fight, love, anger, and hate is very real, and it needs to be articulated in a very real fashion. That is why it appears so real on the page. The readers needed to know what birthed all of this. The words represent the experiences of my people: they are not random events; they are not matter of sheer coincidence. These stories needed to be told, and I'm here to tell it.

I felt explaining some of the context that produced the poems would be a good start to creating this work. I am an artist, writer, poet, and emcee, but I am a freedom fighter first. Every story, word, or phrase is carefully chosen to impart the revolutionary truths that drive me. I wanted to make sure that the pain, heartache, trauma, tension, fear, and struggle that spawned these words was fully articulated. This is what gave me impetus to write, and it was then that I knew this would be my first published work.

The formula of poems and verses, stream of thought reflections and quotes, along with new commentary made me feel I could combine multiple elements in a creative way with relevant contemporary analysis for the benefit of the people. The literature my brothers and sisters create in the guise of music, spoken word, and hip-hop is extremely poignant and valuable, and I wanted to elevate the art form by presenting it in this way. My generation and the generations to come are transfixed by the power of hip-hop music. It has literally taken over the world. Something poor black kids did to express themselves through the pain of their existence is now the most powerful form of media on the planet. This makes it the most powerful medium for communication and education on the planet.

We, who are practitioners of the craft, know it because we learned in the hallowed halls of hip-hop. Be it for better or worse, anybody who considers themselves a hip-hop/rap fan has been changed by the art form. Hip-hop carries deep inside of it the power to inform, and if practiced with the meticulousness of a master alchemist, it wields the power to reform. The world is no longer the same as what it was before hip-hop. We as a people speak and think differently. All because of what some young black kids in the Bronx decided to do in the late '70s. In forty-some odd years, hip-hop has revolutionized the world, and its cultural artifacts can be recognized globally.

I've had the opportunity to perform hip-hop music in several countries throughout the world, many of which have been non-English speaking, and I've been well received everywhere because hip-hop is its own language. Hip-hop is power and when that power is in the hands of those who seek to bring about great change, hip-hop can become revolution.

As an institution, it has traversed a circuitous route to where it is. Money is a powerful narcotic, and hip-hop, like any other institution in the history of mankind is not immune to being co-opted by it for the pursuit of profit. This is where we find the majority of mainstream and underground hip-hop today. The corporate interests' pursuit of profit has led the business of hip-hop to artificially Darwinize its species to self-select "artists" who are more "marketable" from a capitalistic viewpoint. Hence, the preponderance of certain archetypes in the industry. It is what it is. That's the business of music. However, the power in hip-hop is still present, although, somewhat latent at times.

Hip-Hop and Appropriation

A necessary point on hip-hop must be made. My opinion on this issue might be a minority one, but it needs to be said. Hip-hop was birthed out of the pangs and throes of the black experience, which makes hip-hop a precious cultural artifact that belongs to the black experience. This is ours. It belongs to us and only us. We share our cultural inheritance with others in the world, but our sharing does not mean that we are giving you ownership. We are the owners of our culture. This is our art and our expression. It's big, bold, beautiful, and black just like we are.

If you know your history, then you know some of what transpired in order for us to witness the birth of hip-hop in our time. Hip-hop is triumph in the face of tragedy. The tragedy began when our mothers or fathers were captured in their homeland to be enslaved. The tempo of the beat began to quicken on Goree Island at the door of no return. Hip-hop began to form its signature boom when our ancestors who were stolen from their homes survived the middle passage only to reemerge in strange lands to toil their lives away. We began to lament the loss of our homeland, language, culture, religions, and families. The lamentation often took the form of song, which we used to articulate our pain. The bap is a direct result of our ancestors having to watch their fellow brothers and sisters choose death on slave ships by jumping overboard instead of life as a slave. The merging of the boom with the bap happened in the soul of a mother or father contemplating taking the life of their child because they'd rather see them dead then harmed by slavery and white greed. The soul of hip-hop is fortified by all who held dreams of freedom while confined to slave plantations.

Hip-hop's rhythms are bathed in the hopes, dreams, and prayers of the enslaved who only wanted deliverance and freedom for the next generation. Hip-hop is the righteous anger that led to Denmark Vesey, Nat Turner, and Harriet Tubman. Hip-hop is freedmen donning that Union blue uniform to fight gloriously against their Confederate slave masters. Hip-hop is because we as a people were told by the government that we were 3/5ths of a person, and because a Supreme Court justice claimed that although we were human beings, we possessed no rights that white men are bound to respect. That bass hitting your soul is the heavy fear and sorrow in tearful eyes watching crosses being burned on front lawns or seeing men and women who could've easily been you strung up in nooses and hung from trees. The explosive percussive power in our bars and verses is because we watched the sky in Tulsa, Oklahoma, open up, and rain fire down upon us, killing men, women, and children. It's 1985 in Philadelphia watching the skies spit fire on us again. Our beat knocks so hard because we know what it means to stand on a motel balcony on the 4th day of April or in the Audubon Ballroom in front of your daughters and pregnant wife on the 21st day of February. Hip-hop is because we have 12-year-old boys in parks playing with toy guns who meet cops who also play with guns, only theirs fire real bullets. I can go on, but I'm hoping the point is clear enough by now. Hip-hop is only possible because of the strength, resilience, suffering, pain, power, passion, faith, prayer, survival, and pride of black people.

Hip-hop is not new; it is a proud relative prominently placed on the spectrum of African cultural expression. Just like Negro spirituals, blues, funk, jazz, country, soul, and rock and roll, hip-hop is ours. It was manifested out of our sorrow and sacrifice to speak to our people. We are a people who have struggled like none other, and our songs helped guide us through the night to see the morning. We sang our songs like our ancestors taught us to sow seeds of hope for those who would wear our blessed skin tone in the days to come, wishing the burden cast upon the beautiful black of their shoulders would be lighter.

Whites and outsiders don't know this. Some blacks have been taught to ignore this truth that is etched in the most sacred space of their soul. If you are not of this experience, meaning blackness is not your genetic inheritance, then you are not hip-hop. What you are without honoring and respecting our tradition is an interloper, a trespasser currently in the process of bastardizing a sacred ceremony you were never invited to. This is not your place; this is not your language; this ritual was not meant for you.

Is it possible for someone who is not of the black experience to "practice" hip-hop authentically? The overwhelming majority of the time the answer is no; being of the experience is essential for authenticity, but there are exceptions to this rule. For those who aren't the exception their attempt at hip-hop will always be a perverted sloppy imitation devoid of soul, principle, and purpose. The previous non-exception description applies to the overwhelming majority of the folks not of the black experience currently practicing hip hop.

The people of the black experience vary greatly; their individual cultures are nuanced, but they remain connected due to the soil that birthed them. Who are the people of the black experience? Primarily the term is referring to people of African descent who were forced into the diaspora via the slave trades and now make their home in the Americas or other colonial lands. Even more specifically, the term is a direct by-product of the cultural experience of peoples of African descent in what is now known as the United States of America. In its broadest sense, the term refers to all black people of African descent either in the diaspora or still on the continent. Although we differ greatly in look, sound, language, history, religion, and customs, there still exist major commonalities between our artistic, spiritual, and musical expressions throughout many parts of the continent and the world. This would be the closest group of people to whom one might be able to apply the concept of hip-hop being universal.

When hip-hop is removed from its cultural context, it becomes less potent due to a watering down effect resulting from its dislocation. Outsiders approach it without proper knowledge of what and why it is. Their motives are often ill conceived, mainly to exploit it for their own personal reasons, usually fame and fortune. In their hands, our tradition is dumbed down. As of now, many falsely think hip-hop is about bars, ill moves, or the culture. Or they believe hip-hop can be a hobby or pastime. No, hip-hop isn't about trying to prove you are the illest MC, DJ, dancer, or graffiti writer ever. Hip-hop is not about getting signed or getting on. It's not about "money, cars, clothes, and hoes." It ain't.

Peer into the mirror of your soul and see what black people have created before. Hip-hop, like everything black people have produced for themselves in the land of their oppressors, was a means of survival for a stolen people. Lerone Bennett Jr. in his seminal work *Before the Mayflower* said this of African arts and culture: "Art, like religion, was a life expression. There were no art museums or opera houses in pre-white man Africa. Art and aesthetic expression were collective experiences in which all the people participated. Art, in short, was not for art's sake, but for life's sake." This is important to understand because this same spirit crossed the Atlantic Ocean with our ancestors and became the cornerstone of all black artistic expression, eventually finding its way into the foundation of hip-hop. Meaning hip-hop is for life's sake, preserving, fighting, and struggling for the lives of black folks in America and the world over.

And now a mixed group of outsiders being led by the greatest thieves in human history, the ones who stole us initially from Africa, wish to steal even more from us. Those in power and their children look upon us and see something that they were incapable of creating on their own. Out of jealousy and envy, they first attempt to demonize it. They call it jungle music or some other phrase to impugn its greatness. Then their envy forces them to adopt another strategy, which is to take what they can't produce on their own. If they can control it, they can silence the people who are the source of it. They grab it and then run back to their homes and clumsily try to reproduce the magic that naturally occurs in the black soul. Once they feel they understand how it works, they began to show it off among themselves and act as if it belongs to them. Then they use their white magic on the originators of this beautiful thing and tell them, "It belongs to everybody." They say it so much that we begin to believe that what our ancestors were willing to die for to leave for us is actually for everybody, including the thieves.

We know it doesn't work the other way. We could not steal something from them and then claim it belongs to everybody. But when it comes to our sacred possessions, they can pillage what they wish. Like a criminal with no remorse, they begin to parade their looted booty in front of those they stole it from. We watch as they awkwardly misuse our treasures. It's like a child with a new toy; they can't contain themselves and use it so much that we see the sacred wisdoms in rhythms of our ancestors everywhere we look, but the faces using them are not our own. I know y'all have seen commercials and shows where they're using our hip-hop, and there are no black faces anywhere. They use our culture to sell products while we use it to save our lives.

They even have the audacity to claim they know what real hip-hop is in their boardrooms or on their radios, televisions, magazines, and websites. How do you know hip-hop when you haven't been through what our people have survived? Without that knowledge and experience flowing through your veins, you cannot know why we sing. But they don't care; instead they self-select young thieves who have done nothing but poorly imitate those who were blessed to receive their inheritance and put them out in front of everybody, producing the oxymoron of white faces doing black music.

This might be some of what our native brothers and sisters feel when they hear absurd statements like Christopher Columbus discovered America, or when they hear white people claim America is their home and that "foreigners" need to go back to wherever they came from. I don't think I'm the only one who sees the irony in the children of slave owners, children of those who fought to keep blacks segregated, children of the KKK and other white supremacist groups, children of those who went to watch black people lynched from trees, the children of those who used fire hoses and sicced dogs on black bodies, the children of those who witnessed the atrocities heaped upon blacks and did nothing, the children of those who allowed the word nigger to whet their lips regularly and might be on the lips of their offspring now. These very same people now aspire to be hip-hop. They've built an entire nation and culture that has punished black people for being black, but now they want to sing, dance, walk, talk, and act just like us.

Hypothetically speaking if it were possible for outsiders to "practice" hip-hop, what would that look like?

First, they would have to honor, respect, and learn about the people and the culture that produced the art. This has never happened in American or Western society and most likely never will. Without the honor, respect, and true understanding, these outsiders feel they can just take what they want from our cultural experience. They do not value us or our culture when it is in our hands. They only place value on it when it is in their hands.

Second, they would have to study the tradition to be a practitioner of it. That study would have to take place at the hands of a master of the tradition. Like Bennett Jr. pointed out, "Art, in short, was not for art's sake, but for life's sake." If you understand that, then it is obligatory for you to create from a space of honoring life. Our art is not an economic opportunity. They will never understand this, and this is why their presence will only serve to corrupt what was once pure and good.

Third, they would only be able to practice it upon approval from a master of the tradition.

Fourth, if and when an outsider practices, they would always have to pay homage and honor the people who taught them the art form, and be held accountable for how they use the art form by the community.

Those are basic requirements for anyone who seeks to enter the sacred space of black culture and benefit from the hip-hop we've created for ourselves. If this were to happen, then possibly outsiders could practice the tradition, but two key elements are missing from the present context that make it virtually impossible for this to ever occur. White supremacy and white privilege prevent any real equality between cultures and respect for black people and culture. Without equality and true respect for black people and culture, the taking/appropriation becomes theft, especially when the dominant culture uses their power and privilege to insult the native architects of the traditions in order to elevate their fraudulent claim to their misuse of it.

At times, this commonly results in outsiders who have stolen hip-hop from its rightful owners using hip-hop style, language, and culture to insult black people. The insults are done intentionally and unintentionally, but the effect is the same. Furthermore, these people who profit off of black culture often do nothing to support black people in their fight for freedom, justice, and equality in society, which are key ingredients in the recipe that culminated in producing hip-hop. Folks want to talk, dress, walk, rap, dance, and act like black folks but are invisible when we say Black Lives Matter. All that black culture they stole gets tucked away quickly when we talk about police killing black folks in the streets. All that hip-hop spirit they display vanishes when we talk about how the prison industrial complex keeps locking up black men and women, and how the school-to-prison pipeline harvests more black souls daily to satisfy its hunger.

The theft and looting has been going on so long that some black folks actually believe it is okay that the cultural traditions made by our ancestors and passed down to us are now being carried by those our ancestors created it to protect us from. When outsiders attempt our sacred tradition, it hangs off them like an oversized suit. The garment does not sit right on their bodies and flops around all over their flesh. Still they attempt to wear it, even though it will never fit them correctly. Black folks do themselves a disservice when they accept the constant theft of their culture and acquiesce to say it belongs to all. The fact that something happens constantly doesn't make it right. Just because they have stolen from our culture nonstop and then turned around and said they didn't steal it because it's for everybody, does not make them right. They are thieves looking for "justifications" for their devilish actions. I call it how I see it, and I see that we are a proud black people surrounded by a band of hungry ungrateful thieves who attempt to sustain themselves on sucking the blood and marrow from the soul of our culture.

To illustrate the point more clearly, I'll highlight a few cultural artifacts from other peoples who have either been culturally appropriated or been able to keep it at bay. If a person were attempting to learn a martial art, they would have to learn it within the context of the culture that created it. A martial discipline can be from China, Japan, Indonesia, West Africa, Brazil, or the United States. The art will be learned in a way that preserves the integrity and respect for the founders, history, and culture responsible for its development. Forms are learned in the language of the art. Teachers are oftentimes referred to by titles that originate from the native language of the art. In order to practice, you have to learn from the hands of someone who is a certified teacher of the art, who comes from a clear lineage of learning that goes back to the source of the art.

Divorce martial arts from its historical context and you have the new sports phenomenon of mixed martial arts (MMA). There are those in the MMA world who come from a strong background well-rooted in a historical tradition, and there are others who simply want to learn how to kick, punch, and grapple to become famous and win money. That violates almost every core principle in any traditional system of martial arts. MMA keeps making money, and people drift further and further away from the historical roots and purpose of these fighting systems.

Another example is the gross appropriation of yoga, which has become a fad in Western society over the past few years. There are many people who have no idea that yoga originated from what is known as Hinduism. There are multiple types of yogas, but the one that has gained a monopoly in the west is hatha yoga, or what is translated from Sanskrit as force yoga. Hatha yoga is an old spiritual practice, but it is not even considered a mainstream practice in India, the home of Hinduism and yoga. The most common type of yoga is bhakti yoga, and it has nothing to do with stretching and flexibility. However, all the yogic practices originate from historical spiritual traditions of the Indian people. Westerners have cherry-picked what they've felt is important from an entire tradition, which demonstrates a high level of cultural arrogance. The idea that you can simply mute and then eliminate the historical, social, political, religious, and economic context and the people who produced the cultural artifact that you now covet because you only want the stretching part is highly offensive.

They've eliminated almost 2,500 years of history all to fill small yoga studios with white women in yoga pants for a cardio workout. There is no connection to the deeper spiritual and religious truths that hatha yoga or any of the yogas were created for. They've thrown out everything that they deemed of no value, including the people, and this is why I consider it theft. Are these yoga folks at all concerned about the well-being of people in India, the land that gave them their new fitness revolution? For the most part they don't know and don't care. They simply put on a fresh pair of yoga pants, roll out a fresh new yoga mat, and try to perfect their downward dog, completely oblivious to everything else because their privilege allows them to do so. It is wrong for white society to do this to the Indian people and their sacred traditions, just like it would be wrong for it to be done to any martial art, and it is certainly wrong for white folks and other outsiders to do it to black culture, specifically hip-hop. It's theft!

There are those who will think me crazy for saying all of this. Other will agree, I know my opinion represents a minority (no pun intended), but it has to be said. Some may call me a hypocrite because one of my music partners in the production of my music is white. The homie onBEATS is a white dude for real. There is no denying that fact. On our latest Tyson onBEATS album *Tradition* I wrote:

"Just being honest in these sonnets
Some folks be asking how onBEATS responding
because some of these bars are so black
man, it's like they're dipped in onyx
he provides the sonics, I provide the phonics and …"

After recording that verse for the song we were working on, onBEATS wanted to know if folks really asked that question. I told him, yeah, folks often wonder how you feel about me being all black radical on your production. He told me when he was growing up and listening to hip-hop, it was always about black liberation. So when he started producing music, his only point of reference for how the music should be utilized was for the purpose of forwarding the black agenda for black liberation. In his creative heart and mind hip-hop and black liberation were inseparable, and if he was going to create music, it would respect that history and forward that purpose. This is part of the reason why we're a team. He's a John Brown on a beat machine. His example is very different from other white artists and outsiders who loot hip-hop and sell it to white/outsider audiences and have no connection to black people or the black struggle. They bastardize black music for their own personal gain, which is usually fortune and fame in the white world.

I go hard on white people because white supremacy and privilege are so prevalent the world over, but white people are not the only ones who have attempted to steal our legacy. Hip-hop has become a global phenomenon. You'll find people in every country on the planet imitating black culture and attempting to do hip-hop. You have folks in Asia, Europe, South and Central America, Australia, the Malay Peninsula, everywhere on the planet. One other group that needs to be called out is Arabs and Arab rappers. Hip-hop has spread to all parts of the Arab world, and you can see its usage by young folks in Arab countries and folks of Arab descent in parts of the Western world. I would really be hypocritical to go hard on the white supremacist west and not mention Arabs and their false cultural claim to Arab supremacy over blacks. Just like the foundation of Western civilization was largely based on money and resources extracted from the planet via the triangular slave trade, the Arab world profited from a slave trade that primarily traded African bodies for more than 1,000 years. The Arab slave trade moved millions of bodies, the majority women to serve as sex slaves, out of the African continent to slave markets in various parts of the Arab world. A major contributing factor was the expansion of Islam and its allowance of slavery as a legal social and religious practice. A lasting vestige of this horrific historical epoch is the development of the term Abeed (I'm using an English phonetic spelling of the Arabic word). Abeed can be translated in English as slave, and it is exclusively applied to black people because in the Arab cultural psyche black people's only purpose is that of a slave. It doesn't matter who you are, if you have black skin and you're in any part of the Arab world you might hear this term cast down upon you.

This is an interesting fact: Both white Western society and Arab society have produced terms to denigrate black people. White folks call us niggers, and Arabs call us Abeed; they are different words from different languages but in essence they mean the same thing. Both terms are derived from slave trades largely predicated on the exploitation of black peoples. In Western and Arab societies, blacks are considered the lowest of the low in the social hierarchy. Arabs as a people are diverse; they compete amongst themselves as to who is the highest class of Arab. Is it Lebanese, Jordanian, Saudi, Kuwati, and so on and so forth? They also respect their tribal lineages. Arabs are very proud of maintaining their familial bonds, and, like any people with rich history like that, they should be. Their Arabic dialects are different depending on what part of the Arab world you are in, but one thing that is the same across the Arab world is calling black people the racial pejorative Abeed.

I feel this is important because these young people who are produced by a culture that has castigated black people for centuries are now appropriating black cultural heritage. I can't speak on the character of these rappers because I don't know many of them personally. It is possible that maybe some Arab rappers use the term Abeed in their everyday lives when referring to black people; maybe they don't. The point I'm attempting to make is you cannot practice hatred of black people and think you can have access to our cultural artifacts. You cannot belong to a culture that has an age-old practice of demeaning black bodies and think you'll get an invite to use our culture freely. Especially if you aren't doing anything to fight the racial bias that exists in your own culture towards black people. Your taking of our culture without paying homage or respect to black people makes you a thief. Pay homage and respect to the people who created the art form and show that homage and respect by working to support their struggle and ending the racist bigotry alive and well in your cultures today. Do that, and you can come hang out; if not, then you're a thief who is stealing our art form for your own personal gain and you are not welcome here.

Hip-hop as a Tool for Education

Black culture and our artistic expressions have all contributed to the survival of black people here in America. Hip-hop is one of the most recent manifestations of black cultural expression. Hip-hop is many things, but one of the major aspects of its purpose is as a tool for liberation. Mainstream America seeks to blind you to that fact with its corporate takeover. Hip-hop is the backing track to commercials, selling us products we don't need by exploiting our culture. Despite the commodification of our hip-hop, the liberating pulse can still be felt. In spaces that corporate America has yet to pollute, you will find hip-hop being used in its purest form, to nurture, educate, and liberate black people.

I say all this because many young black kids are placed in schools that are designed to fail them. Look at any meaningful metric pertaining to education, and you'll see that blacks are at the bottom of the list. We are the most likely to be pushed out or drop out. We are held back the most. Our children are designated as learning deficient more than any other group. The schools we attend are underfunded when compared to white majority schools. Education is a flawed endeavor when it comes to blacks. There are success stories, but the institution is woefully inequitable when it comes to black students. The bottom line is schools were not designed to educate our youth, and that is why they are doing such a good job of not educating them. We often do not have independent educational services in our communities to help support growth and development for our youth. At this moment in time, we cannot provide an alternative to a system that has been failing our children.

What we do know is that the same child that a counselor may label ADD, ADHD, or learning deficient can have thousands if not millions of rap lyrics memorized. That same child who might not be interested in a third-grade textbook can listen to an entire album of their favorite artist and give you a detailed explanation of why he or she is their favorite artist. Hip-hop has revealed an intelligence in our people that is undervalued by the institution. That hip-hop intelligence needs to be fed with vital information to help the growth and development of our children. This is where the reforming revolutionary power of hip-hop lies, and for those of us who recognize its power, it is incumbent upon us to create the material to give more substance to our audiences.

I'm not saying that other types of songs with other content cannot be made. I strongly feel every artist has to question what they are writing and what they are writing it for. A substantial percentage of artists are writing lyrics that are inspired by mainstream artists. These mainstream artists are all vying for spots offered by the four major record labels. If you're trying to get a deal, there are basically four major record labels that control what is and what is not hip-hop music. They are interested in profit not art. They want "artists" who will sell units and generate views. Therefore, they bank on a formula of finding what sells best and keep putting out more of that to keep money coming in. To do that, these four major companies are tied to the six major corporations that own 90 percent of the U.S. media. These people literally have the power to create any image they want and feed it to the masses. Some artists think they are being innovative and original in what they write and how they carry themselves, when they are actually reproducing what some old white man in a suit at a table deemed is rap or hip-hop. That white man cares nothing about the people who created this art and culture, why they created it, and what they really want and need. It's a cold game.

That's the music side of the equation, and the street side of the equation is similar. White people created the ghetto. The powers that be attempt to fool us and claim we need to be more afraid of Saddam Hussein, Bin Laden, Boko Haram, Al Qaeda, ISIS, The IRA, Chinese, Vietnamese, North Koreans, Russians, Taliban, or anybody else. None of those people or groups have done anything to destroy black folks. On the contrary, the black community has constantly been attacked by white America, and the policies of the white establishment. They are the ones solely responsible for engineering the weapons of slavery, Jim Crow, poverty, mass incarceration, and drugs, which have destroyed the black community. The artists who glorify the pain, trauma, suffering, and ignorance found in places in some of our communities are glorifying the white man's vision for us. The key word is glorify. It is one thing to make commentary on how we live, but it's an entirely different thing to take the pain and suffering and make it the ideal for black existence.

The guns and drugs all came into our communities with government complicity. These things are plagues in our communities, and we've had to find ways to adapt and survive. We tell stories of the world in which we live. Many of us come from places that are not fit for humans to live in. That's very real, and music is an outlet for us to discuss the problems of our existence. This is where some folks in my community will disagree, and that's fine with me, but at no time is the gangster persona, which survives as being a predatory force in the black community, to be celebrated or condoned. There is no excuse for glorifying poor black people killing other poor black people, or selling dope to other poor black people, or pimping black bodies, especially women and children. That is glorifying the work of those who have been responsible for our oppression since 1619. We have to realize that and take back what power we have if we wish to win against this social order that loves to see us either dead or in chains.

Let me also be clear that hip-hop is not the source of the problems in the black community. Some might try to make that philosophical jump with those last statements. The problems blacks face are due to the institutional racist practices America has enacted over the past 400 years. With or without hip-hop, we would still have state-created ghettos and disproportionate representation in jails and prisons. Jim Crow and 'separate but equal' were all created in America prior to hip-hop. The problems that blacks faced in the South or in major urban centers were alive and well without any help from hip-hop. In fact, way before hip-hop, the so-called "deviant" behavior in the black community was blamed on other forms of black cultural expression. Hip-hop is not the problem, but hip-hop can become part of a new way of thinking for black people in America, which can lead to a new way of being.

I'm an educator with a few degrees and a master's in education, but the cultural capital I have as an educator is very limited. I am not bragging about my academic pedigree; I don't really care much about the paperwork attached to my name. I'm not a fool though; I know I can get in some doors, which is extremely valuable, but other doors remain shut in white and black America due to my "education" and being an educator. I'm an emcee, and it is that fact that affords me the ability to walk into almost any urban setting, and because I can spit bars I can have an audience with youth all over. I try to practice humility with my ability, but my skill set is at a level where I can actually spit that hot fire or like we say out here in the bay, your boy be gas'n. That's important because this is the language of the people, and when the people began to hear more than just the clever wordplay they become intrigued and inspired by the message. That is power because hip-hop is consumed in a way where it becomes part of you.

One of my spiritual teachers Zaid Shakir once said, "The fastest way to affect the hearts of the people is through what they hear because the ear has a direct channel to the heart." Hip-hop is the equivalent of sending a message to the heart at light speed. I cannot walk up and drop a book in front of these kids and elicit the same response as I can with hip-hop. I cannot bring in an eloquent speaker who can break down the pathologies of America and solutions to problems in the black community and elicit that same response as I could with it being presented in rap form. This power is found only through hip-hop. That power belongs to hip-hop, and the power is actualized at its highest level by those who command the vernacular of it. We have that power, and it's imperative that we use it to build up our communities and support our youth.

It is imperative for practitioners to develop high quality content and share that with their audience. Again, I'm not advocating censorship. I love to have fun and listen to music that puts me in different moods. Music that reflects love, intimacy, partying, anger, relaxation, and anything else an artist wants to express. I don't believe in censorship, but I am a fan of recognizing the power of your craft and upholding a level of responsibility with what you create. This work here is an attempt at raising the bar with hip-hop, creating a literature that speaks deeper to our time, place, and experience, and providing a reminder and education.

Clarity came to me one day, and I was convinced this had to happen. I was compelled to take my hip hop (the language of the people) and pair it with historical and contemporary political/social/academic analysis to form a unique revolutionary statement. The challenge would be figuring out how to best frame the scope of the conversation. I began to search my catalogue of writings and music and pull out pieces that I felt represented crucial aspects of the black experience. This was the conception point of *Black Boy Poems*.

Beginnings are important, but as a freedom fighter I remain focused on the ultimate objective which is freedom and liberation. Every revolutionary act has to be a step towards obtaining that revolutionary goal. My goal in this work is to spark the fire of revolutionary struggle in the hearts and minds of my people here in America. This is the goal because we are now almost one-fifth of the way through the 21st century, and it is clear to see that we are not free. No one in black skin is free from state sponsored terror, violence, incarceration and the "traditional" obstacles that plague black life.

What does one do? There are myriad ways to attempt to reconcile that oppressive reality. Some push for assimilation and integration, independence, armed rebellion, mass exodus/expatriation and others a mixture of all those ideas. We've seen numerous examples of each idea put into practice. One that speaks to the acuteness of the problem of being black in America is exodus/expatriation. What has to happen in order to make one leave their home? In response to this question we've witnessed a number of our celebrities and leaders expatriating from the United States.

Some by force and others by choice. A portion of the title of this text is an homage to one of my greatest literary influences, Richard Wright, who made a decision to leave the United States in the late 1950s.

In an essay he penned on the subject entitled "I Choose Exile," he spoke candidly about that very decision. For Wright it all came down to one thing, freedom. He honestly believed he could not find freedom as a black man anywhere in the jurisdiction of the United States of America. Wright was very staunch in his understanding that the American system is not made for black people. It was also his understanding that the American system will not allow a way to eventually incorporate black people. He was of the opinion that the system did not have a mechanism in place to reform itself for the sake of guaranteeing justice and equality to blacks. Therefore, his only alternative was to seek freedom for himself and family outside the lands of the United States.

Although that was his opinion and personal decision he did not want his statement to be taken as a call for mass exodus from the continental borders of the United States. I agree with this as well. I have experienced much better treatment as a black man in multiple parts of the world than compared to my homeland. However, I do not think a mass exodus is a practical solution. There will always be black people in America, and they will face the problems that confront black people on a daily basis. The work of liberating blacks in America will always be necessary as long as this American system is in place. So practical steps have to be taken domestically to achieve this goal.

Wright dedicated his entire life to fighting for the liberation of black people. His frustration and disenchantment with America was a byproduct of knowing that fighting for the rights of his people was morally and ethically right. Yet, he, his family, and people were destined to live in a society that chose the wrongs of racism and institutional hatred over liberty and equality.

"I Choose Exile" was written during the 1950s, which coincides with the birth of the Civil Rights Movement. Wright wouldn't have been against the organizing efforts of blacks in America, but he would have questioned their goal of integration and seeking answers from within the system. I say this because he didn't live to see many of the "accomplishments" of the Civil Rights Movement. He died in 1960 at the age of fifty-two, as he suffered from complications from dysentery the last three years of his life. Some believe he was poisoned because of the power and eloquence of his pen. Since he didn't get to see the full flower of many of the changes fought for via the Civil Rights Movement, we have to assume what his feeling would have been.

Although he expatriated, he wasn't a separatist by any stretch of the imagination. He spoke in *Black Boy* about his experience with the Garveyites, the men and women who were the followers of The Honorable Marcus Mosiah Garvey. The founder and leader of one of the most influential Black Liberation groups in American history, the United Negro Improvement Association (UNIA), Garvey preached of "One God, One Aim, One Destiny" and also separation through the Back to Africa movement as well as Item 38 in the UNIA Declaration of Rights of The Negro Peoples of This World.

"We demand complete control of our social institutions without interference by any alien race or races."

The Garveyites were no stranger to demanding complete independence domestically and abroad. They were never able to accomplish this, but Wright saw their zeal for fighting for a new destiny for black people. This desire is what made Wright truly respect them for working towards what they believed in. Although he didn't agree with the aims and goals of the Garveyites, he still respected their mission and did not stand in the way of their attempting to accomplish that mission. This is why I feel Wright wouldn't have objected to the civil rights movement and other aspects of movements that developed in the '50s and '60s. The Nation of Islam, SNCC, SCLC, The Black Panther Party for Self Defense, and other such organizations that took a stand for blacks in America. He would've questioned them all on their true aim, and his questions would've been appropriate. Anyone who is participating in the struggle for freedom and liberation in America has to contend with questions about what they are fighting for, how do they plan on achieving that goal, and if it's even possible to accomplish that goal here. I am of the opinion of Wright that there is no solution for us to be found within the American institution. Our freedom and liberation will only be accomplished by completely overthrowing the system or creating an independent space for black survival outside of the system. I know these represent minority opinions. Some might even claim them defeatist opinions. I don't share that sentiment, but what I truly stand firmly behind is the fact that the American institution is not willing to amend its ways to accommodate black equality.

Hypothetically speaking we could make every politician a black radical, and we would still encounter similar institutional practices because the financial power is still concentrated in the hands of those who are invested in this system functioning the way it does. We would end up with a situation like the Republic of South Africa. South Africans won the battle of apartheid and gained control of the government but whites, who constitute a minority of less than 10 percent of the South African population, still own the majority of all the land and resources. Equality is not simply a ceremonial gifting of rights on paper. It has to be supported with access to quality education, jobs, housing, resources, and strengthened with an infrastructure that puts money behind securing those opportunities for all.

Those with the land and the power and the resources will have to give up some of what they have, and this is something I believe we will never see in this society. It will have to be taken by force. This is also why establishing independent institutions is such an important survival mechanism because the existing institutions are predatory and not interested in equity. They gorge themselves on the labor and money of black and brown folks the world over. This is why the drive for the Garveyites to develop independent institutions appealed to Wright so much. He saw the value in that effort because he viewed it as a means of combating a repressive system.

Here we are, some 42 million of us, and we find ourselves 400 years into the life and times of black people in a land now called America. We are a strong, beautiful, creative people; so much of our power emanates from a place deep in our souls. This power is something we've inherited from those who came before us. We do not always see eye-to-eye, but we all suffer for the same reason whether we accept it or not. Be we atheist, agnostic, Baptist, Methodist, Pentecostal, Catholic, Buddhist, Muslim, Nation Of Islam, Five-Percent Nation, Nuwaubian, Moor, Sovereign, Black Jewish, Mormon, Scientologist, hipster, Afro-Centric, Afro Punk, socialist, communist, capitalist, black radical, vegan, Rastafarian, black Republican, black Democrat, anarchist, Crip, Blood, Piru, Vice Lord, Peoples, Folks, Gangster Disciple, Black P. Stone, Black Guerilla family, Kumi, East Coast, West Coast, Midwest, South, rich, middle class, poor, male, female, young, old, heterosexual, homosexual, bisexual, transgender, or gender neutral, it doesn't matter how we define ourselves, for better or for worse this land is our home, and we are black in this land. Yes, Africa is our motherland, and some of us have been blessed to visit our long-lost home and bathe in the sun and the moon of our people. Not all of us will get that chance. Thus, we must fight for freedom and liberation where our people are and that is here in the wilderness of North America. We are all we have. We are as diverse as we are glorious; there is no victory for our people unless we are able to stand together and confront the evil that has set out to destroy us.

The one lesson that should be painfully clear to us by now is that America will not voluntarily give us our freedom and liberation. Two of our greatest warriors, Dr. Martin Luther King Jr. and Malcolm X differed on many points but one they were unified on is the fact that our oppressor will not voluntarily grant us our freedom; it is the right and responsibility of the oppressed to secure their freedom. In the words of Dr. King, "We know through painful experience that freedom is never voluntarily given by the oppressor; it must be demanded by the oppressed." In the words of Malcolm, "We declare our right to be a man, to be a human being, to be given the rights of a human being ... which we intend to bring into existence by any means necessary!"

Man, woman, or however you identify, you have to bring it into existence. We have to manufacture it or else we will get more of what our experience has been for the past 400 years.

This is what I know. This is part of what I have to offer my people. I am committed with every fiber of my being to the fight for the freedom and liberation of us all. I see the problems that we as a people are faced with daily. In the light of those problems I know that we are the foundation of any solution. We have to build our present and our future if we want something different for black people in America. It won't be an easy fight but there is no path to freedom and liberation of black people that doesn't include the majority of black people directly fighting to make freedom and liberation our reality.

Black Boy Poems is part of that purpose, and part of the purpose of my life. It is one of the many things I was meant to give to my people. This collection represents my words, thoughts, heart, soul, feelings, and everything else I possess as a man displayed proudly upon the battle field leading to our freedom. I have pages and pages of words that describe our pain, hunger, our need to unite and fight, and I will write them and stand in them with all the ferocity I can muster until I am either no more, or I hear the appropriate response from my people. There is no turning back for me. The only question is what will you do? I'm listening very carefully for that response, for when I hear it I will know that my brothers and sisters are ready to join me on the frontline. Our time is now! For our sake and that of our children, don't keep me waiting too long.

Bibliography

ACLU. *Locating the School-to-Prison Pipeline*, 2013.

Anthamatten, Eric Ph.D. "Incarceration, Education, Emancipation." *The Atlantic*, 2015. Permission granted by Eric Anthamatten, Ph.D.

Bailey, Karega. "We're all just one bullet away from being a hashtag," 2014.

Bennett Jr. Lerone. *Before the Mayflower: A History of Black America*, 8th ed. Johnson Publishing Company, 1962. Courtesy of Johnson Publishing Company, LLC. All rights reserved.

"Black Homicide Victimization in the United States: An Analysis of 2013 Homicide Data," Violence Policy Center, accessed March 2016. http://www.vpc.org/studies/blackhomicide16.pdf.

Brooks, Gwendolyn. "We Real Cool." 1959. Reprinted by consent of Brooks Permissions.

Brown v. Board of Education of Topeka, No. 1 (347 U.S. 483).

Bureau of Justice Statistics. *Education and Correctional Populations*. (NCJ 195670, 2003),

Bureau of Justice Statistics. *Prison Inmates at Midyear 2009 Statistical Tables*. (NCJ 230113, 2010).

Coates, Ta-Nehisi. *Between the World and Me*. New York: Spiegel & Grau, 2015.

Craemer, Thomas. "Estimating Slavery Reparations: Present Value Comparisons of Historical Multigenerational Reparations Policies." *Social Science Quarterly,* vol. 96 issue 2 (2015). Permission granted by Thomas Craemer.

Cress Welsing, Dr. Frances. *The Isis Papers: The Keys to the Colors*. Chicago: C.W. Publishing, 1982. Permission granted by Lorne Cress Love.

Second Continental Congress. *Declaration of Independence*. July 4, 1776.

Douglass, Frederick. "The Meaning of July Fourth for the Negro." (speech, Rochester, NY, July 5, 1852).

Dred Scott v. Sandford, 60 US 393 (1857).

Du Bois, W. E. B. "The Souls of Black Folks." Bookbyte Digital Edition, 1903.

Eisen-Martin, Tongo. "Operation Ghetto Storm (Every 28 Hours)." Prepared by Malcolm X Grassroots Movement, 2013. Permission granted by Tongo Eisen-Martin.

Encyclopedia of Virginia, s.v. "An Act Concerning Servants and Slaves, (1705)." (Virginia: Virginia Foundation for the Humanities). (Public Domain)

Feagin, Joe R & Sikes, Melvin P. *Living with Racism: The Black Middle Class Experience*. Beacon Press, 1995. Permission granted by Joe R. Feagin & Beacon Press.

Fish, Hamilton . "Hamilton Fish Papers: Letter from Ulysses S. Grant. (Washington D.C.: Manuscript Division, Library of Congress, 1876).

Hermione Hoby, interview by Toni Morrison 2015. Permission granted by Hermione Hoby.

Independence Police Department, Personnel Records of Timothy Loehmann by Jim Polak (2012).

Jackson, George. *Soledad Brother: The Prison Letters of George Jackson*. (New York: Bantam Books, 1970).

Jefferson, Thomas. "Manners," chap 18 in *Notes on the State of Virginia* (1781).

Jones-DeWeever, Avis Ph.D., ed. "Black Women in the United States, 2014.") Presented at Black Women's Roundtable, National Coalition on Black Civic Participation, March 2014, prepared by Black Women's Roundtable.

Kappeler, Victor E. "A Brief History of Slavery and the Origins of American Policing." (2014). Permission granted by Dr. Kappeler.

King Jr., Martin Luther. "Letter from Birmingham Jail: Why We Can't Wait." 1963.

Knafo, Saki. "When It Comes to Illegal Drug Use, White America Does the Crime, Black America Gets the Time." *Huffington Post*, 2013. Permission granted by Saki Knafo.

"Law Enforcement Leaders to Reduce Crime & Incarceration: Mission Statement," accessed 2015. lawenforcementleaders.org. Permission granted by Law Enforcement Leaders to Reduce Crime & Incarceration.

Lorde, Audre. *I Am Your Sister: Black Women Organizing Across Sexualities*. New York City: Kitchen Table, Women of Color Press, 1985.

McKay, Claude. "If We Must Die." 1919. Permission granted by Claude McKay Literary Estate.

Merriam-Webster OnLine, s.v. "black," accessed 2016. http://www.merriam-webster.com/dictionary/black.

Merriam-Webster OnLine, s.v. "racism," accessed 2016. http://www.merriam-webster.com/ dictionary/racism.

Merriam-Webster OnLine, s.v. "white," accessed 2016. http://www.merriam-webster.com/dictionary/white.

Muhammad, Elijah. *Message to the Blackman in America*. Secretarius Memps Publications, 1965.

Mosenkis, David. "Racial Bias in Pennsylvania's Funding of Public Schools." October 2014.

Newton, Huey P. *Revolutionary Suicide*. New York: Harcourt Brace Jovanovich, 1973.

Nina Simone "Mississippi Goddam," written and performed by Nina Simone, and recorded on *Nina Simone in Concert*. Permission granted by Alfred Music.

Oxford Dictionaries, s.v. "racism," last updated June 21, 2016 by Oxford University Press. http://www.oxforddictionaries.com/us/definition/american_english/racism.

Plessy v. Ferguson, 163 U.S. 537 (1896).

Powell, Prentice. "Being a Black Man in America." YouTube video 3:35 https://www.youtube.com/watch?v=wxew1EMr_v4, posted by PrenticePowell1906 on August 21, 2014.

Prodigy "Survival of the Fittest," recorded 1995 on *Mobb Deep - The Infamous*. The Infamous, permission granted by Hal Leonard.

Robinson, Bert. "SJPD: Use of Force More Likely in Arrests of Blacks." *San Jose Mercury News*, Bay Area News Group, 2009. Permission granted by Bert Robinson.

Rza "Bells of War," recorded 1997 by Wu-Tang Forever. Permission granted by Hal Leonard

"San Francisco Justice Reinvestment Initiative: Racial and Ethnic Disparities Analysis for the Reentry Council." W. Haywood Burns Institute, 2016.

Shaun, King, "Cops are convicted of murder almost as much as whites who lynched blacks." *Daily News*, November 17, 2015. Permission granted by Shaun King.

Tupac Shakur interviewed in prison in 1995. Permission granted by the Amaru Estate.

Tzu, Sun, *Art of War*.

U.S. Const. art I §2, cl. 3

U.S. Const. art. IV § 2, cl. 3

Wessler, Seth. "Education is Not Great Equalizer for Black Americans. *NBC News*, March 16, 2015. Permission granted by Seth Wessler.

X, Malcolm and Goerge Breitman, ed. *By Any Means Necessary: Speeches, Interviews, and a Letter by Malcolm X*. New York: Pathfinder Press, 1970. Permission granted by Richard Hazboun of Pathfinder Press.

West, Cornell . *Race Matters*. Boston: Beacon Press, 1993.

Woodson, Carter. G. *Miseducation of the Negro*. Washington D.C.: The Associated Publisher, Inc., 1933.

About Tyson Amir

Tyson Amir is a freedom fighter, educator, author, activist, emcee, and poet in possession of a powerful pen that allows him to speak directly to the heart and soul of his generation. Being born and raised in the San Francisco Bay Area in a time when America essentially escalated its war on the black community has dramatically shaped his politic and outlook. He's the child of revolutionaries, and in his three decades he has witnessed the birth of hip hop, the U.S. sponsored crack epidemic, the war on drugs, his home state of California becoming a murder capital, the school to prison pipeline, and the emergence of the prison industrial complex. During a more than ten year span encompassing his elementary through high school years, California averaged more than 3,400 murders a year.

These political, historical, social, and economic forces permeate his writing along with the spirit of rebellion that's been passed down the branches of his family tree. This spirit is ever present in his catalogue of music, his collection of poetry, and now in his debut offering as a writer, *Black Boy Poems*. In his most recent work, Tyson skillfully weaves his knowledge, experience, artistic genius, politics, and philosophy to form what can be considered one of the most revolutionary works of literature since the *Autobiography of Malcolm X.*

At times his analysis will bring you face to face with his scholarly side represented by a masters degree in education, a double major/triple minor, and an in-depth study of black revolutionary literature. His poetry and lyrical dexterity clearly displays a mastery of the hip hop art form. The power in his metaphors and vernacular demonstrates the learned experiences of attempting to survive America in black skin. In many ways he's a reporter firmly embedded in the cross sections of every major American problem stemming from the abuses of capitalism, racism, and hatred.

The more you experience his writing the more you're able to witness the degree of commitment to his struggle. His authenticity comes from the fact that he actually lives and breathes what he writes. When he speaks on police violence and brutality, it's punctuated by the fact that in the past 18 months, three of his former students have been killed by law enforcement agents and one was savagely beaten to the point that his hands are now paralyzed.

Tyson has taught in California jails and prisons for more than 13 years. He's said about his experience as an educator behind bars that, "every day is a matter of life and death. This system is eating my people alive, and the effects are felt by families, neighborhoods and the community." Like his teaching, his writing is a weapon which he uses to strike at the heart of the system. The goal is always to win, and that victory means the liberation of his people.

A world traveler but eternally a California boy, Tyson Amir resides in Oakland, CA. where he writes, raps, teaches, organizes, and struggles for his people. You can learn more about his work at TysonAmir.com and BlackBoyPoems.com.